The Companion to British and Irish Cinema

The Companion to British and Irish Cinema

John Caughie
with Kevin Rockett

BFI PUBLISHING

First published in 1996 by
Cassell
Wellington House
125 Strand
London WC2R 0BB
and the
British Film Institute
21 Stephen Street
London W1P 2LN

The British Film Institute exists to promote appreciation, enjoyment, protection and development of moving image culture in and throughout the whole of the United Kingdom. Its activities include the National Film and Television Archive; the National Film Theatre; the Museum of the Moving Image; the London Film Festival; the production and distribution of film and video; funding and support for regional activities; Library and Information Services; Stills, Posters and Designs; Research, Publishing and Education; and the monthly *Sight and Sound* magazine.

British Library Cataloguing-in-Publication Data
A catalogue record for this book is available from the British Library.

ISBN 0 304 34158 4

Cover design by Jamie Tanner
Cover still: *The Crying Game*
courtesy of Artificial Eye

Typesetting by Fakenham Photosetting Ltd
Fakenham, Norfolk

Printed and bound in Great Britain by Redwood Books,
Trowbridge, Wiltshire

CONTENTS

Acknowledgments vii

Introduction ix

The Companion to British and Irish Cinema

Britain: an historical overview 1

Ireland: an historical overview 11

British and Irish cinema: personnel, institutions, key critical concepts 16

British and Irish cinema in Europe 166

Appendix I: European production and audience statistics 193

Appendix II: Select bibliography for European, British and Irish Cinema 201

ACKNOWLEDGMENTS

The Companion to British and Irish Cinema regroups and updates all the British and Irish material written for the Cassell/BFI *Encyclopedia of European Cinema* (1995). Our gratitude therefore goes in the first place to all those who made the *Encyclopedia* possible. We are also grateful to the writers who contributed to the entries on European issues included in the 'British and Irish Cinema in Europe' section: Chris Darke, Richard Dyer, Joseph Garncarz and Simon Horrocks. The following should be thanked for their painstaking editing and checking work: Simon Horrocks, Guy Jowett, Markku Salmi and David Wilson. We also owe special thanks to the staff of the BFI Library, and especially David Sharp and Gillian Hartnoll, and to Sue Bobbermein, Ed Buscombe and Roma Gibson in BFI Publishing.

A work such as this inevitably relies on other sources: trade publications, data provided by embassies and film commissions, journals, filmographies, catalogues, dictionaries, monographs, etc. It is impossible to cite them all, though many appear in the bibliographical notes at the end of some entries and in the final bibliography, as well as with the statistics. May they all be thanked collectively here, including the BFI Library.

Stills were provided by BFI Stills, Posters and Designs.

John Caughie and Kevin Rockett
Ginette Vincendeau, series editor and editor of
The Encyclopedia of European Cinema
London, February 1996

John Caughie is Professor of Film and Television Studies at the University of Glasgow (UK). He is the editor of *Theories of Authorship* and author of *Cinema 2000: a Report on the Future of Public Cinema Exhibition in Britain* and of *Television and Young People*. **Kevin Rockett** is Lecturer in Film at University College, Dublin and co-author of *Cinema and Ireland*.

INTRODUCTION

This introduction is being written in February 1996, in the week in which both *Sense and Sensibility* and *Trainspotting* were released: one, delightfully if ironically English, adapted from Jane Austen by Emma Thompson and directed by the Taiwanese director Ang Lee; the other, scabrously but comically Scottish, adapted by the team which made *Shallow Grave* (1994) – Danny Boyle (director), Andrew Macdonald (producer) and John Hodge (scriptwriter) – from the even more bleakly scabrous novel by Irvine Welsh. In his review column in the *Guardian*, Derek Malcolm began, 'It would seem perverse to like both *Trainspotting* and *Sense and Sensibility*. But that's critics for you.' Still on release and nominated for an Oscar is *Braveheart* (1995), an American film based loosely on the life of a legendary Scottish hero directed by and starring an American, Mel Gibson, who began his career in Australia. Beginning its shoot in Scotland, the film moved to Ireland when the Irish Film Minister offered a more favourable tax environment, a blatant move which provoked complaints by the British Department of Trade and Industry to the European Parliament. *Braveheart* followed *Rob Roy* (1994), an American film with some Scottish development funding, produced, directed and written by Scots (Peter Broughan, Michael Caton-Jones and Alan Sharp), featuring Irish (Liam Neeson), and American (Jessica Lange) stars, with a predictably villainous Englishman (Tim Roth). *The Commitments* (1991) with an English director (Alan Parker), a Scottish producer (Lynda Myles), based on an Irish novel by Roddy Doyle, adapted by two veteran English writers of television sitcoms (Dick Clement and Ian La Frenais), set in Dublin with Irish actors, is an American film. The most successful British film of the last few years has been *The Crying Game* (1992) written and directed by the Irish director Neil Jordan, and starring the Irish actor Stephen Rea, in a film shot in Ireland and London.

If it was ever easy to establish the criteria which makes a film British or Irish or Scottish or American, the last few years seem to have blurred a few more boundaries and confused the map a little further. Add to this the fact that most of the cinematic achievements of the 1990s have involved the substantial participation of television (*The Crying Game*, *Howard's End*, *Naked*, *Backbeat*, *Raining Stones*, *Three Colours Red, White and Blue*, *Four Weddings and a Funeral*, *Ladybird, Ladybird*, *Shallow Grave*, *The Madness of King George*, *Land and Freedom*) and it becomes slightly tricky not only to say what a *British* film is, but also what a British *film* is.

The complexity, diversity and cultural hybridity of recent British and Irish cinema is one of their most encouraging and engaging characteristics, and it is one of the things which this Companion is intended to celebrate. From a distance, British cinema has always looked like a sickly thing: hardly able to walk on its own, stumbling from renaissance to despair, isolated from the great modernist art cinema of mainland Europe, never able to produce the canonical figures of Hollywood, or, when it produced them – from Hitchcock to Ridley Scott – never able to sustain them. The trouble with the image is that, from a certain perspective, it is true; and even more true for Irish cinema where money and investment are even more limited. One response is to mourn; the other is to change the perspective and look a little closer.

This Companion has modest ambitions. It is neither exhaustive in its coverage, nor encyclopaedic in its knowledge. It does, however, attempt to look a little closer at British and Irish cinema. Many will be annoyed by its selectivity: Betty Balfour but not Chrissie White; Phyllis Calvert but not Valerie Hobson; Tilda Swinton but not Helena Bonham-Carter; and Richard Todd is missing. The simple explanation for the absences is pressure of space. Within the constraints of the project, we were aiming for a Companion with around 250 entries covering the significant personalities, movements and institutions in the hundred-year history of British and Irish cinema. The choice of what to include and what to leave out is never innocent. Sometimes it is accompanied by agonising indecision. Sometimes, it is determined by personal taste and judgement. Sometimes it is determined by a desire to promote an argument about what is important, or to open up a corner of the past or the present that is liable to be forgotten. We have tried to make the judgements and the arguments explicit.

British cinema, even more than Irish cinema, has not been exposed to the kind of historical scholarship that has marked American cinema in recent years. There are vast tracts of history which have been surveyed but not explored: the 1920s, for example, or the much-maligned 'quota quickie'. A Companion such as this cannot fill these gaps in scholarship. What we have tried to do, however, is provide a rough guide to the territory, suggesting the major sites of historical interest and the intriguing by-ways. Seen from this perspective, the landscape of British and Irish cinema offers a complexity of detail which cannot be seen from a distance, inviting closer inspection by tourist and explorer alike.

Contents

The Companion to British and Irish Cinema contains the following:

1. Historical overviews of both British cinema and Irish cinema. Readers unfamiliar with these national cinemas are encouraged to read these first, before 'browsing' or looking up entries.

2. The core of the book is made of around 250 alphabetically arranged entries, on personnel (directors, actors, critics, musicians, producers, set designers), critical concepts (e.g. the British New Wave, Irish language film-making) and institutions (e.g. Channel 4). Entries on British cinema were written by John Caughie (signalled by JC at the end of each entry) and those on Irish cinema by Kevin Rockett (KR).
3. A section entitled 'British and Irish cinema in Europe', which draws on material from *The Encyclopedia of European Cinema* and includes entries on pan-European issues (for instance European art cinema, Lesbian and gay cinema in Europe).
4. Two appendices:
– Appendix I: production and audience statistics in Europe.
– Appendix II: select bibliography on European, British and Irish cinema.

Conventions

Personnel entries are classified under their surname or most common name. This is followed by their date and place of birth and, as the case may be, death, as well as their real name. The country of birth/death is only mentioned if it is *not* Britain or Ireland. As a rule, biographical details such as marriage and children are indicated only if considered relevant to the work or achievement of this person.
Film titles and dates, and filmographies. For space reasons, filmographies are not necessarily exhaustive. Three cases apply:
• all films, or all important films, are mentioned in the text, in which case no filmography follows;
• all other films made by the person (and not mentioned in the text) are added at the end. This is indicated by 'Other films', followed by the films in chronological order. If a complete filmography is provided, it is indicated as 'Films';
• a selection of other major films made by the person (and not mentioned in the text) are added at the end. This is indicated by 'Other films include', followed by the films in chronological order.
Whenever possible, the date indicated is that of the release of the film in Britain or Ireland.
Bibliography. Some entries are followed by a single short bibliographical reference (under 'Bib') in an abbreviated form, to direct the reader to further reading. There is also a bibliography on European cinema, as well as British and Irish cinema in appendix II.
Cross-referencing. Throughout the text, persons, institutions and concepts which have their own entry in the rest of the book are signalled by an asterisk placed after the name. Alternatively, an arrow can point to related material. Between entries, other terminologies or related persons may be signalled [e.g. BFI – see British Film Institute]

THE COMPANION TO BRITISH AND IRISH CINEMA

GREAT BRITAIN: AN HISTORICAL OVERVIEW

'... the English cinema remains utterly amorphous, unclassified, unperceived.' (Peter Wollen*, 1969)

The history of British cinema begins promisingly. Victorian enterprise and invention primed the first generation for the new technology, and Victorian entertainment and social improvement prepared an audience in the music halls and the magic lantern shows. Both before and after the first demonstration of the Lumière Cinematograph in Paris in December 1895, moving picture patents were taken out, and Birt Acres had demonstrated his system for the projection of motion pictures on 15 January 1896 to members of the Royal Photographic Society, a month before the first demonstration of the Lumière system to a paying public in Britain on 20 February 1896 at the Regent Street Polytechnic in London. The early cinematographers were portrait photographers, lanternists, instrument makers and businessmen, and they established bases not only in London, but in Yorkshire (Bamforth & Company, the Sheffield Photo Company), Lancashire (Mitchell and Kenyon), and, most famously, in Brighton. From the so-called 'Brighton school', G. A. Smith* corresponded and shared tricks with Georges Méliès, and both he and James Williamson* developed close-ups and multi-shot scenes before Edwin Porter in America.

Britain, then, shares with France many of the pioneering initiatives of early cinema, and by 1900, given its access to an imperial world market, could have been expected to become a (if not the) world leader. The fact that it did not may have more to do with the economic, legislative and cultural conditions in which British cinema developed than with something inherent in the British character. *Pace* Satyajit Ray ('I do not think the British are temperamentally equipped to make the best use of the movie camera') and François Truffaut ('Isn't there a certain incompatibility between the terms "cinema" and "Britain"?'), the amorphousness which Peter Wollen notes in British cinema may be better understood as a product of history than as a state of nature.

Britain and Hollywood

All European cinemas live in the shadow of Hollywood. Britain, however, like Ireland, lives in the same linguistic market. In one transatlantic flow, this has meant that British audiences receive Hollywood films in their own language, without the mediation of dubbing or subtitling, allowing the Hollywood cinema to compete with the national cinema on equal terms. In the other direction, it has meant that major British producers from Alexander Korda* to David Puttnam* have looked to the North American market as the nut they have to crack. In either direction, it gives a particular turn of the screw to the notion of a national cinema in Britain, and gives Britain a particular place in European cinema.

Historically, the American domination of the British market was already in place by the beginning of World War I. The war itself, with many European cinemas out of action, established Hollywood's hegemony, its large domestic market enabling it to construct at an early stage a modern, Fordist mode of production capable of providing mass entertainment for a world market. By 1926, with around 3,500 cinemas operating in Britain and approximately 40 per cent of cinemagoers attending twice a week, only 5 per cent of the films shown in Britain were produced in Britain, and Britain represented over a third of Hollywood's foreign earnings.

During the silent period the possibility of Britain being part of a European cinema was still open. It was an easy matter to retitle or remake films for different national languages and French films were popular in the cinemas. Alfred Hitchcock* directed his first films for Michael Balcon* in Germany, Michael Powell* had his first job with Rex Ingram in the south of France, directors like Victor Saville* and Graham Cutts* worked in France and Germany, and even a star like Betty Balfour* made films with Louis Mercanton and Marcel L'Herbier. The arrival of sound, however, reshaped the world market around language, placed Britain firmly in the same linguistic market as Hollywood, and severed the links with the European mainland.

But British audiences' infatuation with Hollywood was not simply a matter of markets, and Jeffrey Richards in *The Age of the Dream Palace* (1984) suggests some of the irrational, cultural reasons which shaped preferences. Of particular relevance is a split which emerged in the audience not around language but around accent, with a marked preference for American films among the working-class audience and satisfaction with British films among the middle classes. Richards quotes a 1937 survey of exhibitors in *World Film News* which reports on the difficulties that exhibitors in working-class areas had with British films:

> British films, one Scottish exhibitor writes, should rather be called English films in a particularly parochial sense: they are more foreign to his audience than the products of Hollywood, over 6,000 miles away. Again and again exhibitors of this category complain of 'old school tie' standards inherent in so many British films. They describe the 'horse laughs' with which the Oxford accents of supposed crooks are greeted and the impatience of their patrons with the well-worn 'social drama' type of filmed stageshow.

This working-class audience (which most surveys put at around 80 per cent of the total) preferred 'the more vigorous American films'. Exhibitors from middle-class areas, however, reported a preference for British films, 'especially in places like Bournemouth, Dorking, the Isle of Wight etc.'

Good clean comedy and society drama with interesting dialogue, something people can think about and discuss afterwards, seems to sum up the most frequent attitude to what is wanted. The Gaumont (Matthews–Hitchcock) and Wilcox (Anna Neagle) type of British film seems to go down particularly well. History is often stated to be popular, as are mystery films. American gangster, crime or police films are frowned upon.

In a country as divided as Britain by class and region, with their separate tastes, preferences and prejudices, American films may have occupied neutral territory for the mass market on which the box office depended, and Jimmy Cagney may have been more recognisable as a working-class hero than Michael Redgrave. The popular British films with the working-class audience of the 1930s were, of course, those of George Formby* and Gracie Fields* with their roots in northern music hall. Critics, on the other hand, voted with Bournemouth and Dorking, and the opposition was established between a 'quality' British cinema, based on the supposedly 'English' characteristics of reality and restraint, and the frivolities and melodramas of the Hollywood dream factory, an opposition which revolved around Michael Balcon's* distinction of 'realism and tinsel'.

World War II provided the conditions for such a quality cinema. Feature film output dropped and imports were restricted, but audiences increased, and, in the Crown Film Unit and the Ministry of Information, the government had established a support mechanism not only for documentaries and information films, but also for feature production, as part of the war effort at home and overseas. The war also provided British themes and narratives which offered an emotional intensity to a British audience primed for patriotism. Films like *Target for Tonight* (1941) and *49th Parallel* (1941) were top box-office draws, and in the early stages of the war, realism with its roots in documentary established itself not only as a quality cinema, but also as a popular national cinema.

Much of the history of Britain's immediate postwar relations with Hollywood concerns a series of negotiations by Rank for a share of the American market, and a series of bunglings by government on the imposition and repeal of import taxes on films, which resulted in boycott skirmishes across the Atlantic. The requirement for American companies to remit more of their profits for investment in British production intensified the pressure on them to form subsidiaries in Britain, advancing the process of turning British commercial cinema into a branch industry dependent on American investment and distribution.

Domestically produced feature films clearly targeted at British audiences continued to be produced by teams like Basil Dearden* and Michael Relph, Frank Launder* and Sidney Gilliat, or the Boulting Brothers*, well into the 1960s, the British New Wave* continued to send out echoes into the 1970s, and the *Carry On** films went on until 1978. But as Margaret Dickinson and Sarah Street suggest in *Cinema* *and State* (1985), 'After 1961 it became increasingly difficult to define any part of the industry as British rather than Anglo-American', and the generation of successful film-makers which emerged in the late 1970s and 1980s – Ridley Scott*, Alan Parker*, David Puttnam* – have been explicit, with varying degrees of satisfaction, that their kind of success is dependent on the American market.

The impact of Hollywood on British culture has been by no means wholly negative, and there have been good reasons for audiences to prefer American films. Its economic dominance in mass entertainment, however, in production, distribution and, increasingly, exhibition, has progressively closed down the possibilities of a national popular cinema in Britain, while the lure of the American box office has shaped the possibilities which remain, commodifying culture as marketable images.

Regulation and support

For most other European countries the arguments for a national cinema could be bound up with the defence of a national culture in the national language. In many countries, these were arguments which governments could recognise, producing systems of legislation and support that provided the conditions for some kind of relatively coherent cultural strategy. In Britain, the language argument did not apply, and culture was not regarded as a proper concern of government. British government policy towards cinema has been dedicated much more significantly to the regulation of the market and the protection of the manufacturing industry than to the sustenance of a national film culture.

The first significant legislation of cinema in Britain was the 1927 Cinematograph Films Act, which instituted a quota on foreign imports. The quota provision required exhibitors to increase the percentage of domestic product shown in the cinemas from the 5 per cent of 1927 to 20 per cent by 1935. The initial effect was indeed to boost production: new companies appeared, large companies like Gaumont-British and Gainsborough reorganised to take advantage of quota requirements, and the largest company, British International Pictures, built its studios at Elstree. The later effect, when it was discovered that audiences still preferred American films, was to produce 'quota quickies' at minimum cost to satisfy the quota requirement. Very little critical work has been done on the 'quota quickie', and the judgment that they were uniformly dreadful may be the result of assumption rather than analysis. They did achieve at least some of the requirements of an industrial quota by maintaining employment levels in the industry, and they provided conditions in which directors like Carol Reed* and Michael Powell*, and actresses like Margaret Lockwood* and Googie Withers*, could work on a large number of films in a relatively short space of time. They did not, however, win over audiences to British films.

The quota was a protective measure, designed to create a market for

British films. Without investment, however, it was apparent that the only market which would be created was the British one, and that was not sufficient to guarantee the quality which critics increasingly demanded. In the postwar period, government, and particularly the Attlee Labour government with future Prime Minister Harold Wilson at the Board of Trade, began to develop systems of economic support for the production of 'quality' British films.

The first such initiative was the establishment in 1949 of the National Film Finance Corporation (NFFC) with a rolling fund of £5 million from the Treasury. While the NFFC was a limited resource in an increasingly difficult climate, over the thirty-five years of its existence it helped to fund over 750 films, including *The Third Man* (1949), *The Small Back Room* (1949), *The Happiest Days of Your Life* (1950), *Saturday Night and Sunday Morning* (1960) and *Gregory's Girl* (1981). It also supported the establishment of the short-lived Group 3, which produced twenty-two feature films between 1951 and 1955 with John Baxter* as managing director and John Grierson* as executive producer, a unique Griersonian attempt to develop a government-supported feature film production company.

In much the same spirit of doing something for the film industry, in 1951 the Labour government introduced the Eady Levy, a levy of one-twelfth of the ticket price at the box office, which was to be returned mainly to the producers of eligible British films but with some funds reserved for the British Film Institute* Experimental Film Fund (later the BFI Production Board), the National Film School and the Children's Film Foundation. While the support of the Experimental Film Fund (under the chairmanship of Michael Balcon*) clearly recognised the cultural dimension of film, as far as the return to producers was concerned there was no requirement as to the type of film, and the definition of a British film was a version of the one which had been developed for quota regulation: a film 75 per cent of whose production costs was spent on British labour and British materials. The Eady Levy did indeed provide an incentive to production, making the difference between profit and loss for many films and attracting overseas production to Britain. By the 1970s, the Hollywood majors were making increasing use of British studio space, exploiting British special effects skills to make a number of the new space age spectaculars. The result was that films like *Superman*, *Star Wars* and *Batman*, which were made in British studios with 75 per cent of their production costs going to British labour and materials, were defined by the Department of Trade and Industry as British films and qualified for Eady support. Both the logic and the absurdity of the situation are apparent. Following an industrial logic, the Levy attracted production to Britain which provided a continuation of skilled employment. The absurdity was that, while indigenous British producers struggled to survive, a government levy was subsidising what were already hugely successful films made by competitors in the linguistic market. The industrial logic produced a cultural absurdity.

By the end of the 1970s, a major difficulty for domestic production was in securing investment for British films which seemed increasingly to be high-risk investments. The brief flurry of renaissance at the beginning of the 1980s, associated mainly with Goldcrest* and hailed at the time as a resurgence of the national spirit, is attributable, at least in part, to a change in tax law. The Inland Revenue Statement of Practice SP9/79 was a tax arrangement, introduced in 1979, which allowed such institutions as banks and pension funds to consider films as the equivalent of industrial machinery, and claim tax relief against investment in films. It offered an incentive to financial houses and holding companies like Pearson-Longman and Crédit Lyonnais to invest in the film industry. The most visible result of this was *Chariots of Fire* (1981), much of whose initial funding came from the National Union of Mineworkers' Pension Fund. The success of *Chariots of Fire* was followed by that of *Gandhi* (1982), *Local Hero* (1983) and *A Passage to India* (1985), and the renaissance was on. The flurry looked like a change in the climate.

Unfortunately the climate changed again in 1986, and the late 1980s and early 1990s were marked by more traditional British weather. In line with removing public support from sections of industry which the Thatcher government thought should be 'liberated', the budget of 1985 not only withdrew tax incentives, it also terminated the Eady Levy and closed down the NFFC. It replaced the NFFC with British Screen, a consortium of major film and television interests – including Channel 4, Rank and Granada Television – with at least pump-priming support from the Treasury. While the initial record of British Screen under Simon Relph was impressive and often enlightened, funding sources which were themselves exposed to the uncertainties of the market were not capable of protecting the film industry from the devastations of recession. The number of films produced has fluctuated, but the levels of investment have shown a fairly steady downward trend: more films are struggling to find less money.

The historic lack of long-term forms of public support for cinema, either through subsidy or incentives, may not be unique to Britain in Europe, but it is a major determining condition. The discourse of economic liberalism proclaims that if British people freely choose to support American films, then they are exercising their sovereignty as consumers and it is not for governments to intervene. But without effective government intervention there is a narrowing range of popular British cinema to exercise choice upon, and mainstream British cinema is driven more and more into dependence on American investment.

Television

Since at least the early 1980s it has been impossible to discuss British cinema without also discussing British television: the 'least worst television in the world', as Milton Schuman tagged it; or in another tag popular at the beginning of the 1980s, 'British cinema is alive and well, and its name is television.' The most apparent and dramatic effect of television has been the wooing of the mass audience away from public forms of entertainment towards private, domestic entertainment. In Britain this happened more dramatically than elsewhere in Europe, partly because British television was able to meet the need for native forms of entertainment which cinema had failed to satisfy, and partly because postwar cinema was in the stranglehold of near monopolistic or duopolistic conditions in distribution and exhibition. The two factors together created a downward spiral in which cinema admissions declined from a peak of 1,635 million in 1946 to a low of around 70 million in 1984. In weaning the audience from public entertainment, television also prepared the way for video, with Britain, by the beginning of the 1980s, running second only to Japan in per capita ownership of video recorders, demonstrating that Britain had not lost its appetite for films but had transferred its affections to the small screen.

The initial reaction of the film industry to television's popularity was self-protection and non-cooperation. Since 1982, however, with the arrival of Channel 4 and increasingly with the Films Act of 1991 – which requires all broadcasters to commission at least 25 per cent of their domestically produced programmes from independent producers – the film industry and the television industry have been on converging tracks. In particular, television has become the one remaining hope of an indigenous low to medium-budget feature film industry.

The increasing interdependency of television and cinema transforms not only the economics of British film but also the cultural and aesthetic expectations which the national audience and the international market have of it. Directors like Ken Loach* and Mike Leigh* have brought what is essentially a British television aesthetic into cinema, to considerable international acclaim, challenging to some extent the critical antipathy to British cinema and chipping away at its amorphousness. More insidiously, television has primed the world audience for the prestige of Britain's literary and theatrical heritage, finding a market through such sumptuous literary adaptations as *Brideshead Revisited* (1981) and *The Jewel in the Crown* (1984) for the 'Heritage' film [> HERITAGE CINEMA IN EUROPE], one of Britain's more dubious contributions to world culture. The rediscovery in the films of Merchant/Ivory* *et al.* of Edwardian England and its waning Empire – the ironic ambivalence towards class and sexuality of E. M. Forster or Evelyn Waugh softened by the warm, elegiac tones of national nostalgia – seems to have reshaped what is meant by 'quality' in British cinema into period detail, melancholic languor and the evocation of loss. At a time when Britain has difficulty selling much else, it has been remarkably successful at selling its past.

An art cinema?

These are some of the conditions which give shape to the 'official' British cinema, and particularly to the British 'quality' cinema. The place of the art cinema, however, as a component of the national culture like Italian neo-realism or the French New Wave, was occupied by the British Documentary Movement*. It is somehow appropriate to the empirical and utilitarian traditions of British thought that documentary should be its contribution to world art cinema: an art cinema, as Alan Lovell suggests (*Studies in Documentary* [1972]), which was ambivalent about art. The Documentary Movement is, however, a more complex phenomenon than critical discourses have sometimes supposed, and the experimentalism of Len Lye* or Norman McLaren*, the lyricism of Basil Wright*, or the links to Surrealism through Humphrey Jennings* and Alberto Cavalcanti*, were not wholly suppressed by the no-nonsense Calvinism of John Grierson*. Parallel to the 'official' art cinema of the Documentary Movement, there was an 'unofficial' cinema in the avant-gardism of the group around *Close Up**, the internationalism of the London Film Society*, and the political radicalism which developed around the Progressive Film Institute, the Workers' Film and Photo League, and Kino. This latter constituted a Workers' Film Movement which shadowed the official Documentary Movement through the 1930s, offering a less consensual critique of British society and politics during the Depression, and engaging directly in the politics of class, the international arms industry, the international working-class movement, and the Spanish Civil War. The documentary attitude which was appropriated by critics and producers during and after the war for the discourse of quality cinema contained the official Documentary Movement and forgot the rest.

What was contained or forgotten in particular was modernism, and the documentary as art cinema which was promoted after the war (after the death of Jennings, with Lye in New York, McLaren in Canada and Cavalcanti back in Brazil) was an art cinema without the avant-garde* impulse of much European modernism. This lack of sustained engagement with modernism makes Britain's art cinema almost unique in Europe, and provides the distinction between an art cinema and a 'quality' cinema.

The currents of modernism and the avant-garde present in the unofficial cinema of the 1930s seem to have been extinguished by the patriotic needs of wartime cinema, and there is no continuous tradition. The current resurfaced, however, in the 1960s and 1970s in the Workshop Movement*, the London Film-makers Co-op, and the Independent Filmmakers Association. This very heterogeneous movement emerged from the aesthetics of the American avant-garde, pop art, the politics of 1968 and feminism as both an alternative cinema and an oppositional cinema; it was fostered by the BFI* Production Board, the Arts Council and the Greater London Council; and it was given an infrastructure by Channel 4* in the 1980s. Placed, and placing itself, on the margins, with no intention of being absorbed into the mainstream, it was nevertheless a remarkably vigorous and vigorously diverse current. In the 1980s and 1990s, with the emergence out of this current of directors like Peter Greenaway*, Derek Jarman*, Sally

Potter* and Isaac Julien*, there is the first appearance of a British art cinema which has engaged not only with modernism, but with popular culture, pop art and the other avant-garde movements of American and European culture, combining them with a more localised politics of race, gender and sexuality. With the continuing infirmity or uncertainty of indigenous mainstream cinema, the eddies on the edge of the mainstream begin to suggest what a national cinema might look like, the amorphousness which Wollen complains of beginning to redefine itself more positively as diversity.

Critical perspective

It seems possible that some of the shapelessness of British cinema is a trick of critical perspective. Certainly, it is not a *cinéma d'auteurs*, and many of those who have been quickest to bury it – Truffaut, *Movie** – have been those who are most committed to the creative, self-expressive *auteur* as the guarantee of value. In a cinema which lacks stable systems of support, the producer has to create the structures in which expression can happen, continually reinventing the wheel, and it may be those structures, rather than the individual artist, which give the cinema its shape. If, as Andrew Sarris claims, the history of American cinema is a history of directors, then the history of British cinema is one of producers and producer-directors – Hepworth*, Balcon*, Korda*, Grierson*, Puttnam*, Attenborough* – and of production teams – Powell* and Pressburger, Dearden* and Relph, Launder* and Gilliat, Muriel and Sidney Box*, the Boulting Brothers*, Merchant-Ivory*. The individual director as *auteur*, the self-expressive artist who allowed critics to shape American popular cinema and European art cinema, is a more elusive figure in British film culture. This is not to suggest that all that is required to make British cinema fall into place is a substitution of the producer for the director, or even the replacement of one critical paradigm by another – genre studies, say, instead of authorship. No single paradigm seems adequate to the specificities and diversities of a national cinema. Without a means of classification or a test of value, criticism is faced with the choice of abandoning the theory or abandoning the cinema. It may be, however, that it is not the shape of the cinema which is the problem but the shape of the criticism.

In the 1990s, in a Britain which is no longer Great and a Kingdom which is no longer United, there are again signs of a cinema staggering towards resurgence, still without consistent support and still uncertain about what constitutes success. Like Dr Johnson's dancing dogs, it is not always that they do it well but that they do it at all that seems to invite – and deserve – attention. *Four Weddings and a Funeral* (1994) is undoubtedly an international phenomenon, but it does not in itself constitute a renaissance: it may, in fact, be an example of a film which is only famous for being famous. More significant is the tentative emergence of an infrastructure which allows films to be produced in unexpected places and at a variety of levels. If British cinema as a complex whole begins to seem something more than a contradiction in terms, and if criticism finds new ways of charting its history, it may be because both cinema and criticism are beginning to recognise and reflect the fault lines, divisions and diversities which disunite the culture into differences and identities rather than imposing on it the unity implicit in the desire for a National Cinema. JC

[> BOND FILMS, EALING COMEDY, FREE CINEMA, GAINSBOROUGH MELODRAMA, HAMMER HORROR, CLOSE UP, SCREEN, SEQUENCE, SIGHT AND SOUND].

IRELAND: AN HISTORICAL OVERVIEW

Cinema in Ireland, in both its pre-colonial and post-colonial formations, has been dominated by foreign films. For some years films from Britain, France and Italy were the most frequently seen in Ireland, but since the early 1910s the vast majority of films screened have been American, while most of the rest have been British. Only rarely have indigenous Irish films had more than peripheral status. Indeed, the first fiction films made in Ireland were by the American company, Kalem, which visited Ireland between 1910 and 1912, and whose director, Irish-Canadian Sidney Olcott, returned during the following two years to produce the first fictional representations of Irish history and culture. These productions had more to do with the potential income from the urban ethnic Irish cinema audience in America than with the relatively modest income available from the still largely rural Irish population.

It was not until 1916 that professional indigenous film-making began with the Film Company of Ireland*, but this development did not encourage the independent Irish state, established in 1922, to support Irish films. Indeed, nationalist policies towards the cinema and popular culture in general were propelled by xenophobia and a conservative Catholic morality that was already clearly evident before independence. The new state expended its energies on a cultural protectionist policy that sought to exclude from Ireland any influences which might challenge the pre-modern official Gaelic and Catholic cultures. The cinema, music (especially jazz), literature and popular publications were restricted in a policy as much Catholic as it was 'Gaelic'.

The Official Film Censor operates under the Censorship of Films Act, 1923, which restricts any film from public exhibition if it is deemed indecent, obscene or blasphemous, or is 'contrary to public morality'. Subjective assessments by conservative censors led to a policy of restricting anything which infringed Catholic morality. As a result, films which dealt with contraception and abortion, or represented in any sympathetic way extramarital affairs or divorce (on which a constitutional ban was introduced in 1937), or depicted rape or homosexuality, were either banned or cut. The result was that during the first four decades of independence about 3,000 films were banned, while another 8,000 were cut, with many other films never submitted to the Official Film Censor, a government employee, as their fate would have been well known to the distributors. Among the films banned were *Brief Encounter* (1945, UK) and *The Postman Always Rings Twice* (1946, US). The adaptations of Tennessee Williams plays in the 1950s were also banned, while the cycle of British 'social problem' dramas of the late 1950s and early 1960s were either banned or severely cut. The administrative explanation for such extensive banning and cutting was that the censors pursued a policy, approved by the Minister for Justice, of rarely issuing limited certificates, such as the British 'X' which was introduced in 1951. Thus almost all films released could be seen by all age groups. This policy did not change until 1965 after a sustained campaign by distributors and exhibitors concerned about declining product availability, with the support of liberal journalists and other anti-censorship campaigners.

Against this background of official hostility to the foreign cinema the Irish state might have been expected to encourage an alternative indigenous Irish cinema. Far from it; but the reason for this is as much economic as it is cultural. Ireland occupies a peripheral economic space in world cinema, with box-office accounting for only about 0.5 per cent of the global market. In European terms, it represents 1.1 per cent of the market; its 2.3 admissions per person per annum puts it around the European average, but the ability to generate a surplus on a film within its own territory is not possible except for the most modestly budgeted films. Total box-office income in 1992 was a mere IR£21 million, while video wholesale was worth IR£15 million and video rental and sell-through about IR£40 million. As a result, private investors have only rarely put money into Irish films, while the Irish state did not commit any significant resources to an Irish cinema in the decades after independence. The policy that emerged was integrated within general economic parameters.

The decades after independence had seen an attempt to build an Irish economic base through protecting the native bourgeoisie from foreign competition and through state intervention in unprofitable areas of the economy. While the state made significant strides in the development of natural resources and the building of an infrastructure, the bourgeoisie remained generally inefficient even in a protected home market. In the postwar years a gradual shift in policy occurred which led to the embracing of foreign capital as the means of developing an Irish industrial base. In this context film was viewed as another industry which could generate employment and produce foreign earnings. As a result, state policy for film production became firmly linked to industrial policy, with little or no concern with a cultural programme for film. When this policy culminated in the belated opening of Ardmore Studios* in 1958, no provision was made for an Irish, let alone a cultural, policy at the studios. The exception to this had been to utilise the players of the Abbey Theatre, the Irish National Theatre and other Irish theatres in film productions, though they were usually confined to supporting roles in non-Irish films. Thus players as various as Cyril Cusack*, Barry Fitzgerald*, Noel Purcell and Jimmy O'Dea combined their theatre work with often inconsequential film parts. Alfred Hitchcock*, John Ford and others adapted Abbey Theatre plays as films, though before the establishment of Ardmore these were usually studio productions made in Britain or the USA. The consequence of this policy of encouraging foreign capital to make films in Ireland, and of providing financial aid for the studios, was that support for indigenous production was minimal until the early 1980s.

By then the struggle had shifted from concern with the direct and indirect subsidising of foreign productions in Ireland towards debate within the Irish film community between those who favoured a committed indigenous cinema and those who championed a commercial Irish film 'industry'. The outcome of this debate is that all sides are now relatively satisfied: tax-based investments allow for large private investment in films, while the rejuvenated Bord Scannan na hEireann* (Irish Film Board), and increased sums from Irish television for independent productions, have resulted in such an expansion of native and foreign productions that 1994 was the most active year ever for film production in Ireland. This further shift in film policy is part of a broader redefining of the position of the native bourgeoisie in the international economy. It is in the context of these changes that the struggle for an Irish cinema can be most usefully viewed.

During the barren decades of the 1940s, 1950s and 1960s Irish film-makers were largely confined to servicing information campaigns for government departments and state agencies through making documentaries and drama-documentaries on public health, farming modernisation or tourism. Ironically, these campaigns were indirectly part of the modernisation process which was to lead to a dramatic shift from the inward-looking protectionist policies of the early decades of independence, to an outward-looking, international focus in Irish society and culture from the late 1950s onwards. However, it is Peter Lennon's documentary, *The Rocky Road to Dublin* (1968), that stands out as the most challenging film made in Ireland in the 1960s. Though based as a journalist in Paris, Lennon, working with French cinematographer Raoul Coutard*, interviewed a number of Irish 'modernisers', while adding an acerbic commentary which was highly critical of independent Ireland. When the film was adopted by activists during the May 1968 'Events' in France as evidence of a committed critical cinema, it was assured of both notoriety and extensive audience interest in Ireland.

In the inter-war period only a small handful of fiction films were made by Irish film-makers. Culturally and economically, the most successful of these were *Irish Destiny* (1926, retitled *An Irish Mother*) and *The Dawn* (1936), both set during the final military phases of the struggle for independence. These films, and their American and British counterparts like *The Informer* (1935), *Ourselves Alone* (1936) and *The Plough and the Stars* (1936), all proved popular with Irish audiences. But a film industry and the allegiance of audiences cannot be built on such (uncritical) nostalgia. It was not until the social and cultural effects of the internationalisation of Irish society began to manifest themselves in the late 1960s and early 1970s that a new generation of Irish film-makers began to look with a critical eye at aspects of Irish culture and society previously unexplored on film.

In this new cinema a more complex notion of the past was explored by such film-makers as Bob Quinn*, Pat Murphy*, Robert Wynne-Simmons (*The Outcasts*, 1982), and Tommy McArdle (*It's Handy When People Don't Die*, 1980), with the pious platitudes of nationalist historiography being interrogated for their simplistic formulations. The bastion of Catholic and state ideology, the family, was shown to have fissures at its heart: the fragmented family in all classes and in all periods was explored. Such film-makers as Kieran Hickey* (*Exposure*, 1978; *Criminal Conversation*, 1980), who looked at middle-class mores, or Joe Comerford*, who focused on the opposite end of the social spectrum, brought out themes such as infidelity and incest which had been long buried by Irish society. Catholic institutions – especially education, as in Cathal Black's* *Our Boys* (1980) – celibacy in Bob Quinn's *Budawanny* (1987) and *The Bishop's Story* (1994), and teenage pregnancy in Margo Harkin's *Hush-A-Bye-Baby* (1989), did not escape scrutiny. The city made its cinematic presence felt for the first time in films such as Comerford's *Withdrawal* (1974) and *Down the Corner* (1978), and in Black's *Pigs* (1984), where marginal social groups are represented.

Many of these films were informed by a realist aesthetic in their perhaps unconscious rejection of earlier romantic representations of Ireland by foreign film-makers. Some film-makers, however, by locating their films in the west of Ireland, have consciously sought to subvert that cinematic and cultural tradition. Quinn's *Poitin* (1978), where greed, drunkenness and attempted rape are centred in a traditional Irish lakeside cottage, and Comerford's *Reefer and the Model* (1988), in which two gay men dance at a ceilidh in a pub, suggest that the most powerful inheritances are being challenged. While many of these films posed a realist opposition to the romantic tradition, other film-makers were exploring new formal parameters, especially Thaddeus O'Sullivan*, whose innovative *On a Paving Stone Mounted* (1978) drew on avant-garde traditions to examine Irish migration. By contrast, those who try to work within mainstream commercial genres, such as City Vision's *The Courier* (1987), discover that Dublin's cityscape is not readily adaptable to the thriller format. This problematic of genre is most clearly evident in the formal schizophrenia of *Reefer and the Model*, where the first half of the film has the feel and resonance of a European art film but much of the rest is informed by Hollywood chase movies.

Reefer suggests that Ireland, like other European countries, is grappling with the dominance of American culture, as some of its film-makers embrace Hollywood while others search for a critical, subversive relationship to it. Among those who have chosen to embrace international commercial cinema, Neil Jordan* (*The Crying Game*, 1992), Jim Sheridan* (*My Left Foot*, 1989, and *In the Name of the Father*, 1993), and Pat O'Connor*, have opened up spaces and possibilities of which previous generations of Irish film-makers might only have dreamed: not least the total of nineteen Oscar nominations for

Jordan's and Sheridan's films, with three wins, while Irish make-up artist Michelle Burke is the only contemporary Irish person to have won two Oscars, for *La Guerre du feu/Quest for Fire* (1981, Fr./Canada) and *Bram Stoker's Dracula* (1992, US). While Irish-born directors such as Herbert Brenon and Rex Ingram became successful in Hollywood, neither of them made a film in Ireland. The present generation of commercial cinema directors have successfully straddled the Irish and non-Irish cinema worlds and in the process have helped place indigenous Irish film-making in the international arena. KR
[> IRELAND AND OTHER CINEMAS, BORD SCANNAN NA hEIREANN, IRISH-LANGUAGE FILMS, FILM INSTITUTE OF IRELAND]

BRITISH AND IRISH CINEMA: PERSONNEL, INSTITUTIONS, KEY CRITICAL CONCEPTS

ALLGOOD, Sara
ALWYN, William
ANDERSON, Lindsay
ANSTEY, Edgar
ARDMORE STUDIOS
ARNOLD, Malcolm
ASHCROFT, (Dame) Peggy
ASQUITH, Anthony
ATTENBOROUGH, (Sir) Richard
BAKER, (Sir) Stanley
BALCON, (Sir) Michael
BALFOUR, Betty
BARKER, (Sir) William G.
BARRY, John
BATCHELOR, Joy
BAXTER, John
BLACK BRITISH INDEPENDENT FILM
BLACK, Cathal
BOGARDE, (Sir) Dirk
BOND FILMS
BOORMAN, John
BORD SCANNAN NA hEIREANN (IRISH FILM BOARD)
BOULTING, Roy and John
BOX, Muriel, Sidney and Betty
BRANAGH, Kenneth
BRITISH BOARD OF FILM CENSORS
BRITISH DOCUMENTARY MOVEMENT
BRITISH FILM INSTITUTE (BFI)
BRITISH NEW WAVE
BUCHANAN, Jack
BURTON, Richard
BYRNE, Eddie
BYRNE, Gabriel
CAINE, Michael
CALVERT, Phyllis
CARDIFF, Jack
CAREY, Patrick
CARROLL, Madeleine
'CARRY ON ...' FILMS
CAVALCANTI, Alberto
CHANNEL 4
CHRISTIE, Julie
CLARKE, T. E. B.
CLEESE, John
CLOSE UP
COLMAN, Ronald
COMERFORD, Joe
CONNAUGHTON, Shane
CONNERY, Sean
CORK FILM FESTIVAL
COWARD, Noël
CRICHTON, Charles
CUSACK, Cyril
CUTTS, Graham
DALRYMPLE, Ian
DAVIES, Terence
DAY-LEWIS, Daniel
DEAN, Basil
DEARDEN, Basil
DEL GIUDICE, Filippo
DICKINSON, Thorold
DILLON, Carmen
DONAT, Robert
DORS, Diana
DOUGLAS, Bill
EALING COMEDY
EDINBURGH INTERNATIONAL FILM FESTIVAL
ELLIOTT, Denholm
ELVEY, Maurice
EVANS, (Dame) Edith
FIELDS, (Dame) Gracie
FILM COMPANY OF IRELAND
FILM INSTITUTE OF IRELAND
FILM SOCIETY, The
FINNEY, Albert

FISHER, Terence
FITZGERALD, Barry
FLAHERTY, Robert
FORBES, Bryan
FORMBY, George
FORSYTH, Bill
FRANCIS, Freddie
FREARS, Stephen
FREE CINEMA
FRICKER, Brenda
GAINSBOROUGH MELODRAMA
GIELGUD, (Sir) John
GILLIAM, Terry
GILLIAT, Sidney
GODFREY, Bob
GOLDCREST
GRANGER, Stewart
GREENAWAY, Peter
GREENE, Graham
GREENWOOD, Joan
GRIERSON, John
GUINNESS, (Sir) Alec
HALAS, John
HAMER, Robert
HAMMER HORROR
HARRIS, Richard
HARRISON, (Sir) Rex
HAWKINS, Jack
HAY, Will
HEPWORTH, Cecil
HICKEY, Kieran
HILLER, (Dame) Wendy
HITCHCOCK, (Sir) Alfred
HOPKINS, (Sir) Anthony
HOSKINS, Bob
HOWARD, Leslie
HOWARD, Trevor
HURST, Brian Desmond
HURT, John
IRELAND AND OTHER CINEMAS
IRISH LANGUAGE FILM-MAKING
IRONS, Jeremy
JACKSON, Glenda
JARMAN, Derek
JENNINGS, Humphrey
JOHNSON, (Dame) Celia
JORDAN, Neil
JULIEN, Isaac
KERR, Deborah
KILLANIN, (Lord) Michael
KORDA, (Sir) Alexander
KORDA, Vincent
KUBRICK, Stanley
KUREISHI, Hanif
LAUGHTON, Charles
LAUNDER, Frank
LEAN, (Sir) David
LEIGH, Mike
LEIGH, Vivien
LEJEUNE, C. A.
LESTER, Richard
LOACH, Ken
LOCKWOOD, Margaret
LONDON FILM-MAKERS CO-OP
LOSEY, Joseph
LUCAN, Arthur
LYE, Len
McANALLY, Ray
McDOWELL, Malcolm
MACKENDRICK, Alexander
McKENNA, Siobhan
McLAREN, Norman
MALLESON, Miles
MASON, James
MATHIESON, Muir
MATTHEWS, Jessie
MERCHANT-IVORY
MILLS, (Sir) John
MIRREN, Helen
MONTAGU, Ivor
MORE, Kenneth
MORRISON, George
MOVIE
MULVEY, Laura
MURPHY, Pat
NEAGLE, (Dame) Anna
NEESON, Liam
NEWTON, Robert
NIVEN, David
NORTHERN IRELAND AND FILM
NOVELLO, Ivor

O'CONNOR, Pat
O'LEARY, Liam
O'SULLIVAN, Thaddeus
O'TOOLE, Peter
OBERON, Merle
OLIVIER, (Sir) Laurence
PARKER, Alan
PAUL, R. W.
PEARSON, George
PINTER, Harold
PLEASANCE, Donald
POTTER, Sally
POWELL, Dilys
POWELL, Michael and PRESSBURGER, Emeric
PUTTNAM, David
QUINN, Bob
RADIO TELIFIS EIREANN (RTE)
RANK, J. Arthur
REA, Stephen
REDGRAVE, Michael
REDGRAVE, Vanessa
REED, (Sir) Carol
REED, Oliver
REISZ, Karel
RELPH, Michael
RICHARD, Cliff
RICHARDSON, (Sir) Ralph
RICHARDSON, Tony
ROBERTS, Rachel
ROBESON, Paul
ROBSON, (Dame) Flora
ROEG, Nicolas
ROTHA, Paul
RUSSELL, Ken
RUTHERFORD, (Dame) Margaret
SABU
SAVILLE, Victor
SCHLESINGER, John
SCOTLAND AND FILM
SCOTT, Ridley
SCREEN
SELLERS, Peter
SEQUENCE
SHERIDAN, Jim
SIGHT AND SOUND
SIM, Alastair
SIMMONS, Jean
SLOCOMBE, Douglas
SMITH, G.A.
SMITH, (Dame) Maggie
STAMP, Terence
SWINTON, Tilda
TERRY-THOMAS
THOMPSON, Emma
TODD, Ann
TOYE, Wendy
UNSWORTH, Geoffrey
USTINOV, (Sir) Peter
WALES AND FILM
WARNER, Jack
WATT, Harry
WHITELAW, Billy
WILCOX, Herbert
WILLIAMSON, James
WISDOM, Norman
WITHERS, Googie
WOLLEN, Peter
WORKSHOP MOVEMENT
WRIGHT, Basil
YOUNG, Freddie

ALLGOOD, Sara

Dublin 1883 – Los Angeles, USA 1950

Irish actress. At a young age, Allgood became a successful actress at the Abbey Theatre, playing in J. M. Synge's 1904 play *Riders to the Sea*, and as Pegeen Mike in Synge's *The Playboy of the Western World* (1907). Other high points of her theatrical career included the Sean O'Casey plays *Juno and the Paycock* (1924), in which she played Juno to Barry Fitzgerald's* Paycock, and *The Plough and the Stars* (1926). Though she made one film, *Just Peggy*, while on tour in Australia in 1918, her first British feature was in Alfred Hitchcock's*, and Britain's, first film with synchronous sound, *Blackmail* (1929). The following year she played Juno in Hitchcock's version of O'Casey's play. She settled in Hollywood after receiving enthusiastic reviews for her performances while touring with the Abbey Theatre in America. Her career there, though, was not a success; she was offered only minor Irishwomen roles as cooks, landladies and other matronly figures. KR

Other Films Include: *That Hamilton Woman/Lady Hamilton, How Green Was My Valley* (1941); *The Lodger* (1944); *My Wild Irish Rose* (1947).

ALWYN, William

Northampton 1905 – Southwold 1985

British composer. As well as being Professor of Composition at the Royal Academy of Music with a number of symphonic works to his credit, Alwyn scored more British films than any other composer (he was also, incidentally, the second cousin of Gary Cooper). He began film composition as part of the British Documentary Movement* and worked particularly with Paul Rotha* and Humphrey Jennings*, for whom he scored *Fires Were Started* (1943). After the war, he composed scores for around eighty feature films, forming particular associations with Carol Reed* and with Frank Launder and Sidney Gilliat*. JC

ANDERSON, Lindsay

Bangalore, India 1923 – London 1994

British director and critic. Anderson's importance to British cinema was both as a director and as a critic and polemicist. As one of the editors of *Sequence** from 1947 to 1951, Anderson introduced the concept of the director as poet of the cinema, and when the Western was still a despised genre in British criticism, offered John Ford as a prime example. As a writer for *Sight and Sound**, the *New Statesman* and the *Observer* in the 1950s he argued for a socially engaged cinema and for the poetry of everyday life, and as one of the organisers of and contributors to Free Cinema* in 1956, he put his polemics into practice with a number of social documentaries which developed from the Humphrey Jennings* poetic tradition rather than the sociological tradition of the John Grierson* school. (He received his only Oscar, for Best Short Subject, for *Thursday's Children*, 1953.) From 1956 Anderson was closely associated, as assistant director, with the theatre revolution which was going on at London's Royal Court Theatre under the banner of the 'angry young men' and directed his first production there in 1957.

Discussing his first feature, *This Sporting Life* (1963), one of the key films of the British New Wave*, Anderson rejected the notion of a representative social realism in favour of the poet's sense of the unique: 'We were not making a film about a "worker", but about an extraordinary (and therefore more deeply significant) man, and about an extraordinary relationship. We were not, in a word, making sociology.' This sets Anderson in opposition to the naturalistic 'kitchen sink' tag under which British social realism is often subsumed, an opposition which becomes even more apparent with the allegorical nature of the trilogy centred round the character Mick Travis (played by Malcolm McDowell*): *If....* (1968), which was awarded the Palme d'Or at Cannes, *O Lucky Man!* (1973), and *Britannia Hospital* (1982).

In a famous article written for *Sight and Sound* in 1956, 'Stand Up! Stand Up!', Anderson says, 'Fighting means commitment, means believing what you say, and saying what you believe. It will also mean being called sentimental, irresponsible, self-righteous and out of date by those who equate maturity with scepticism, art with amusement, and responsibility with romantic excess.' In his last years, Anderson seemed to have become irascible rather than angry – irritated by lack of recognition, lack of support, lack of a British film industry, by the need to make pop promos to support himself, by the British Film Institute*, and, particularly, by 'pernicious' film studies. JC

Bib: Jonathan Hacker and David Price, *Take 10: Contemporary British Film Directors* (1991).

Other Films Include: **Documentaries** – *Meet the Pioneers* (1948); *Idlers That Work* (1949); *Three Installations, Trunk Conveyor, Wakefield Express* (1952); *O Dreamland* (1953); *Green and Pleasant Land, Henry, The Children Upstairs, A Hundred Thousand Children, £20 a Ton, Energy First, Foot and Mouth* (1955); *Every Day Except Christmas* (1957); *Raz, dwa, trzy/The Singing Lesson* (1967, Poland); **Features** – *The White Bus* (1967); *In Celebration* (1976); *Chariots of*

Fire [as actor] (1981); *The Whales of August* (1987, US); *Glory! Glory!* (TV/1988, Canada/US).

ANSTEY, Edgar

Watford 1907 – London 1987

British director/producer, who joined John Grierson's* documentary unit at the Empire Marketing Board in 1931. His most significant contribution was *Housing Problems* (1935), co-produced with Arthur Elton, and with Ruby Grierson, Grierson's sister, directing the to-camera interviews which gave the film its distinctive innovation. A similar approach was adopted in *Enough to Eat?* (1936), a documentary on malnutrition. Anstey was associated with the *March of Time* documentaries in New York and London from 1937 to 1939, and with propaganda documentaries during the war. He established the British Transport Film Unit in 1949, and used it as a documentary training unit until his retirement in 1974. JC

Bib: Elizabeth Sussex, 'Basil Wright and Edgar Anstey', *Sight and Sound* (Winter 1987/88).

ARDMORE STUDIOS

Irish film studios. Ardmore (near Dublin, a three-stage studio), was established in 1958 with a mixture of private and state capital. Its initial policy of adapting Abbey Theatre plays as films quickly gave way to a policy of encouraging foreign producers to make films at the studios. Productions based there have included *Shake Hands With the Devil* (1959), *A Terrible Beauty* (1960) and *Excalibur* (1981; made during the time director John Boorman* was the studios' chairman). The use of state funding to subsidise Ardmore while under state ownership during 1975–82 was a major target in the campaign for an indigenous Irish cinema by independent film-makers, which led to the setting up of the Irish Film Board*. No state funds have been allocated to Ardmore since 1982. KR

ARNOLD, Malcolm

Northampton 1921

British composer, whose best-known work was on *The Bridge on the River Kwai* (1957), a score which won him an Academy Award. Arnold had previously scored *The Sound Barrier* (1952) and *Hobson's Choice* (1954) for David Lean*, varying the tempo with the 'St. Trinian's' films for Launder and Gilliat*. He has around fifty distinguished British films to his credit, and is the composer of a number of orchestral works, including incidental music for ballet and theatre. JC

ASHCROFT, (Dame) Peggy

Croydon 1907 – London 1991

British actress, who made her London stage debut in 1927, and was the leading theatrical dame for more than half a century. Unlike the triumvirate of theatrical knights – John Gielgud*, Laurence Olivier*, Ralph Richardson* – Ashcroft made very few films. She made her debut in *The Wandering Jew* (1933) and had a cameo role in Hitchcock's* *The 39 Steps* (1935), but during the 'golden years' of the 1940s and 1950s, when men were being men, she concentrated on her stage career. It was in the 1980s (and her seventies) that her strength as a supporting actress on screen became widely recognised, first on television and then in the cinema. Her Barbie in *The Jewel in the Crown* (Granada, 1984) was one of the understated delights of British acting, and her Oscar for Best Supporting Actress for *A Passage to India* (1985) was only surprising because it was not clear who she was supporting. JC

Other Films Include: *Quiet Wedding* (1941); *The Nun's Story* (1958, US); *Secret Ceremony* (1968); *Sunday Bloody Sunday* (1971); *Der Fussgänger/The Pedestrian* (1974, Ger./Switz).

ASQUITH, Anthony

London 1902–68

British director. Son of Lord Herbert Asquith, the Liberal Prime Minister, and educated at Winchester and Balliol College, Oxford, 'Puffin' Asquith was a founder member of the London Film Society* in 1925, was wooed by John Grierson* for the documentary unit, and was president of the ACT, the leading film trade union, from 1937 until his death in 1968. His early films, *Shooting Stars* (co-dir. A. V. Bramble, 1928) and *A Cottage on Dartmoor* (1929), were compared favourably to Alfred Hitchcock's*. An actor's director, his films from the late 1930s adopt a highly literate approach to dialogue well suited to stage adaptations, and he is credited with the best adaptation of Shaw in *Pygmalion* (1938) and of Wilde in *The Importance of Being Earnest* (1952). He developed an association with the playwright Terence Rattigan, adapting such stage successes as *French Without Tears* (1939), *The Winslow Boy* (1948) and *The Browning Version* (1951), and using Rattigan's scripts for *The Way to the Stars* (1945) and *The Yellow Rolls-Royce* (1964). For Gainsborough*, somewhat surprisingly, he directed the costume melodrama *Fanny by Gaslight* (1944).

His *Times* obituary said of Asquith, 'He holds a minor but secure place among the world's best film directors.' 'The world' may be an exaggeration, but he holds an honourable place in British cinema. JC

Bib: J. R. Minney, *Puffin Asquith: A biography of the Hon. Anthony Asquith* (1973).

Other Films Include: *Tell England* (1931); *Moscow Nights* (1935); *Channel Incident* (1940); *Freedom Radio, Quiet Wedding, Cottage to Let* (1941); *Uncensored* (1942); *We Dive at Dawn, The Demi-Paradise* (1943); *While the Sun Shines* (1947); *The Woman in Question* (1950); *The Net* (1953); *The Young Lovers, Carrington V.C.* (1954); *Orders to Kill* (1958); *The Doctor's Dilemma* (1959); *The Millionairess* (1960); *The V.I.P.s* (1963).

ATTENBOROUGH, (Lord) Richard — Cambridge 1923

British actor, director and producer. Attenborough made his film debut in 1942 in *In Which We Serve*. Though the part was small it established him as the juvenile funk whose upper lip began to quiver when all around were stiffening theirs. An interesting coward in a cinema full of heroes, Attenborough was the alter ego of John Mills* – the same milieu, but lacking fibre and simple, working-class decency. In civilian clothes, his characters were delinquent before teenagers were invented, and his fresh young face brought a compelling and ambivalent menace to the 17-year-old psychotic, Pinky, in *Brighton Rock* (1947). In the late 1950s, he said, 'I decided for all intents and purposes to give up acting, to go into production and wait until this idiotic cherubic face had sunk sufficiently to allow me to do something else.' From 1959 he was involved in production with Bryan Forbes*, working behind the cameras of *The Angry Silence* (1960) as well as acting in it, receiving his first producer credit on *Whistle Down the Wind* (1961), and co-producing *The L-Shaped Room* (1962). He claims that he wanted to direct in order to make *Gandhi* (1982), a project he nurtured for twenty years. His directorial debut, which he also produced, was *Oh! What a Lovely War* (1969), a screen adaptation of Joan Littlewood's dramatised documentary, where he persuaded a complete roll-call of British stars to give their services for a daily rate. As a director, particularly on *Gandhi* and *Cry Freedom* (1987), he has gone for the grand scale, the broad emotional wash and the high ethical tone rather than the intimate and ambivalent observation which makes his acting memorable, but at least in *Magic* (1978, US) the menace of the William Goldman script survives.

Attenborough has won British Academy Best Actor awards for *Guns at Batasi* and *Seance on a Wet Afternoon* (both 1964), Golden Globe awards for Best Supporting Actor in *The Sand Pebbles* (1966, US) and *Doctor Dolittle* (1967, US), and a host of awards, including the Oscar for Best Film, for *Gandhi*. Since the 1970s, he has been at the centre of the British cultural establishment, and has become one of the leading figures in the attempt to refloat British cinema. He was knighted in 1976 and received a life peerage in 1993. JC

Bib: Jonathan Hacker and David Price, *Take 10: Contemporary British Film Directors* (1991).

Other Films Include: **As Actor** – *A Matter of Life and Death* (1946); *London Belongs to Me* (1948); *Morning Departure* (1950); *The Magic Box* (1951); *The Ship that Died of Shame* (1955); *Private's Progress* (1956); *Brothers in Law, The Scamp* (1957); *Sea of Sand* (1958); *I'm All Right Jack, Jet Storm, The League of Gentlemen* (1960); *The Great Escape* (1963, US); *The Flight of the Phoenix* (1965, US); *A Severed Head, Loot* (1970); *10 Rillington Place* (1970); *Rosebud* [US], *Conduct Unbecoming* (1976); *Shatranj ke khilari/The Chess Players* (1978, India); *The Human Factor* (1980); *Jurassic Park* (1993, US); *Miracle on 34th Street* (1994, US). **As Director** – *Young Winston* (1972); *A Bridge Too Far* (1977); *A Chorus Line* (1985, US); *Chaplin* (1992); *Shadowlands* (1993).

B

BAKER, (Sir) Stanley

Ferndale, Wales 1927 – Malaga, Spain 1976

British actor. Robert Murphy suggests that 'Stanley Baker is the key figure in 60s crime films, just as Jack Hawkins* had been in the 50s.' Where Hawkins is avuncular, honest and domesticated, Baker is tough, ambiguous and solitary. The contrast can be traced back to *The Cruel Sea* (1953), where Hawkins' concerned and caring Captain is opposed to Baker's car salesman become First Lieutenant, a sadistic bully who cowers before Hawkins' confident authority and is invalided out (of the war and the film) with a duodenal ulcer. As so often in British cinema, the distinction is played out around class, but Baker's characteristic persona also suggests a much more threatened masculinity which is later exploited in a series of films with Joseph Losey*: *Blind Date* (1959), *The Criminal* (1960), *Eva/Eve* (1962, Fr./It.) and *Accident* (1967).

Baker was knighted in 1976, a month before he died of cancer at the age of 49. JC

Other Films Include: *Obsession* (1949); *The Red Beret* (1953); *Helen of Troy* (1955, US); *Hell Drivers, Campbell's Kingdom* (1957); *Violent Playground* (1958); *Jet Storm* (1960); *The Guns of Navarone* (1961); *Zulu* (1963); *Robbery* (1967).

BALCON, (Sir) Michael

Birmingham 1896 – Sussex 1977

British producer. Less of a showman than Alexander Korda* or Herbert Wilcox* and less of a missionary than John Grierson*, Balcon is a key figure not only for the British film industry, but also for projecting an image of Britishness, and particularly of Englishness, in the years immediately after the war.

Balcon's career began in partnership with Victor Saville*, with whom he founded a distribution company, Victory Motion Pictures, in 1919. He produced his first film, *The Story of Oil*, a documentary directed by Saville, in 1921. In 1923, he produced Graham Cutts'* film *Woman to Woman*, and in 1924 Cutts and Balcon founded Gainsborough Pictures, from which came *The Rat* (1925) with Ivor Novello*, and Alfred Hitchcock's* *The Lodger* (1926). Balcon remained with the studio when it was taken over by Gaumont-British, and during the 1930s he produced some of the most successful films of the decade, including Saville's films with Jessie Matthews*, Robert Flaherty's* *Man of Aran* (1934), and Hitchcock's *The Man Who Knew Too Much* (1934) and *The 39 Steps* (1935). From 1936 until 1938 he was head of production for MGM-British, and in 1938 he took over from Basil Dean* as head of production at Ealing* Studios.

It was at Ealing that Balcon left his most distinctive mark on British cinema and on the representation of Britishness. The image which Balcon cultivated was of the 'team spirit', a self-regulating community like the ones they created in the films. Balcon, however, was the man in charge, and his values and tastes are written all over the output. 'By and large we were a group of liberal-minded, like-minded people,' he told John Ellis in 1975. 'We voted Labour for the first time after the war; that was our mild revolution.' When the studio was sold to the BBC in 1955, Balcon erected a plaque which read, 'Here during a quarter of a century were made many films projecting Britain and the British character.'

Balcon spent the rest of his career as an influential elder statesman, still at the heart of things. He served as chairman of Bryanston (the production company which became a significant force in the British New Wave*), a director of Border Television, and chairman of the British Film Institute Experimental Film Fund (subsequently the BFI Production Board) from its founding in 1951 until 1972. Of the three men who exerted the greatest influence on the shape of British cinema – Grierson, Korda and Balcon – all were producers, but only Balcon was English. JC

Bib: Michael Fleugel (ed.), *Michael Balcon: The Pursuit of British Cinema* (1984).

BALFOUR, Betty London 1903 – Weybridge 1978

British actress. 'Betty Balfour,' says Anthony Slide, 'was without doubt the most popular and most adorable film star that this country has ever produced, or ever will produce.' In the 1920s, though other stars like Alma Taylor, Chrissie White or Stewart Rome had strong local followings, only Betty Balfour and Ivor Novello* ranked in the international popularity polls along with the stars of Hollywood. She was known as the 'British Mary Pickford' or as 'Britain's Queen of Happiness', her popularity based on her comic gamine charm and common touch rather than on her sexual allure. Prefiguring Gracie Fields*, her most popular creation, Squibs, was based on a music-hall sketch featuring her as a pert, Cockney flower girl. Under contract till 1925 to the Welsh-Pearson company and directed by George Pearson*, Balfour made no attempt to break into Hollywood, but like Novello she was able to export her talents to mainland Europe, working with Louis Mercanton on *La Petite bonne du palace* (1926, Fr.) and *Croquette* (1927, Fr.), and with Marcel L'Herbier on *Le Diable au coeur* (1926, Fr.). Her popularity waned with the coming of sound, though she played a supporting role to Jessie Matthews* in *Evergreen* (1934) and appeared with John Mills* in *Forever England* (1935). JC

Bib: Anthony Slide, 'Britain's Queen of Happiness', *Silent Picture* 2 (Spring 1969).

Other Films Include (Directed by Pearson except where indicated): *Mary-Find-the-Gold, Squibs* (1921); *The Wee MacGregor's Sweetheart, Squibs Wins the Calcutta Sweep* (1922); *Squibs' Honeymoon, Squibs, MP, Love, Life and Laughter* (1923); *Reveille* (1924); *Satan's Sister* (1925); *The Sea Urchin* [Graham Cutts] (1926); *Paradise* [Denison Clift] (1928); *Die Regimentstochter* [Hans Behrendt] (Ger.); *Champagne* [Alfred Hitchcock] (1928); *Squibs* (1935); *29 Acacia Avenue* [Henry Cass] (1945).

BARKER, (Sir) William G. London 1867 – [?] 1951

British producer and director of the early silent cinema. A travelling salesman, whose early interest in cinema was as a cameraman on 'topicals', Barker became manager of the successful Warwick Trading Company in 1906 and formed his own company, Barker Motion Photography, in 1909, building the first studios at Ealing. For his first major success, *Henry VIII* (1911), he hired Sir Herbert Beerbohm Tree at a reputed fee of £1,000 for a day's shooting, and then boosted his rentals by announcing that he would publicly burn all circulation copies after a release of six weeks. Rachael Low compares him with Cecil Hepworth*, ascribing to Hepworth 'the greatness of dignity' and to Barker 'the greatness of the preposterous, the larger-than-life'. He retired from the cinema in 1916. JC

Bib: Rachael Low, *The History of British Film, 1906–1914* (1948).

Other Films Include: *The Fighting Parson* (1912); *The Tube of Death/The Anarchist's Doom, The Battle of Waterloo, Sixty Years a Queen, East Lynne, The Great Bullion Robbery, In the Hands of the London Crooks* (1913); *The Lights O' London* (1914); *Jane Shore* (1915).

BARRY, John

York 1933

British composer. Unlike the other distinguished names of British film music – William Alwyn*, Malcolm Arnold*, Walton, Vaughan Williams – Barry's roots were in popular music. He played in a military band during National Service, was a rock and roll trumpeter, worked with Johnny Dankworth and Jack Parnell, and had his own group, the John Barry Seven, in the 1960s. Best known for his work on the James Bond* films, most of which he scored, he is also responsible for such memorable scores as *Midnight Cowboy* (1969, US), *A Clockwork Orange* (1972) and *Body Heat* (1981, US). He received an Oscar for *Born Free* (1965), and a British Academy award for *The Lion in Winter* (1968). JC

BATCHELOR, Joy and HALAS, John

Watford 1914 – London 1991

Budapest, Hungary 1912 – London 1995

British animators, forming Halas-Batchelor cartoons in 1940, who made many information and propaganda cartoons for the Ministry of Information during the war. Halas-Batchelor became the largest animation unit in postwar Britain, making shorts for information and educational uses and for entertainment. Their most successful film was the animated feature-length version of *Animal Farm* (1954), which took three years to make. Their only other feature-length film was a version of *Ruddigore* (1966). JC

Other Films Include: *Carnival in the Clothes Cupboard* (1941); *Dustbin Parade, Digging for Victory* (1942); *Jungle Warfare* (1943, also *Six Little Jungle Boys*); *A Modern Guide to Health* (1946); *The Owl and the Pussycat* (1953); *History of the Cinema* (1956); *Dam the Delta* (1960); *Automania 2000* (1963); *What is a Computer?* (1970).

BAXTER, John

Foots Cray, Kent 1896 – [?] 1975

British director and producer. A theatre manager and agent before he came to the cinema in the early 1930s, Baxter brought with him a love of music hall and a commitment to the victims of the Depression. The love of music hall was expressed in his work with Arthur Lucan* in two films featuring Old Mother Riley (a popular cross-dress 'dame'), *Old Mother Riley in Society* (1940) and *Old Mother Riley in Business* (1940), and in three films with Flanagan and Allen, *Theatre Royal* (1943), *Dreaming* (1944) and *Here Comes the Sun* (1945). His commitment to society's victims is expressed in a series of not particularly elegant but hard-hitting films in the 1930s and 1940s, beginning with his debut semi-documentary *Doss House* (1933). His best-known film, *Love on the Dole* (1941), adapted from Walter Greenwood's best-selling novel, presents a rather different image of life in the Northern slums than had been circulated by Gracie Fields*.

Described by Richard Dyer McCann as a 'poor man's Mick Balcon*', Baxter took up production after the war. He was instrumental in the establishment of the National Film Finance Corporation (NFFC) in 1948, and he became the Managing Director of Group 3, an attempt to establish a government-supported feature film unit, during its brief life from 1951 until 1957. JC

Bib: Geoff Brown and Tony Aldgate, *The Common Touch: the Films of John Baxter* (1989).

Other Films Include: *Say It With Flowers, Music Hall, Flood Tide* (1934); *A Real Bloke, The Small Man* (1935); *Men of Yesterday, Hearts of Humanity* (1936); *Song of the Road* (1937); *Crook's Tour* (1940); *The Common Touch* (1941); *Let the People Sing, We'll Smile Again* (1942); *The Shipbuilders, When We Are Married* (1943).

BBFC – see BRITISH BOARD OF FILM CENSORS

BFI – see BRITISH FILM INSTITUTE

BLACK BRITISH INDEPENDENT FILM

British movement. In his introduction to *Questions of Third Cinema* (Pines and Willemen, eds., 1990) Paul Willemen argues that black film-makers 'now constitute the most intellectually and cinematically innovative edge of British cultural politics'. Institutionally, black independent film-making in Britain owes its existence to a combination of factors in the late 1970s and early 1980s – 'race riots' and inner city unrest, resulting in a politics of containment on the part of local authorities and more focused demands for access and representation from the black communities; the enlightened cultural policies of the Greater London Council before its dissolution; the commitment of the new Channel 4* to previously unfranchised cultural voices; and the development of the Workshop Movement*. The Workshop Movement in particular established the infrastructure for the emergence of black workshops such as Sankofa and Black Audio Film/Video Collective, whose films – *Territories* (Sankofa, 1984), *Passion of Remembrance* (Sankofa, 1986) and *Handsworth Songs* (Black Audio, 1986) – formed canonical reference points, and whose founders – Isaac Julien*, Maureen Blackwood, Martine Attille, Nadine Marsh-Edwards, Lina Gopaul, John Akomfrah – were identified as the directors, producers, writers and theorists within what was essentially a collective movement. Aesthetically, black film-making was influenced by a conjunction of 'Third World' debates around Third Cinema, debates about representation and subjectivity developed by *Screen**, and debates about race, identity, hybridity and diasporic cultures articulated by such black theorists as Stuart Hall, Paul Gilroy and Homi K. Bhabha. In the 1990s, the collective spirit has been replaced to some extent by an attention to individual directors like Isaac Julien and feature films like *Young Soul Rebels* (1991). New voices, however, continue to emerge – Gurinder Chadha, whose first film, *I'm British But. . .* (1989), was supported by the BFI New Directors scheme, went on to make the first Asian feature film in Britain, *Bhaji on the Beach* (1993) – and black film-makers associated with the workshops continue to develop a debate about a multicultural British cinema. JC

Bib: *Black Film, British Cinema*, ICA Documents no. 7 (1988).

BLACK, Cathal born 1952

Irish director and writer. Though Black has made only a few films, they have displayed a visual richness which is not always evident in the work of other Irish film-makers. His first film, *Wheels* (1976), was an adaptation of a short story by Irish writer John McGahern. It explores the relationship of a son to his father who remains on the family farm after the son has migrated to the city. *Our Boys* (1980) was the first sustained look at Irish Catholic education. Using actuality material, documentary interviews and drama sequences, Black examined the often brutal legacy of Christian Brothers education. Sensitivity to its subject matter led RTE*, one of the film's backers, to shelve the film for a decade before broadcasting it. *Pigs* (1984) focuses on a disparate group of outsiders, including the first representation of a gay man in an Irish film, who live in a Dublin squat. Black's visual resonances are within the European art cinema tradition, with few concessions to mainstream commercial cinema. KR

BOGARDE, (Sir) Dirk London 1921

British actor, whose strikingly varied career makes him both a figure of unique respect in British cinema and a critical problem. The popular view is of a 1950s male pin-up, reaching stardom in such films as *Doctor in the House* (1954), who was rescued from a crippling seven-year contract with Rank* to become a serious actor in the European art cinema* of Joseph Losey* – *The Servant* (1963), *Accident* (1967) – and Luchino Visconti – *La Caduta degli Dei/The Damned* (1969), *Morte a Venezia/Death in Venice* (1972). Certainly, the respect which he commands has something to do with his surprising ability to reinvent himself. More systematic criticism (notably by gay critics) recognises in this ability a testing of male sexuality which extends across his work – a striking feature in a national cinema which is apparently so certain its masculinity. It appears in the sexualised delinquency of *The Blue Lamp* (1950), it is explicit in the homosexuality of *Victim* (1961) – both 'social problem' films directed by Basil Dearden* – and it is most playfully camp in *Modesty Blaise* (Losey, 1966). It also surfaces in a consistent strain of erotic sadism which is exploited by Losey in *The Servant*, by Visconti in *The Damned*, and by Liliana Cavani in *Il portiere di notte/The Night Porter* (1974). If there is a case for considering actors as *auteurs*, Bogarde is probably one of the more interesting and complex of British *auteurs*.

For a leading British actor he has made remarkably few American films – *Song Without End* (1960), *The Fixer* (1968) and *Justine* (1969) – but since the 1970s he has become one of the most European of British actors, with important roles in films by Visconti, Cavani, Henri Verneuil (*Le serpent/The Serpent/Night Flight from Moscow* (1973, Fr.), Alain Resnais (*Providence*, 1977, Fr.), Rainer Werner Fassbinder (*Despair/Eine Reise ins Licht*, 1978, Ger.), and Bertrand Tavernier (*Daddy Nostalgie/These Foolish Things*, 1990, Fr.).

Bogarde received British Film Academy awards for *The Servant* and for *Darling* (1965), and a BAFTA award for 'outstanding contribution to world cinema' in 1990. He was knighted in 1992. JC

Bib: Andy Medhurst, 'Dirk Bogarde', in Charles Barr (ed.), *All Our Yesterdays* (1986).

Other Films Include: *Dancing with Crime* (1947); *Esther Waters, Once a Jolly Swagman* (1948); *So Long at the Fair* (1950); *Blackmailed* (1951); *Hunted, The Gentle Gunman* (1952); *The Sleeping Tiger* (1954); *Simba, Doctor at Sea* (1955); *Ill Met by Moonlight* (1956); *Doctor at Large, Campbell's Kingdom* (1957); *A Tale of Two Cities* (1958); *The Doctor's Dilemma, Libel* (1959); *The Mind Benders* (1962); *Doctor in Distress* (1963); *King & Country* (1964); *A Bridge Too Far* (1977).

BOND FILMS

British film series. Somewhat predictably, the package for the most commercially successful series of films in postwar British cinema was put together by an Italian-American ('Cubby' Broccoli) and a Canadian (Harry Saltzman, who had previously been involved in Woodfall*) with American money (United Artists). The success itself was less predictable: Ian Fleming's James Bond novels, though Philip Larkin and Kingsley Amis were fans, had not been best-sellers, Sean Connery* was an unknown, and United Artists were only prepared to invest $900,000 in *Dr No* (1962). Connery, however, brought to the part an accent which was foreign to the embarrassments of English class, and a style which allowed space for the audience to share the joke; the one-liners and double entendres of the dialogue allowed the audience not to take the violence too seriously ('sado-masochism for all the family'); Ken Adam's design chimed with the pop culture and pop art of the 1960s; and the narratives were based on routines on which infinite variations could be played, rather than on logical or psychological development. (Bond films are like *Carry On* films* in that people remember incidents rather than stories.) More fundamentally, James Bond offered playful fantasies to men, 'an assembly kit for fantasists' (Alexander Walker). While the 'angry young men' were vituperating against women as the agents of conformity, Bond offered sublimation and conquest. The formula ran on into the 1990s, surviving changes of cast with increasing self-reflexiveness, measuring the political temperature after the Cold War, and charting a history of male fantasy from sex to technology to techno-sex, and from playful sadism (the golden girl of *Goldfinger*, 1964) to body horror with special effects (the exploding of Grace Jones in *A View to a Kill*, 1985).
JC

Bib: Tony Bennett and Janet Woollacott, *Bond and Beyond: The Political Career of a Popular Hero* (1987).

BOORMAN, John

Shepperton 1933

British director. 'For me,' says John Boorman, 'movie-making is a way of exploring the hidden places.' Despite coming from television documentary (he was head of BBC television documentaries from 1960 to 1964), Boorman is interested in a cinema of myth, a mythic interest which focuses on the Grail legend, and leads at its most interesting to modern 'quest' films like *Point Blank* (1967, US) and *Deliverance* (1972, US), or, more traditionally, to *Excalibur* (1981, US). It can also lead to *The Exorcist II: The Heretic* (1977, US), which Boorman describes as a 'human and healing film' but which others thought a disaster. His autobiographical film, *Hope and Glory* (1987), gives a rather cute but visually dazzling account of boyhood in the London Blitz, and won Best Director and Best Screenplay awards from the New York Film Critics.

Taking up residence in Ireland, Boorman was made Chairman of the Board of the National Film Studios of Ireland (formerly Ardmore Studios*) in 1975 until it went into receivership in 1982, and was a member of the Irish Film Board* from 1980 to 1982. He was Executive Producer of Neil Jordan's* first feature, *Angel* (1982). JC

Bib: John Boorman, *Money into Light: The Emerald Forest, A Diary* (1985).

Other Films: *Catch Us If You Can* (1965); *Hell in the Pacific* (1968, US); *Leo the Last* (1970); *Zardoz* (1974); *The Emerald Forest* (1985); *Where the Heart Is* (1990, US); *Beyond Rangoon* (1995, US).

BORD SCANNAN NA hEIREANN (IRISH FILM BOARD)

Irish organisation. Bord Scannan na hEireann is the statutory body, established in 1981, charged with aiding Irish film production. With the exception of minimal amounts from the Irish Arts Council, it was the first state body to invest directly in indigenous productions. It made culturally significant investments in pre-production and took minority stakes through loans in films from an annual budget of only about IR£500,000 until 1987 when the Board was wound down as part of government cutbacks. It was reactivated in 1993 under Lelia Doolin, with an initial budget of IR£1.1m, rising to annual sums of £2–3 million in subsequent years. The Board membership includes film director Neil Jordan*. Films supported by the Board include Jordan's first feature, *Angel* (1982), Pat Murphy's* *Anne Devlin* (1984), and Joe Comerford's* *Reefer and the Model* (1987). KR

BOULTING, Roy — Bray 1913
and
BOULTING, John — Bray 1913 – Sunningdale 1985

British directors, writers and producers, and twin brothers, who produced most of their films together. During the war, John directed *Journey Together* (1945) for the RAF Film Unit, and Roy directed *Desert Victory* (1943), *Tunisian Victory* (1944) and *Burma Victory* (1945) for the Army Film Unit. In Charter Films, which they established in 1937, roles were fluid. 'As producers and directors,' said John Boulting, 'we generally worked on the basis that the one who wrote the script should direct the film and be the arbiter of the film's creative development.' In the 1940s they produced such tough dramas and melodramas as *Pastor Hall* (1940), *Thunder Rock* (1942), *Fame is the Spur* (1947), and, probably their best film, *Brighton Rock* (1947). From the 1950s they switched to comedy, social satire and farce, producing one classic in *I'm All Right Jack* (1959), and a few amusing swipes at British manners and institutions in such films as *Private's Progress* (1956), *Brothers in Law* (1957) and *Carlton-Browne of the F.O.* (1959). JC

Other Films Include: *The Guinea Pig* (1948); *Seven Days to Noon* (1950); *The Magic Box* (1951); *Seagulls over Sorrento* (1954); *Lucky Jim* (1957); *Suspect* (1960); *Heavens Above!* (1963); *The Family Way* (1966); *Twisted Nerve* (1968); *There's a Girl in my Soup* (1970).

BOX, Muriel — Violette Muriel Baker; Tolworth 1905 – London 1991,
Sydney — Beckenham 1907 – Perth, Australia 1983
and
Betty — Beckenham 1920

British directors, producers and writers. Muriel and Sydney Box began as a prolific husband and wife writing team, writing one-act plays in the 1930s, and formed a company during the war, with Sydney's sister Betty as assistant, to produce government instructional films. Moving to feature film writing, Sydney and Muriel received an Oscar in 1945 for the original script of *The Seventh Veil*. In 1946, Sydney was placed in charge of Gainsborough by J. Arthur Rank*, with Muriel in charge of the script department, and Betty in charge of Islington Studios. Together they were responsible for almost forty films in a four-year period. In the early 1950s, Muriel began directing, and has directed more films than any other British woman, *Sight and Sound** condescendingly describing them as 'women's pictures ... part of the magazine fiction of the screen – and no less competently organised than most magazine fiction.' Sydney and Muriel's working partnership broke up in 1958 when Sydney became a television executive. They separated in 1969. Betty has had a director-producer relationship with Ralph Thomas, resulting in over thirty films, including the *Doctor* ... series, since 1954. She is married to Peter Rogers, who produces the *Carry On* series with Ralph's brother, Gerald Thomas. Of the trio, Muriel has a particularly strong claim to a place in British film history as one of an extremely small group of women feature film directors. Her work has recently been reassessed by feminist critics. JC

Films Directed By Muriel Box: *The Happy Family* (1952); *A Prince for Cynthia* [short], *Street Corner* (1953); *The Beachcomber, To Dorothy a Son* (1954); *Simon and Laura* (1955); *Eyewitness* (1956); *The*

Passionate Stranger (1957); *The Truth About Women* (1958); *Subway in the Sky, This Other Eden* (1959, Ir.); *Too Young to Love* (1960); *The Piper's Tune* (1962); *Rattle of a Simple Man* (1964).

BRANAGH, Kenneth — Belfast 1960

British/Irish actor and director, whose significance for British cinema may be in his revival of the tradition of popular Shakespeare on film. His first film as actor/director, *Henry V* (1987), offered an opportunity to reassess the patriotism of Laurence Olivier's* 1945 version in the age of Thatcherite English nationalism, but the political edge was blunted by what Branagh has called 'life-enhancing populism'. *Much Ado About Nothing* (1993) plays out the Olivier/Vivien Leigh* fantasy of the 'fabled couple' with a rather 'laddish' Branagh playing Benedict to the Beatrice of his then wife, Emma Thompson* (from whom he has subsequently separated). The film's undoubted popularising success relies on its charm, its settings and its all-star cast (including Hollywood's Keanu Reeves and Denzel Washington), rather than its challenge or new perception. While the comparison with Olivier may be too obvious, it allows us to chart a shift in stardom from heroism and dangerous romance to a rather resistible brashness, and from Shakespeare as national myth to Shakespeare as national theme park.

Branagh has also directed and acted in non-Shakespearean films, the sub-Hitchcockian *Dead Again* (1991), the sub-*Big Chill*, *Peter's Friends* (1992), and the not completely sub-Coppola *Mary Shelley's Frankenstein* (1994). *Frankenstein* had Branagh as the scientist and many of the usual directorial mannerisms (a lot of running actors and wheeling cameras), but something awesome was preserved from the relentless gothic horror of the book – and not all the credit can go to Coppola, who produced, De Niro, who played the monster, or even Mary Shelley, who put it there in the first place. He directed *In the Bleak Midwinter* (1995) from his own screenplay, and played Iago in Oliver Parker's *Othello* (1995). JC

Bib: Alison Light, 'The Importance of Being Ordinary', *Sight and Sound* (September 1993).

BRITISH BOARD OF FILM CENSORS (BBFC) [now BRITISH BOARD OF FILM CLASSIFICATION]

British institution. 'This film is so cryptic as to be meaningless. If there is a meaning it is doubtless objectionable.' Thus the 1930 BBFC examiner in rejecting Germaine Dulac's *La Coquille et le clergyman/The Seashell and the Clergyman* (1928). The Board was established in 1913 as an industry response to the eccentricities of the Local Authority licensing of films. Technically, it was an industry-run advisory body, financed by the fees levied on applications, 'advising' Local Authorities on the suitability of films for public exhibition, and the submission of a film for certification was voluntary. In effect, it was virtually impossible for a film to be shown commercially without a BBFC certificate. The Board has been served in its time by some legendary 'old duffers' (though John Trevelyan, BBFC Secretary in the 1960s and 1970s brought a more liberal approach) and the archives are full of equally legendary inanities which reflect at best a conservative and at worst a dangerously reactionary view of class relations, sexual relations, religion, and international affairs. In 1975 a more 'rational' system of regulation was introduced when films were removed from the common law offence of indecency and brought under the Obscene Publications Act, which allowed a defence of context (on the grounds, for example, of artistic context) and gave some protection from arbitrary prosecution. In 1982, the BBFC changed its name to the British Board of Film Classification, and in 1985, in response to anxieties about 'video nasties', it was given statutory authority for the certification of videos under the Video Recording Act. JC

Bib: James C. Robertson, *The Hidden Cinema: British Film Censorship in Action 1913–1975* (1989) and *The British Board of Film Censors: Film Censorship in Britain, 1895–1950* (1985).

BRITISH DOCUMENTARY MOVEMENT

British movement. Internationally, the documentary movement is frequently identified as Britain's major contribution to world cinema, while domestically its influence on both the aesthetics and the institutions of cinema is regarded as decisive. As a movement, its home base lay in a sequence of state-sponsored bodies in the 1930s and 1940s: the Empire Marketing Board (EMB) Film Unit (1927–33) established by John Grierson* and Stephen Tallents; the General Post Office (GPO) Film Unit (1933–39), which operated from the disbandment of the EMB until it became the Crown Film Unit (1939–52) under the Ministry of Information, with responsibilities for wartime and postwar propaganda. The movement, however, had loose boundaries, and incorporated at various points the Shell Film Unit, the British Transport Film Unit, the Realist Film Unit, the Strand Film Unit, and Films of Scotland. Grierson was the driving force throughout, recruiting to the various units such personnel as Basil Wright*, Edgar Anstey*, Arthur Elton, Stuart Legg, Paul Rotha*, Harry Watt*, Humphrey Jennings*, Alberto Cavalcanti*, Len Lye*, Norman McLaren*, Pat Jackson, and his two sisters, Ruby and Marion Grierson.

Institutionally, the continuing significance of Grierson's achievement in the establishment of a government-sponsored sector was in blurring the lines between state and independence, where independence came to mean dependence on the state as a way of ensuring independence from commerce. It was the same achievement, with the same contradictions, which another Scot, John Reith, was simultaneously negotiating with the incorporation of the BBC. In both, there were ideological and moral values at stake as well as institutional ones: institutionally, non-commercial cinema and broadcasting were established within the framework of public service in opposition to commerce; ideologically, cinema and broadcasting with a serious purpose were regarded as morally superior to the Hollywood dream factory. In this way, the documentary movement gave institutional form to a bias against 'mere' entertainment which came to define what was meant by 'quality' cinema.

Aesthetically, the 'documentary attitude' is credited with (or blamed for) the dominance of social realism and an ambivalence towards 'artiness' in British cinema. Certainly, a reading of Grierson might confirm such a view: the origins, he declares, 'lay in sociological rather than aesthetic ideas'. Michael Balcon* extended the influence of social realism when he claimed the patrimony of the documentarists for Ealing*: 'More and more,' he said, the feature film 'makes use of characters and action arising out of contemporary problems, such as were handled by the documentarists: labour problems, class problems, problems of psychology. More and more it is prepared to break away from the studio and its hothouse plots, to use real places and real people.' All this, however, is to create a myth of the documentary movement, unifying a set of diverse practices and aesthetic strategies under a homogenised 'realism', collapsing together the reportage of *Housing Problems* (1935) with the lyricism of *Song of Ceylon* (1934) and the modernism of *Night Mail* (1936), *Pett and Pott* (1934), or Len Lye's experiments in animation. While Grierson himself undoubtedly had little time for aesthetic debate, it is reasonable to conjecture that had it not been for the pressures of wartime propaganda, he might not have been able to keep the lid on experimentation and debate for ever. It is the mythology of the documentary movement, a mythology which Grierson promoted, which has formed the decisive critical discourse in British film culture rather than an attentiveness to the films themselves. JC

Bib: Ian Aitken, *Film and Reform: John Grierson and the Documentary Film Movement* (1990).

BRITISH FILM INSTITUTE (BFI)

British institution, established in 1933 to 'encourage the use and development of the cinematograph as a means of entertainment and instruction'. From the beginning, the BFI occupied an uncertain territory between culture, education and industry. As a potential instrument of cultural regulation, it evoked the suspicion of the industry, who attempted to restrict its sphere of influence to instructional films, and of educationalists, who resented its subservience to the industry. By the late 1940s its future was in doubt, but the Radcliffe Committee of 1947 attempted to give it a more clearly cultural remit.

An information service was established in 1934, particularly for the support of education and culture, and the National Film Archive (initially the National Film Library) in 1935, with a distribution library from 1938. The Scottish Film Council was established in 1934, initially as a committee of the BFI but subsequently as an autonomous body. In 1952, the BFI took over the Festival of Britain's Telekinema as the National Film Theatre, building its own theatre in 1957, and instituting the London Film Festival the same year. In the 1960s it began to build up a chain of Regional Film Theatres. The Education Department reached the peak of its influence in the 1970s, when it was central to many of the debates in film culture and initiated the development of Film Studies in higher education, and in the 1980s, when it made important advances in establishing Media Studies in the school curriculum. By the 1980s the BFI Library was the largest collection of books and periodicals on film and television in the world. The Institute has published *Sight and Sound** since 1933, and BFI Publishing has become a major force in media publishing. In production, the BFI Experimental Film Fund was established in 1951 under the chairmanship of Michael Balcon*, changing its name to the BFI Production Board in 1966.

Recession and the contortions demanded of cultural institutions by a market economy have left their mark on the BFI, and it still occupies the same uncertain territory between culture, education and industry, attempting to address an increasing number of constituencies with decreasing resources, torn between a new entrepreneurial desire to be a major player in the British film and television industries and old public service responsibilities to research, archives, education and culture. Its record of achievement, however, is impressive, and it has been one of the few resources of British film culture which might be envied from outside. JC

BRITISH NEW WAVE

British movement. The films usually associated with a 'British New Wave' between 1959 and 1963 had their roots in Free Cinema*, in the journal *Sequence**, and in the documentaries of Humphrey Jennings* and the neo-realism of Roberto Rossellini and Vittorio De Sica. More immediately, they had their roots in British theatre and literature. Woodfall, the main production company, was formed by Tony Richardson*, John Osborne and the producer Harry Saltzman, with the explicit intention of exploiting the success of the Royal Court Theatre, and the films are – without exception – adaptations of novels, stories or plays, mostly written in the mid-1950s. The new wave in the cinema can be read as the backwash of a wave which had happened elsewhere. (Lindsay Anderson* attributed this dependence on adaptation to the reluctance of British backers to put money into anything which had not proven its success elsewhere.)

What was new, however, was that the key directors (Anderson, Tony Richardson, John Schlesinger*, Karel Reisz*) all directed their first features between 1959 and 1963, translating to the cinema some of their generation's revolt against the complacency of the older generation and the metropolitan bourgeoisie, and finding in the northern working class a vitality and toughness which the postwar cinema of Ealing* had not reflected. They brought with them a new sense of place and observation – 'the poetry of everyday life' – which they had learned from their own documentary experience. What was not new about the new wave was that the directors were all 'Oxbridge' men. Their identification with northern working-class men was from the outside, characteristically refracted through a romantic individualism (which they shared with the French New Wave) which sought out rough, alienated heroes at odds with their society, and punished the women who trapped them into conformity. In translating the celebrated anger and vitality of the new culture they also translated some of the misogyny which fuelled it.

The British New Wave was short-lived, most of its directors working in America from the mid-1960s. Its descendants might be traced in television rather than cinema, where the progressive realist drama of the 1960s and 1970s kept a small domestic flame alive. JC

Bib: John Hill, *Sex, Class and Realism: British Cinema, 1956–1963* (1986).

Films Include: *Room at the Top, Look Back in Anger* (1959); *The Entertainer, Saturday Night and Sunday Morning* (1960); *A Taste of Honey* (1961); *The Loneliness of the Long Distance Runner, A Kind of Loving* (1962); *This Sporting Life, Billy Liar* (1963).

BUCHANAN, Jack

Helensburgh, Scotland 1891 – London 1957

British actor associated with the top-hat-and-tails school of musical comedy in the 1930s. Following success on both sides of the Atlantic in musical revue (including a Broadway success with Jessie Matthews*), Buchanan made his first talkies in Hollywood, where he partnered Jeanette MacDonald in Ernst Lubitsch's *Monte Carlo* (1930, US), before returning to Britain to become one of the most popular and debonair leading men of the sophisticated British musical. He partnered Anna Neagle* in *Goodnight Vienna* (1932), Fay Wray in *When Knights Were Bold* (1936), and starred with Maurice Chevalier in René Clair's *Break the News* (1938), a film which Buchanan also produced. Unfortunately for the British musical, he never partnered Jessie Matthews on film. He was often claimed as Britain's answer to Fred Astaire, and the two can be seen together to excellent effect in Vincente Minnelli's *The Band Wagon* (1953, US). JC

BURTON, Richard

Richard Jenkins; Pontrhydfen, Wales 1925 – Switzerland 1984

British actor. Burton's career is rather too conveniently divided into two periods: Before and After *Cleopatra*. Before *Cleopatra* (1963, US) he is characterised as an actor of great power and passion; after, he is merely a celebrity. The fact that the Fall turns around a woman – and not only *a* woman, but Elizabeth Taylor – and around an abandonment of theatrical integrity in favour of Hollywood stardom, strengthens the suspicion that Burton may be the most mythologised of British actors. Certainly, his stage career in the 1940s and 1950s suggests a theatrical potential never fully realised. But his cinema career was always uneven, and much of the best was saved to the last. In his prelapsarian phase, he was suitably heroic (if unchallenged) in a number of Hollywood epics, notably *The Robe* (1953, US) and *Alexander the Great* (1956, US); he was miscast in *Look Back in Anger* (1959) in an attempt to bring some of his acquired Hollywood glamour to the 'kitchen sink'; while Nicholas Ray in *Amère victoire/Bitter Victory* (1957, Fr./UK) perhaps recognised a kindred spirit in Burton's characteristic blend of insolence, sensitivity and sadness. After the Fall, he produced some of his best cinematic performances in roles which were far removed from the heroism of his youth – the disillusioned, self-destructive and weary cynicism of *Who's Afraid of Virginia Woolf?* (1966, US), *The Night of the Iguana* (1964, US) and *The Comedians* (1967, US). He played the aging Trotsky in Joseph Losey's* *L'Assassinio di Trotsky/The Assassination of Trotsky* (1972, It/Fr); and in *The Spy Who Came in from the Cold* (1965) and, poignantly, in his last film, Mike Radford's *Nineteen Eighty-Four* (1984), completed just before his death, he exposed some of the more fragile qualities which the strength of his famous theatrical voice had often concealed. JC

Bib: Melvyn Bragg, *Rich: A Biography of Richard Burton* (1988).

BYRNE, Eddie

Dublin 1911–1981

Irish actor. Byrne was already an experienced variety theatre performer at Dublin's premier venue, the Theatre Royal, before playing in *I See a Dark Stranger* (1946), the first of more than twenty films he acted in. He usually played Irish character roles in British films, having the lead in only one film, *Time Gentlemen Please!* (1952), in which he was a tramp who disturbs the equanimity of a sedate English village. His later career included roles in *Mutiny on the Bounty* (1962, US) and *Star Wars* (1977, US), his last film. KR

Other Films Include: *Captain Boycott* (1947); *The Gentle Gunman* (1952); *Happy Ever After* (1954); *Rooney* (1958).

BYRNE, Gabriel

Dublin 1950

Irish actor, who began his career at the Dublin Shakespeare Society in 1974 and thereafter worked at the Project Theatre when Jim Sheridan* was in charge. His first television appearances were in *The Riordans*, a rural soap, and its successor, *Bracken*. His first film role was in Thaddeus O'Sullivan's* *On a Paving Stone Mounted* (1978), and his first commercial cinema roles in *The Outsider* (1979) and *Excalibur* (1981, US). Thereafter, he began to carve out a career as an international star through memorable roles as an investigative journalist in *Defence of the Realm* (1985), an Irish-American gangster in the Coen brothers' *Miller's Crossing* (1990, US), and as a traveller/gypsy in *Into the West* (1992). His good looks and screen presence would seem to make him ideal material as a potential commercial cinema star, but his career has yet to achieve megastar status, a result perhaps of a string of less than memorable roles in such films as Michael Mann's *The Keep* (1983, US), Costa-Gavras' *Hanna K* (1983), Ken Russell's* *Gothic* (1986), and Frank Deasy and Joe Lee's *The Courier* (1987). He has continuing theatrical interests, and was executive producer of *Into the West*. Byrne lives mainly in the USA and was married until 1993 to actress Ellen Barkin, opposite whom he starred in *Siesta* (1987, US). KR

Other Films Include: *A Dangerous Woman* (1993, US); *Trial by Jury* (1994, US); *A Simple Twist of Fate* (1995, US); *The Usual Suspects* (1995, US).

C

CAINE, Michael

Maurice Micklewhite; London 1933

British actor, who came to prominence as one of the representative figures of London's 'swinging 1960s' (when he shared a flat with Terence Stamp* in the King's Road). A graduate of Joan Littlewood's Theatre

Workshop, he played bit parts in such films as *Carve Her Name with Pride* (1958) and *The Wrong Arm of the Law* (1962), attracted attention in *Zulu* (1963), and achieved stardom as Harry Palmer in *The Ipcress File* (1965). His persona as a crafty Cockney Lothario was established in *Alfie* (1966), a film which was surprisingly successful in the US and which won him his first Oscar nomination. Never a romantic star, marked indelibly as basically an 'ordinary bloke' by his accent (a trademark as well as a mark on which he trades), Caine is an intensely professional cinematic actor, whose performances are carefully measured and whose stardom is based on craft as much as charisma. 'In a play,' he says, 'the person who's speaking is getting all the attention. You're not looking at the other person. But in a movie, the person who's speaking doesn't exist unless someone reacts. Movies are about reacting, and that's what I do particularly well.' He did it well enough to steal the Oscar nomination from Laurence Olivier* in their two-hander, *Sleuth* (1973), and to win an Oscar for Best Supporting Actor in Woody Allen's *Hannah and Her Sisters* (1986, US). Not always wise in his choice of films, he gave one of his best performances in partnership with Sean Connery* in John Huston's *The Man Who Would Be King* (1975, US). JC

Bib: Michael Caine, *Acting in Films: An actor's take on movie making* (1990).

Other Films Include: *The Wrong Box, Funeral in Berlin, Hurry Sundown* [US] (1966); *Billion Dollar Brain* (1967); *The Magus* (1968); *The Italian Job* (1969); *Get Carter* (1970); *Kidnapped, Zee & Co* (1972); *The Black Windmill* (1974); *The Romantic Englishwoman/Une Anglaise romantique* (1975, UK/Fr.); *California Suite* (1978, US); *Dressed to Kill* (1980, US); *Victory/Escape to Victory* (1981, US); *Deathtrap* (1982, US); *The Honorary Consul* (1983); *Educating Rita* (1983); *Mona Lisa* (1986); *On Deadly Ground* (1994, US).

CALVERT, Phyllis London 1915

British actress, who became a star in the Gainsborough* melodramas of the 1940s. Previously she had played an effective lead to George Formby* in *Let George Do It!* (1940), and had worked with Carol Reed* on *Kipps* (1941) and *The Young Mr Pitt* (1942), but it was *The Man in Grey* (1943) which brought wide popular appeal. Typecast as the virtuous victim, and caught between Margaret Lockwood's* scheming, James Mason's* cruelty and Stewart Granger's* swashbuckling, Calvert was able to make virtue interesting, and, in *Fanny by Gaslight* (1944) in particular, there is nothing insipid about her femininity. By the 1950s she was playing more varied dramatic parts, with her performance as the mother in *Mandy* (1952) her most satisfying role. JC

Other Films Include: *Two Thousand Women, Madonna of the Seven Moons* (1944); *They Were Sisters* (1945); *Men of Two Worlds, The Magic Bow* (1946); *Time Out of Mind* (1947, US); *The Golden Madonna* (1949); *Appointment with Danger* [US], *Mr Denning Drives North* (1951); *The Net* (1953); *Indiscreet* (1958, US); *Twisted Nerve* (1968).

CARDIFF, Jack — Great Yarmouth 1914

British cinematographer and director, who became an expert on colour cinematography with Technicolor in the 1930s. He was a camera assistant at the age of 13, graduating to camera operator for René Clair's *The Ghost Goes West* (1936), and for Europe's first Technicolor film, *Wings of the Morning* (1937). In the late 1930s he made a series of documentary shorts, shot mainly in India, to gain experience of the new colour system, returning to Britain as co-cinematographer on *The Great Mr Handel* (1942). He was snapped up by Michael Powell and Emeric Pressburger* for *The Life and Death of Colonel Blimp* (1943), *A Matter of Life and Death* (1946), *Black Narcissus* (1947) – for which he won an Academy Award – and *The Red Shoes* (1948). For Alfred Hitchcock*, he photographed *Under Capricorn* (1949), with its exceptionally long takes. Cardiff turned to directing in the late 1950s, with *Sons and Lovers* (1960) as his most successful film, but he remained primarily a cinematographer. JC

Other Films Include: **As Cinematographer** – *Western Approaches* (1944); *Scott of the Antarctic* [co-ph] (1948); *The African Queen* (1952); *The Barefoot Contessa* (1954, US); *War and Peace* (1956, US); *The Prince and the Showgirl* (1957); *The Vikings* (1958, US); *Death on the Nile* (1978); *Conan the Destroyer* (1984, US); *Rambo First Blood Part II* (1985). **As Director** – *Intent to Kill* (1958); *Young Cassidy* [completed for John Ford] (1965).

CAREY, Patrick — London 1917

Irish director and cameraman. From a theatrical family, Carey worked for several years on the Dublin stage, but from 1945 he began working in films in Britain, shooting his first film, a documentary, in 1947. Working mainly in Asia during the following six years, he was one of the crew that filmed the 1953 ascent of Mount Everest. Continuing to work in Britain, and for the National Film Board of Canada, he specialised in 'nature documentaries'. He won an Oscar in 1967 for his photography on *Wild Wings* (1967), after three earlier films had been nominated for the award. One of these was Carey's most admired film, *Yeats Country* (1965), which drew on the Sligo landscape to evoke W. B. Yeats' poetry. Carey rarely worked in feature production, though he was second unit director-cameraman on *A Man for All Seasons* (1966). KR

CARROLL, Madeleine

Marie Madeleine Bernadette O'Carroll; West Bromwich 1906 – Marbella, Spain 1987

British actress, who became one of a few British stars to achieve international stardom in the 1930s. Originally a French teacher, she made her stage debut in 1927, only a year before she appeared in film. Her lack of the usual theatrical background may account for her unmannered performances. She made an international impact in Victor Saville's* *I Was a Spy* (1933), in which she played the Belgian nurse Marthe Cnockhaert, who simultaneously spied for the Allies and tended the German wounded. Alfred Hitchcock* ensured her stardom, pairing her, as one of the first of his cool blondes, with Robert Donat* in *The 39 Steps* (1935) and with John Gielgud* in *Secret Agent* (1936). Her particular appeal was more attuned to Hollywood, and it is no surprise that she moved there in 1936, starring with Ronald Colman* in *The Prisoner of Zenda* (1937, US). She retired from film in 1949, and subsequently worked for UNESCO. JC

Other Films Include: *The Guns of Loos, The First Born* (1928); *The Crooked Billet, L'Instinct* [Fr.], *The American Prisoner, Atlantic* (1929); *The 'W' Plan, Young Woodley, French Leave, Escape, The School for Scandal* (1930); *Fascination* (1931); *Sleeping Car* (1933); *The Dictator* (1935); *White Cradle Inn* (1947).

'CARRY ON . . .' FILMS

British series, which began unthreateningly with *Carry On Sergeant*, intended as a one-off in 1958, initiated the series with *Carry On Nurse* (1959), continued with up to four films a year through the 1960s, appeared intermittently in the 1970s until *Carry On Emmannuelle* (1978), and then reappeared in 1992 with its salute to the quinquennial celebrations, *Carry On Columbus*. The thirty films in the series were produced by Peter Rogers and directed by Gerald Thomas, with a core cast which included Kenneth Williams, Sid James, Kenneth Connor, Charles Hawtrey, Joan Sims, Hattie Jacques and Barbara Windsor. The films belong in the music-hall tradition of George Formby* and Max Miller, and their humour is in the tradition of the seaside postcard ('pinched bums, big tits, screaming queens and henpecked husbands are the conditions of their existence'; 'their most celebrated feature, their great comic glory, is the reliance on innuendo' – Andy Medhurst). In the early films, the objects of the carryings on were institutions, but by the mid-1960s the series had discovered a rich seam in the send-up of film genres – Bond movies* (*Carry On Spying*, 1964), epics (*Carry On Cleo*, 1964), and empire (*Carry On ... Up the Khyber*, 1968). By the end of the permissive 1970s cinemagoers were harder to scandalise, and the '*Carry On ...*' films were consigned to endless repeats on weekend afternoon television. JC

Bib: Andy Medhurst, 'Carry On Camp', *Sight and Sound* (August 1992).

CAVALCANTI, Alberto

Rio de Janeiro, Brazil 1897 – Paris, France 1982

British/Brazilian director. Educated in law in Brazil, and in art in Geneva, Cavalcanti became an art director in Paris in the 1920s, associating himself with the avant-garde art movement, and particularly with Surrealism. His first major film was *Rien que les heures* (1926), a 'city film' which anticipated Walther Ruttmann's *Berlin: Symphony of a Great City* (1927). In 1934 he was invited by John Grierson* to join the GPO Film Unit, to which he brought a concern with technical innovation and experiment that often ran counter to Grierson's more social reformist agenda. Relations between the two were strained. Harry Watt*, however, credits him with training his generation of documentary film-makers: 'I believe fundamentally,' he said, 'that the arrival of Cavalcanti in the GPO Film Unit was the turning point of British documentary.' Cavalcanti's best known directed films with the Unit, *Pett and Pott* (1934) and *Coal Face* (1935), are distinctive in their intricate editing of sound and image, and his productions (for which he also supervised sound) include *Night Mail* (1936), *North Sea* (1938) and *Spare Time* (1939).

Cavalcanti left the Grierson group when it became the Crown Film Unit and joined Ealing Studios, where he directed two of the studio's best films of the early 1940s, *Went the Day Well?* (1942) and the 'Ventriloquist's Dummy' episode of *Dead of Night* (1945). But his real importance at Ealing was in training and developing new directors like Robert Hamer*, Charles Frend and Charles Crichton*, and in production. Michael Balcon* credits Cavalcanti with a special role in establishing the 'trademark' of Ealing*: 'The whole of the Ealing output had a certain stamp on it. Whether I would have done it on my own I don't know. But most certainly I acknowledge ... that of all the help I got his is the help that was most important.' From 1949, Cavalcanti divided his time between Brazil, where he founded the Brazilian Film Institute; Europe, where he directed in Britain, France, Italy, Austria and Romania; and the US, where he taught at UCLA. JC

Bib: Elizabeth Sussex, 'Cavalcanti in England', *Sight and Sound* (August 1975).

Other Films Include: *Le Train sans yeux* (1925, Fr.); *La P'tite Lilie* (1927, Fr.); *La Jalousie du barbouillé* (1928, Fr.); *Le Petit Chaperon rouge* (1929, Fr.); *Coralie et Cie* (1933, Fr.); *We Live in Two Worlds, The Line to Tschierva Hut* (1937); *The Chiltern Country* (1938); *La Cause commune* [made in UK for showing in France] (1940); *Champagne Charlie, Trois Chansons de la résistance/Soup Before Sunrise* [made in UK for Free French Army] (1944); *Nicholas Nickleby, They Made Me a Fugitive* (1947); *Simão o coalho/Simon the One-Eyed* (1952, Brazil); *Herr Puntila und sein Knecht Matti* (1955, Aus.); *La Prima notte* (1958, It.); *Thus Spake Theodor Herzl* (1967, Israel).

CHANNEL 4

British institution, whose establishment in 1982 signalled a change in the relationship between British cinema and television. Channel 4 was conceived as a publisher-broadcaster rather than a producer-broadcaster like the BBC or the ITV companies, with the Channel commissioning its original work rather than producing programmes itself. Under this system, the series 'Film on Four' was established, commissioning films for television from independent producers, with investment set at around £500,000. In operation the system became a form of patronage for the low- to medium-budget feature film, with Channel 4 holding back transmission of some films to give them life in the cinema, entering into partnerships with the BFI* Production Board or British Screen, or investing in (continental) European films. Out of this came such films as *The Draughtsman's Contract* (1982), *A Letter to Brezhnev* (1985), *My Beautiful Laundrette* (1985), and investment in, for example, *Paris, Texas* (1984, Ger./Fr.). In addition, the legislation which established Channel 4 wrote into its remit that it should experiment and innovate and cater for audiences not previously addressed. Accordingly, the commissioning editor for Independent Film and Video had the responsibility of seeking new production from oppositional groups like Cinema Action, from small regionally based companies, and from the Workshop Movement* which the Channel helped to develop. The remit was extended to include investment in Third World cinema. At the beginning of the 1980s, at one level Channel 4 seemed to provide the context for a medium-budget art cinema, and at another level it was creating a diversity of access to film production – and, as a national broadcaster, to film viewing. Government legislation in 1991 made Channel 4 more dependent than it had been on advertising revenue, and the accountants had to count the costs of patronage more carefully. While support of the Workshops was cut off at the beginning of the 1990s, and much of the radical excitement soured into scepticism, Channel 4 still deserves credit for fostering such directors as Terence Davies*, Isaac Julien* and Derek Jarman*. In the 1990s, it has surprised many by its success in an increasingly commercial broadcasting environment, and it is still a major part of the infrastructure of a new British art cinema. JC

Bib: John Pym, *Film on Four: A Survey, 1982–1991* (1992).

CHRISTIE, Julie — Chukua, India 1941

British actress, who emerged as a star in the 1960s, representing the liberated woman before women's liberation was formally recognised. In *Billy Liar* (1963), in her first major role, she is the free spirit in the grim northern city who cuts through the male dreams of leaving, and actually escapes, leaving Tom Courtenay's bags on the station platform as monuments to lost desire. 'With Julie Christie,' says Alexander Walker, 'the British cinema caught the train south.' The train was heading for the swinging 1960s, for which Christie became an icon. In *Darling* (1965), the iconic movie of the period, her character is both celebrated for her freedom and punished for her independence, playing out the ambivalence of the sexual revolution. Her performance won her an Oscar, and awards from the New York Critics and the British Film Academy. Carrying her independence into her personal life and career, Christie has been discriminating and her filmography contains few of the clunkers which pepper the careers of most British stars of her generation. She has been as successful in Hollywood as in Britain in securing interesting projects, including her role in Altman's *McCabe & Mrs. Miller* (1971) for which she received an Oscar nomination. Her recent work has included a number of voice commentaries on television documentaries on political issues, and her commitment to feminism led her to accept a lead role in Sally Potter's* *The Gold Diggers* (1983), a low-budget film with an all-women crew on which all participants were paid the same wage. JC

Other Films Include: *Young Cassidy, Doctor Zhivago (*1965); *Fahrenheit 451* (1966); *Far from the Madding Crowd* (1967); *Petulia* (1968, US); *In Search of Gregory* (1969); *The Go-Between* (1970); *Don't Look Now* (1973); *Shampoo* (1974, US); *Nashville* [cameo as herself] (1975, US); *The Demon Seed* (1977, US); *Heaven Can Wait* (1978, US); *Memoirs of a Survivor* (1981); *The Return of the Soldier, Heat and Dust* (1983); *Power* (1986, US); *Miss Mary* (1987, Argentina); *La Mémoire tatouée/Secret Obsession* (1988, Fr/Tunisia); *Fools of Fortune* (1990).

CLARKE, T. E. B.

Thomas Ernest Bennett Clarke; Watford 1907 – Surrey 1989

British scriptwriter, who was a contract writer at Ealing from 1943 until 1957, responsible for a number of the films by which Ealing* comedy came to be defined: *Hue and Cry* (1947), *Passport to Pimlico* (1949), *The Lavender Hill Mob* (1951) and *The Titfield Thunderbolt* (1953). Clarke was mainstream Ealing, the Ealing of the self-regulating community in its 'gentle revolution' (Michael Balcon's* phrase) against postwar bureaucracy, as opposed to the sharper comedy of Robert Hamer* or Alexander Mackendrick*. Though his characteristic form was comedy, he also co-wrote for Basil Dearden* the moralising fantasy *The Halfway House* (1944), and the police drama *The Blue Lamp* (1950) which created the character of P.C. George Dixon for Jack Warner*. Clarke won an Oscar and an award at Venice for *The Lavender Hill Mob*. JC

Bib: T. E. B. Clarke, *This is Where I Came In* (1974).

Other Films Include: *For Those in Peril* (1944); *Who Done It?* (1956); *Barnacle Bill* (1957); *A Tale of Two Cities, Gideon's Day, Law and Disorder* (1958); *Sons and Lovers* (co-sc., 1960).

CLEESE, John

Weston-super-Mare 1939

British actor. It is difficult to dissociate Cleese, a graduate of the Cambridge Footlights comedy revue, from his television work on *Monty Python's Flying Circus* (1969–74) and *Fawlty Towers* (1975, 1979). His comic brilliance in those series, owing as much to physical routines as to the nuances of dialogue or character development, makes it difficult to see him without expecting the hysteria to burst through, a funny walk to take over, or a dead parrot to be slapped on the table. Many of his most popular film performances derive from routines – the Monty Python films or *The Secret Policeman's Ball* (1980) – but in *A Fish Called Wanda* (1988), which he scripted and on which he collaborated with Charles Crichton*, he showed the potential of his basic persona for more sustained comic development with a performance that won him a BAFTA Best Actor award. JC

Other Films Include: *Interlude* (1967); *The Best House in London, The Rise and Rise of Michael Rimmer, The Magic Christian* (1969); *And Now for Something Completely Different* (1971); *Monty Python and the Holy Grail* (1975); *Monty Python's Life of Brian* (1979); *Time Bandits* (1981); *The Secret Policeman's Other Ball, Monty Python Live at the Hollywood Bowl*; *Monty Python's The Meaning of Life* (1983); *Silverado* [US], *Clockwise* (1985); *The Secret Policeman's Third Ball*

(1987); *Erik the Viking* (1989); *Mary Shelley's Frankenstein* (1994, US).

CLOSE UP

British/Swiss film journal, published in English in Switzerland from 1927, edited by Kenneth Macpherson and Winifred Bryher, with articles in the early issues by H. D. (Hilda Doolittle), Dorothy Richardson, Gertrude Stein and Eisenstein, and contributions to the later issues from John Grierson*, Ralph Bond and Paul Rotha*. Financed by Bryher's personal fortune, *Close Up* was aimed at a cinephile readership. Intellectually, it belonged to the same contradictory current of English modernism as the London Film Society*, arguing passionately for the art of the film and the avant-garde, pessimistic about the arrival of sound, but defending the right of the masses to entertainment ('as long as they desire eyewash and bunk they must have it'). *Close Up* was against censorship and cosmopolitan in its interests, with a special issue on 'Black cinema and race' in 1929, and sophisticated articles on psychoanalysis and the cinema. In 1930, Macpherson directed what Peter Wollen* calls 'the one outstanding British avant-garde film of the period', *Borderline*, starring H. D., with Paul and Eslanda Robeson* in the cast. The journal folded in 1933.

The interest of *Close Up* for an intellectual history of the cinema was revived in the 1980s by feminist work (especially by Anne Friedberg) that looked in particular at the work of H. D., Bryher and Richardson on psychoanalysis and issues of spectatorship. JC

COLMAN, Ronald

Richmond, Surrey 1891 –
Santa Barbara, California 1958

British actor. Colman emigrated to America in 1920 and his most popular starring roles belong to the history of Hollywood cinema, but while his British cinema career was brief, it is noteworthy. He was recruited for film from the London stage, and was one of the actors placed under contract by Cecil Hepworth* in his attempt to develop a stable of British stars. He made two films with Hepworth: *Sheba* (1919) and *Anna the Adventuress* (1920). His career in Hollywood was slow to start, but after he was chosen by Lillian Gish to star opposite her in *The White Sister* (1923, US), it never looked back. One of the most popular stars of both the silent and the sound screen over three decades, he was, after Chaplin, the cinema's best loved Englishman. 'Ronald Colman,' wrote one of his contemporaries, 'is good for humanity. Doctors might prescribe a dose of him for depressed patients or for those with acute melancholia. He should be encouraged for a world that is too humdrum and too respectable.' JC

Other British Films: *The Toilers, A Daughter of Eve, Snow in the Desert, A Son of David* (1919); *The Black Spider* (1920). **American Films Include**: *Stella Dallas* (1925); *Beau Geste* (1926); *Bulldog Drummond* (1929); *Bulldog Drummond Strikes Back* (1934); *Clive of India, A Tale of Two Cities* (1935); *Lost Horizon, The Prisoner of Zenda* (1937); *The Light That Failed* (1940); *The Talk of the Town, Random Harvest* (1942); *Kismet* (1943).

COMERFORD, Joe — Born 1949

Irish director and writer. Comerford is one of the main contributors to recent developments in Irish cinema. His films have brought to the screen previously ignored or excluded marginal social groups: drug addicts in *Withdrawal* (1974), working-class teenagers in *Down the Corner* (1978), travellers in *Traveller* (1982), and IRA renegades in *Reefer and the Model* (1988), a film which won the Europa prize for best film in 1988. Comerford's films are often informed by a gloomy, dark image of the Irish, with the inarticulate incest victim, Angela, in *Traveller* an extreme example. Among his other films is *High Boot Benny* (1993). KR

CONNAUGHTON, Shane — Born 19[?]

Irish writer. Connaughton trained as an actor, but became a writer of stage and television plays and films. He was nominated, with Jim Sheridan*, for Best Adapted Screenplay for the Oscar-winning *My Left Foot* (1989). Though he did not win an award for that film, he had already collected an Oscar in 1981 for writing the short, *The Bottom Dollar*. His writing, especially in the linked stories published as *A Border Station* (1989), and in his original script for *The Playboys* (1992), centres on his own childhood. Connaughton's work is usually set in and near the village of Redhills, Co. Cavan, where he was brought up and where *The Playboys* was shot. KR

Bib: Kevin Rockett, 'From Atlanta to Dublin', *Sight and Sound* (June 1992).

CONNERY, Sean — Edinburgh 1930

British actor. The accepted myth of Connery casts him as an Edinburgh milkman, body builder and art school model, entering a stage career through the chorus line of *South Pacific*, appearing in films from 1956, and becoming a star 'accidentally' when he was chosen to play James Bond* in *Dr No* (1962). There is, however, a concealed history in his career in television drama in the late 1950s.

Among a number of distinguished roles, including Vronsky in an adaptation of *Anna Karenina* and Hotspur in *The Age of Kings*, Connery played the demanding lead role of the derelict boxer in a live BBC version of Rod Serling's *Requiem for a Heavyweight* (1957), a role created by Jack Palance in one of the key plays of American live television drama.

Bond, however, made Connery a star, and the association was so strong that he could have been trapped in the part. Always unpretentious as an actor, he seemed destined to play interesting variations on the theme of sardonic sexuality. What is remarkable, however, is the increasing depth which his basic persona has acquired with age. Always good to look at, with enough irony to translate good looks into playful sexual danger, his later screen presence has developed the contours of a landscape embedded with history. Since *Robin and Marian* (1976, US), and increasingly in films like *Highlander* (1986), *Der Name der Rose/The Name of the Rose* (1986, Ger./It./Fr.), *The Untouchables* (1987, US) and *Indiana Jones and the Last Crusade* (1989, US), he has claimed, like Clint Eastwood and John Wayne, the prerogative of the aging male star to play against his own legend. Liberated from the romantic lead, he has been able to counterpoint age and experience against youth and vigour, using his own mythic persona to give the counterpoint an elegiac tone.

Connery won an Oscar as Best Supporting Actor for *The Untouchables*, and a BAFTA award as Best Actor for *The Name of the Rose*. JC

Other Films Include: *No Road Back, Hell Drivers* (1957); *Darby O'Gill and the Little People* (1959, US); *The Longest Day* (1962, US); *From Russia with Love* (1963); *Marnie* [US], *Goldfinger* (1964); *The Hill, Thunderball* (1965); *A Fine Madness* (1966, US); *You Only Live Twice* (1967); *Shalako* (1968); *La tenda rossa/Krasnaya palatka/The Red Tent* (1969, It./USSR); *The Molly Maguires* (1970, US); *The Anderson Tapes* [US], *Diamonds are Forever* (1971); *The Offence* (1973); *Zardoz, Murder on the Orient Express* (1974); *The Wind and the Lion* (1975, US); *A Bridge Too Far* (1977); *The First Great Train Robbery* (1978); *Time Bandits, Outland* (1981); *Five Days One Summer* (1982); *Never Say Never Again* (1983); *The Russia House, The Hunt for Red October, Highlander II – The Quickening* (1990, US); *Robin Hood: Prince of Thieves* (1991, US); *Rising Sun* (1993, US); *A Good Man in Africa* (1993, US); *Just Cause, First Knight* (1995, US).

CORK FILM FESTIVAL

Irish film festival. Established in 1956, the Cork Film Festival was the first film festival in Ireland. Its traditional strength has been its eclectic selection of short films. After a period of indecisiveness in the 1970s, it began to engage more fully with the changing Irish film cul-

Stephen Rea in *Angel* (Neil Jordan, 1982).

Hitchcock, John Longden, Anny Ondra (right) in *Blackmail* (Alfred Hitchcock, 1929).

Richard Attenborough and Carol Marsh in *Brighton Rock* (John Boulting, 1947).

Terence Longdon, Kenneth Connor, Leslie Phillips, Cyril Chamberlain, Kenneth Williams in *Carry On Nurse* (Gerald Thomas, 1959).

David Hemmings in *The Charge of the Light Brigade* (Tony Richardson, 1968).

Ben Cross and Nigel Havers in *Chariots of Fire* (Hugh Hudson, 1981).

Jack Hawkins and Donald Sinden in *The Cruel Sea* (Charles Frend, 1953).

Forest Whitaker and Stephen Rea in *The Crying Game* (Neil Jordan, 1992).

Saskia Reeves, Brenda Bruce, Donal McCann, Ciaran Hinds in *December Bride* (Thaddeus O'Sullivan, 1990).

Julie Christie and Dirk Bogarde in *Darling* (John Schlesinger, 1965).

Freda Dowie, Dean Williams, Angela Walsh, Lorraine Ashbourne in *Distant Voices, Still Lives* (Terence Davies, 1988).

Ursula Andress and Sean Connery in *Dr. No* (Terence Young, 1962).

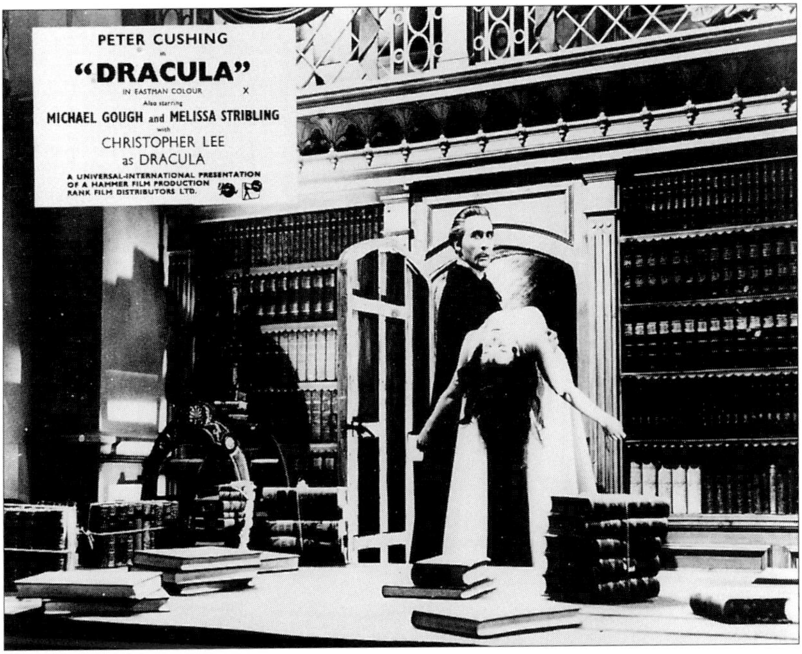

Christopher Lee in *Dracula* (Terence Fisher, 1958).

Drifters (John Grierson, 1929).

Jessie Matthews in *Evergreen* (Victor Saville, 1934).

John Hurt and Richard Harris in *The Field* (Jim Sheridan, 1990).

tural environment of the 1980s. It was for thirty years the only Irish film festival, but there are now five others: the successful Dublin Film Festival, which began in 1986, the pleasurable Galway Film Fleadh (Festival), the modest Derry Film Festival, and two children's film festivals, in Dublin and Belfast. KR

COWARD, Noël

Teddington 1899 – Blue Harbor, Jamaica 1973

British playwright, actor, scriptwriter and producer. An actor since the age of 12, Coward is primarily known as a leading actor and writer of the prewar British theatre. Many of his plays were adapted for the screen in the 1930s: *Cavalcade* (1933), *Bitter Sweet* (1933 and 1940) and *Design for Living* (1933). His first screen acting credit was for two bit parts in D. W. Griffith's *Hearts of the World* (1918), and in the 1950s and 1960s he played cameo roles in such films as *Our Man in Havana* (1960) and *The Italian Job* (1969). Conventionally identified in the theatre as a writer of sparkling dialogue and sophisticated society comedy, a musical lyricist of wit and brilliance, and an actor who took haughtiness to the brink of self-parody, Coward's work in the cinema shows a range of craft, sensitivity and technique. His most significant contri-bution was in the four films on which he worked with David Lean*: *In Which We Serve* (1942), co-directed with Lean, for which he wrote the screenplay and the music, and played a lead part; *This Happy Breed* (1944) and *Blithe Spirit* (1945), both adapted from his stage plays; and *Brief Encounter* (1945), co-written by Lean and Coward and based on Coward's original stage play, *Still Life*. Coward received a Special Academy Award for *In Which We Serve*. JC

Bib: Sheridan Morley, *A Talent to Amuse: A Biography of Noël Coward* (1969).

CRICHTON, Charles

Wallasey 1910

British director, best known for his three classic Ealing comedies*, *Hue and Cry* (1947), *The Lavender Hill Mob* (1951) and *The Titfield Thunderbolt* (1953). He began his career as an assistant editor at London Films, where he cut such films as *The Private Life of Henry VIII* (1933), *Elephant Boy* (1937) and *The Thief of Bagdad* (1940). He began directing at Ealing with *For Those in Peril* (1944) and continued to direct with the studio until *The Man in the Sky* (1957). He made one successful comedy after Ealing closed, *The Battle of the Sexes* (1959), and a low-key thriller, *He Who Rides a Tiger* (1965), but his career in the 1960s was not particularly distinguished. In 1988, however, John Cleese*, with whom he had made a number of training videos, persuaded him to co-script and direct the very successful comedy *A Fish Called Wanda*. JC

Bib: Charles Barr, *Ealing Studios* (1977).

Other Films Include: *Dead of Night* ['The Golfing Story'] (1945); *Against the Wind* (1948); *Dance Hall* (1950); *Hunted* (1952); *The Divided Heart* (1954); *Law and Disorder* (1958).

CUSACK, Cyril

Durban, South Africa 1910 – Dublin 1993

Irish actor. Though born in South Africa, Cusack lived most of his life in Ireland. His first film role was as an evicted child in the Film Company of Ireland's* *Knocknagow* (1918), but he did not come to prominence as a film actor until he played a member of an IRA gang in Carol Reed's* *Odd Man Out* (1947). By then he was a well-established actor at the Abbey Theatre, where he had worked since 1932. He appeared in more than fifty film and television productions. Like most Irish actors, he was rarely given the lead role in films, and his theatrical career was more important artistically. KR

Other Films Include: *Shake Hands with the Devil* (1959); *A Terrible Beauty* (1960); *Fahrenheit 451* (1966); *Poitin* (1978).

CUTTS, Graham

Brighton 1885–1958

British director, who began his career as a northern exhibitor and moved into direction with the apparently sensational *Cocaine* (which had to be retitled *While London Sleeps*) in 1922. Cutts formed a partnership with Herbert Wilcox* and his brother Charles in the early 1920s, before moving to Gainsborough where he was Michael Balcon's* main director at Gaumont-British before the emergence of Alfred Hitchcock. Cutts was a stylist, achieving success with Ivor Novello* on *The Rat* (1925) and its sequel, *The Triumph of the Rat* (1926), with Jack Buchanan* on *Confetti* (1927), and with Betty Balfour* on *The Sea Urchin* (1926). He did not manage the transition to sound with equal success. JC

Other Films Include: *Paddy the Next Best Thing, Woman to Woman* (1923); *Die Spielerin/Chance the Idol* [Ger.], *The Queen was in the Parlour* (1927); *Return of the Rat* (1929); *The Sign of Four* (1932); *Three Men in a Boat* (1933); *Just William* (1939); *Combined Operations* [doc], *Food Manufacture* [doc] (1946).

DALRYMPLE, Ian

Johannesburg, South Africa 1903 – London 1989

British writer, director and producer, described by Roger Manvell as 'one of several enlightened and highly educated young British university men attracted to adopt film-making as a profession during the 1920s and 1930s'. Dalrymple wrote screenplays – many of them adaptations – for some of the most significant films of the 1930s, including two of Michael Powell's* 'quota quickies', *Her Last Affaire* (1935) and *The Brown Wallet* (1936), *The Good Companions* (1933) and *South Riding* (1938) for Victor Saville*, *The Citadel* (1938) for King Vidor, and *Pygmalion* (1938), for which he received an Academy Award. He also co-directed with Saville the excellent *Storm in a Teacup* (1937), which he adapted from James Bridie's stage play. During the war, after scripting *'Pimpernel' Smith* (1941) for Leslie Howard*, he became head of the Crown Film Unit, his productions including *London Can Take It!* (1940), *Target for To-night* (1941) and *Listen to Britain* (1942). He formed his own company, Wessex, in 1946, where he directed one of his most interesting adaptations, *Esther Waters* (co-dir. Peter Proud, 1948), from George Moore's novel, and continued to produce until the late 1960s. JC

DAVIES, Terence

Liverpool 1945

British director, whose small but perfectly formed output over an almost twenty-year period – three shorts and two features between 1974 and 1992 – is one more testimony both to the aesthetic possibilities and the financial difficulties of a British art cinema. Davies' work to date has been largely autobiographical. Both his trilogy, released in 1984 and comprising *Children* (1974), *Madonna and Child* (1980) and *Death and Transfiguration* (1983), and his two features, *Distant Voices, Still Lives* (1988) and *The Long Day Closes* (1992), return to the experience of growing up in Catholic, working-class Liverpool in a family which was both nurturing (the mother) and brutalising (the father). The films are highly formal in their composition, recreating the past like a family album, using studio settings to maintain control, and evoking memory with a soundtrack of radio voices and popular songs. Davies' celebration of the working-class community and the enduring 'mam' has been criticised for its sentimentalising nostalgia, but has been defended as a highly formalised and self-reflexive exploration of male memory. *The Neon Bible* was shown in Cannes (1995) to a mixed reception. JC

DAY-LEWIS, Daniel

London 1957

British actor. Son of the poet Cecil Day-Lewis and Jill Balcon and grandson of Michael Balcon*, Daniel Day-Lewis' film career is marked by a remarkable range and a willingness to take risks in his choice of roles. Apparently carved out for the effete or brooding masculinity of an earlier age, which he plays in *A Room with a View* (1987) and Martin Scorsese's *The Age of Innocence* (1993, US), or for the unrestrained eroticism of *The Unbearable Lightness of Being* (1987, US), Day-Lewis stretches his physical versatility from the athletic dash of Hawkeye in Michael Mann's *The Last of the Mohicans* (1992, US) to his Oscar-winning performance as Christy Brown, the writer confined to a wheelchair by cerebral palsy, in Jim Sheridan's* *My Left Foot* (1989). First achieving recognition as the gay punk in Stephen Frears'* and Hanif Kureishi's* *My Beautiful Laundrette* (1985), Day-Lewis, now on the edge of international stardom, took the same risks with public and box-office acceptability when he played the not particularly attractive Gerry Conlon, one of the Guildford Four who were wrongly imprisoned as IRA bombers, in Sheridan's *In the Name of the Father* (1993). JC

DEAN, Basil

Croydon 1888 – London 1978

British producer and director, who founded Associated Talking Pictures in 1929 and extended Ealing* studios in 1931. Dean was a major figure in London theatre in the 1920s, coming to film as an extension rather than a replacement of his theatre activities. He adapted his own co-authored play, *The Constant Nymph*, twice (in 1928 and 1933), and directed adaptations of Galsworthy's *Loyalties* (1933) and Dodie Smith's *Autumn Crocus* (1934). He also saw the potential of music hall as popular entertainment, signing up Gracie Fields* and George Formby*. He produced Gracie Fields' first film *Sally in Our Alley* (1931) and directed several others, including her best, *Sing As We Go* (1934). For Formby, he established the director/producer team of Anthony Kimmins and Jack Kitchin. Dean was committed to a national cinema, and was opposed to the internationalism which Korda* sought: 'Better that the vulgarity should be our own,' he said, 'and not someone else's.' He returned to the theatre in 1938, handing over Ealing studios to Michael Balcon*. JC

Bib: Basil Dean, *Seven Ages: An Autobiography 1888–1927* (1970), and *The Mind's Eye: An Autobiography 1927–1972* (1972).

Other Films Include: **As Director and Producer** – *The Return of Sherlock Holmes* (1929); *Escape, Birds of Prey* (1930); *Lorna Doone,*

Look Up and Laugh (1935); *The Show Goes On, The First and the Last* (1937).

DEARDEN, Basil

Basil Dear; Westcliffe-on-Sea 1911 – London 1971

and

RELPH, Michael

Broadstone, Dorset 1915

British director, producer, writer team, who worked together from the mid-1940s until Dearden's death in a car accident in 1971. Basil Dearden had joined Basil Dean* as a stage manager in the West End theatre, and accompanied him to Ealing in 1936. At Ealing, he assisted on George Formby* films and co-directed Will Hay* comedies with Hay. His solo directorial debut was *The Bells Go Down* (1943), a film on which Michael Relph was art director. Relph had entered films in 1932 as an art director for Michael Balcon*. He joined Ealing in 1942, working as designer on all Dearden's films and as associate producer on others. Their director-producer-writer team was formed in 1949.

Dearden and Relph, both at Ealing and after, are associated with the social problem film, dealing with issues such as delinquency (*Violent Playground*, 1958), race (*Sapphire*, 1959) and closeted homosexuality (*Victim*, 1961). Critical commentary has tended to treat them as decent but dull, and certainly the cautious narrative form of their films often cocoons the problem they are addressing. But it also throws up difficulties in the way of resolution, and the social (and sexual) tensions in their films are often more interesting than the Big Moral Statement they are trying to make. *Frieda* (1947), directed by Dearden with Relph as associate producer, about a small postwar community adjusting to the idea of a good German, is one of the most interesting, and least discussed, Ealing films, and a brilliant dissection of postwar society. JC

Bib: 'Dearden and Relph: two on a tandem', *Films and Filming* (July 1966).

Other Films Include: **Dearden –** *The Black Sheep of Whitehall* [co-dir. Hay] (1941); *The Goose Steps Out* [co-dir. Hay] (1942); *My Learned Friend* [co-dir. Hay] (1943); *The Half-way House, They Came to a City* (1944); *Dead of Night* ['The Hearse Driver'] (1945). **Dearden/Relph –** *The Captive Heart* (1946); *Saraband for Dead Lovers* (1948); *The Blue Lamp* (1950); *Pool of London* (1951); *The Gentle Gunman* (1952); *The Square Ring* (1953); *The Ship that Died of Shame* (1955); *The Smallest Show on Earth* (1957); *Rockets Galore* (1958); *The League of Gentlemen* (1960); *The Secret Partner* (1961); *The Mind Benders* (1962); *Woman of Straw* (1964); *Khartoum* (1966); *The Assassination Bureau Limited* (1969); *The Man Who Haunted Himself* (1970).

DEL GIUDICE, Filippo

Trani, Italy 1892 – Florence, Italy 1961

British producer, who arrived in Britain as a refugee from Mussolini in 1932, established the Two Cities production company with the director Mario Zampi in 1937, and produced some of the most critically acclaimed films of the 1940s. In an article in *The Quarterly Review of Film and Television* (Summer 1952), Geoffrey Wagner writes, 'It can be claimed that one man [...] effectively created the British prestige cinema. This was Filippo del Giudice who, over a very few years, produced thirty-five films, including *In Which We Serve* (1942), *The Way Ahead* (1944), *The Way to the Stars* (1945), *Odd Man Out* (1947), *Men of Two Worlds* (1946), *School for Secrets* (1946), *Blithe Spirit* (1945), *Henry V* (1945), and *Hamlet* (1948) ... Including *Henry V*, all these films, constituting a remarkable record of quality, were made for an average of £200,000, about half the amount spent by most English producers operating at that time [...]. All these movies were powerful commercial successes; *Henry V* has grossed fifteen million dollars in its limited specialised release in the United States.'

Del Giudice retired to a monastery in 1958. JC

DICKINSON, Thorold

Bristol 1903 – London 1984

British director, who had a richly varied career in the British film industry and in film culture over more than half a century. In the 1920s he was assistant director and editor for George Pearson*, and in the early 1930s he edited *Sing As We Go* (1934) for Basil Dean* and *Midshipman Easy* (1935) for Carol Reed*. He went to Spain during the Civil War and directed two short documentaries, *Spanish ABC* and *Behind the Spanish Lines* (both co-dir. Sidney Cole, 1938). He directed his first feature, *The High Command*, in 1937, and continued to direct feature films consistently though not prolifically throughout the 1940s. As a director, his films are marked by a strong visual imagination which places him outside the mainstream of British cinema of the period, but which at its richest, as in his adaptation of Pushkin, *The Queen of Spades* (1949), rivals the work of Michael Powell* and Emeric Pressburger. He was also programme controller of the London Film Society* throughout the 1930s, and Vice-President of the Association of Cine-Technicians (the industry trade union) from 1936 to 1953. He was an adviser on film in Israel in the early 1950s, and from 1956 to 1960 he directed the film service of the United Nations Office of Public Information. In 1960 Dickinson took up the post of Lecturer in Film Studies at the Slade School of Fine Art, and became Britain's first Professor of Film in 1967. He published *A Discovery of Cinema* in 1971. JC

Bib: Jeffrey Richards, *Thorold Dickinson: The man and his films* (1986).

Other Films Include: *The Arsenal Stadium Mystery* (1939); *Gaslight* (1940); *The Prime Minister* (1941); *The Next of Kin* (1942); *Men of Two Worlds* (1946); *Secret People* (1952); *Hill 24 Doesn't Answer* (1955, Israel).

DILLON, Carmen

London 1908–95

British art director. Trained as an architect and working mainly with Two Cities, Rank and Disney, Dillon established her reputation with the Laurence Olivier* Shakespeare adaptations: *Henry V* (asst. art dir., 1945), *Hamlet* (1948) and *Richard III* (1955). She won an Oscar for *Hamlet* and an Art Direction award at Venice for *The Importance of Being Earnest* (1952). Associated particularly with period reconstruction, she was flexible in her approach. She breaks exuberantly with historical naturalism in *Henry V*, where she combines theatricality with a vivid colour scheme drawn from illuminated manuscripts, but in Joseph Losey's* *The Go-Between* (1970) or Fred Zinnemann's *Julia* (prod. des., 1977) she builds the feel of the period out of closely researched detail. JC

Other Films Include: *The Gentle Sex* (1943); *The Way to the Stars* (1945); *School for Secrets* (1946); *The Browning Version* (1951); *Doctor in the House* (1954); *The Prince and the Showgirl* (1957); *A Tale of Two Cities* (1958); *Sapphire* (1959); *Kidnapped, Carry On Constable* (1960); *Accident* (1967); *Lady Caroline Lamb* (1973); *Butley* (1976).

DONAT, Robert

Manchester 1905 – London 1958

British actor. Gaining international recognition for his supporting role as Culpepper in Alexander Korda's* *The Private Life of Henry VIII* (1933), Donat's performance as Edmond Dantès in *The Count of Monte Cristo* (1934, US) confirmed his stardom. His wry wit in *The 39 Steps* (1935) and *The Ghost Goes West* (1936), combined with the affectionate idealism of *The Citadel* (1938) and *Goodbye, Mr. Chips* (for which he won an Oscar in 1939), made him the most popular male romantic lead of the late 1930s in Britain. Reviewing his performance in Jacques Feyder's *Knight Without Armour* (1937), Graham Greene* said, 'Mr Donat is the best film actor – at any rate in star parts – we possess; he is convincing, his voice has a pleasant roughness and his range is far greater than that of his chief rival for film honours, Mr Laurence Olivier*.' During the war he gave one of his finest performances in Carol Reed's* *The Young Mr. Pitt* (1942), and he continued to extend his range after the war with *The Winslow Boy* (1948). A chronic asthmatic throughout his career, he was only able to complete his last film, *The Inn of the Sixth Happiness* (1958), with the aid of oxygen, and was given a Special Citation by the Academy 'for the valour of his last performance'. JC

Bib: Jeffrey Richards, *The Age of the Dream Palace: Cinema and Society in Britain, 1930–1939* (1984).

DORS, Diana

Diana Fluck; Swindon1931 – London 1984

British actress. 'I was the first sex symbol this country ever had,' Diana Dors claimed in 1966. 'Before me female stars were either pretty or matronly. Sex was just an incidental – best left to the Continentals.' Dors' career began with Rank with an underage debut in *The Shop at Sly Corner* (1946), cameos in the Huggetts series, and appearances in one or two social problem films – notably *Good-time Girl* (1948) and *I Believe in You* (1952) – in which her sexual precociousness was one of the problems. She was a memorably unglamorous kitchen maid in Lean's* *Oliver Twist* (1948), but her most satisfying and critically successful performance was as the condemned murderer Ruth Ellis in *Yield to the Night* (1956). The success of the film failed to ignite the Hollywood career she sought, and her career as a star effectively ended in the 1960s. She returned in 1984 for one final sensitive performance in Losey's* *Steaming*, a film released (in 1985) after the death of both Losey and Dors.

Christine Geraghty compares Dors' sex symbol role to that of Marilyn Monroe and Brigitte Bardot, finding in the construction of each the same public private life, the difficult marriages, the emphasis on the body and body parts (the pout, the lips, the wiggle), the same mixture of knowingness and vulnerability, and the same final retreat – into suicide, privacy, or, in Dors' case, bankruptcy, professional decline and tours of working men's clubs to maintain her lifestyle. The peculiarly British characteristic which Dors added to the sex goddess was humour and a knowing kind of vulgarity.

In an interview, she claimed to have turned down the Shirley Ann Field part in *Saturday Night and Sunday Morning* (1960), a piece of casting which might have left its mark on the masculinity of the social realist cinema. JC

Bib: Christine Geraghty, 'Diana Dors', in Charles Barr (ed.), *All Our Yesterdays: Ninety Years of British Cinema* (1986).

DOUGLAS, Bill

Newcraighall, Scotland 1937-
Barnstaple 1991

British director. Douglas made only four features: the autobiographical trilogy, *My Childhood* (1972), *My Ain Folk* (1974) and *My Way Home* (1979), and his film on the Tolpuddle Martyrs, *Comrades* (1986). The films, however, give evidence of a major European director whom the British film industry was unable to support. *My Childhood* lasts fifty minutes and cost around £4,000 to make. It is, however, one of the most intense and artistically condensed expressions of experience in British cinema. Almost painful in the unsentimental rigour of its style, the trilogy, in the semi-autobiographical tradition of Mark Donskoi, the Soviet director much admired by Douglas, traces Douglas' childhood in a mining village in Scotland during and immediately after the war, through institutionalisation in a children's home and relative liberation in the inanities of National Service, to his first glimpses of a sustaining male relationship. The merits of the films were recognised by critics both at home and overseas, but Douglas failed to gain financial support for further projects until Channel 4* put up the balance to make *Comrades* four years after the script had been completed. Douglas's script of James Hogg's *Confessions of a Justified Sinner*, on which he had worked for twelve years and which was believed by those who had read it to be his best work, had failed to find financial backing at the time of his death at the age of 54. JC

Bib: Eddie Dick, Andrew Noble and Duncan Petrie (eds.), *Bill Douglas: A Lanternist's Account* (1993).

EALING COMEDY

British genre. While Ealing comedy should include the films which Basil Dean* produced with George Formby* and Gracie Fields* in the 1930s, the term usually refers to those comedies made under Michael Balcon* in the postwar period – from *Hue and Cry* (1947) to *Barnacle Bill* (1957) – directed mainly by Charles Crichton*, Henry Cornelius, Charles Frend, Alexander Mackendrick* and Robert Hamer*, and scripted most characteristically by T. E. B. Clarke*. Nostalgia has often imposed a unity on Ealing comedy which misses the variations between the films themselves, and the term 'Ealing comedy' has a certain mythical status, identifying not simply a collection of films but a way of being English. Charles Barr relates this to Michael Frayn's distinction between Herbivore and Carnivore elements in British culture around the time of the Festival of Britain in 1951: 'Festival Britain was the Britain of the radical middle-classes – the do-gooders; the readers of the *News Chronicle*, the *Guardian* and the *Observer*; the signers of petitions; the backbone of the BBC. In short, the Herbivores, or gentle ruminants.' Ealing comedies belonged with the Herbivores.

The ingredients of the mythical genre involve a set of oppositions between settled communities and soulless progress. The herbivorous communities can be represented by the crew of a West Highland puffer, a small business, or a London borough; carnivorous progress can be represented by an American, big business, or Whitehall: respectively, *The Maggie* (1954), *The Man in the White Suit* (1951), *Passport to Pimlico* (1949). The outcome is invariably a triumph of community and consensus over capitalism and bureaucracy. Identified in spirit with the memory of the Blitz and the herbivore Attlee Labour government in its early years, the Carnivores were coming, and by the time of *The Maggie* (1954) the opposition has developed sharp edges.

The genre may have died with Ealing, but the spirit lives on. JC

Bib: Charles Barr, *Ealing Studios* (1977).

EDINBURGH INTERNATIONAL FILM FESTIVAL

British festival, established in 1947 as the first British film festival and then only the third in the world (after Venice and Cannes). It was established by Norman Wilson, editor of *Cinema Quarterly*, the journal of the British Documentary Movement*, and Forsyth Hardy, John Grierson's biographer. Its first advisory committee included Basil Wright* and Paul Rotha*, and its early focus was on screening and discussing world documentary. Under the direction first of Murray Grigor and then of Linda Myles, in the 1970s and early 1980s the festival became an important focus of theoretical discussion, with the first Women and Film conference in 1972; retrospectives and publications on Sam Fuller, Roger Corman, Douglas Sirk and others; special events on psychoanalysis and cinema, history/popular memory, and avant-garde cinema; and 'Scotch Reels', an influential debate on Scottish film culture. In the 1980s, other festivals appeared in Britain – Tyneside, Leeds, Birmingham, Nottingham, for example – with their own distinctive edge and equal claims on subsidy. It remains to be seen whether Edinburgh will discover a distinctive direction for the latter part of the 1990s. JC

ELLIOTT, Denholm London 1922 – Ibiza, Spain 1992

British actor, distinguished as a consistently watchable supporting actor since his film debut in 1949. Elliott's characterisation of the vulnerable, and sometimes shifty, loser was played with enough sensitivity to win him sympathy. He was rewarded with recognition in the 1980s, winning BAFTA awards for his supporting roles in *Trading Places* (1983, US), *A Private Function* (1984), and *Defence of the Realm* (1985). He became part of the Merchant-Ivory* stable in *A Room with a View* (1985) and *Maurice* (1987), and had fun in cameo roles in the Hollywood blockbusters *Raiders of the Lost Ark* (1981, US) and *Indiana Jones and the Last Crusade* (1989, US). JC

Other Films Include: *The Sound Barrier* (1952); *The Cruel Sea, The Heart of the Matter* (1953); *King Rat* (1965); *Alfie* (1966); *A Doll's House* (1973); *Robin and Marian* (1976, US); *Bad Timing* (1980); *Killing Dad* (1989).

ELVEY, Maurice William Seward Folkard; Darlington 1887 – Brighton 1967

British director, distinguished more for the quantity of his work than its quality. Between 1913 and 1957, with around 300 features and innumerable shorts, he is reputed to have made more feature films than any other director in Britain, and may have few rivals anywhere in the world. 'Elvey's position,' says Rachael Low, 'as one of the most important film-makers in England cannot be questioned, whatever the artistic qualities of his work. [...] Although not an originator himself, he was quick to adopt new ideas and to sense what the public liked.' JC

Bib: Rachael Low, *The History of British Film, 1914–1918* (1950), and *The History of British Film, 1918–1928* (1971).

Films Include: *Maria Marten* (1913, also *The Murder in the Red Barn*); *When Knights Were Bold* (1916); *Dombey and Son* (1917); *Adam Bede, Hindle Wakes* (1918); *Comradeship* (1919); *Bleak House* (1920); *The Hound of the Baskervilles* (1921); *The Passionate Friends* (1922); *The Sign of Four* (1923); *Hindle Wakes* (1927); *Sally in our Alley* (1931); *This Week of Grace* (1933); *The Gentle Sex* [co-dir., Leslie Howard], *The Lamp Still Burns* [completed by Elvey after Howard's death] (1943); *Is Your Honeymoon Really Necessary?* (1953); *You Lucky People* (1955).

EVANS, (Dame) Edith

London 1888 – Cranbrook, 1976

British actress, and theatrical dame, who made relatively few films but left her mark as a character actress on those she made. She secured her place in history (and the place of handbags) with her Lady Bracknell in Anthony Asquith's* *The Importance of Being Earnest* (1952). The almost operatic nature of her performance was well suited to Thorold Dickinson's* expressionistic *The Queen of Spades* (1949), and she gave a memorable cameo in *Tom Jones* (1963). Her performance in Bryan Forbes'* *The Whisperers* (1966) as an eccentric old woman, down but not quite out, won her Best Actress awards from the Berlin festival, the British Academy and the New York Film Critics. JC

F

FIELDS, (Dame) Gracie

Grace Stansfield; Rochdale 1898 – Capri, Italy 1979

British actress. By the time she made her film debut in 1931, 'Our Gracie' was already a star of the music hall and a major recording star, with an audience that had followed her progress since 1915 when she left Rochdale and the Lancashire cotton mills to join musical revue. By 1936 she was the most popular British film star and remained among the top three until 1940. Though her popularity dipped during the war, when she elected to remain in Hollywood (where she made three modestly successful films), it recovered afterwards and she continued into retirement abroad as a British national institution, created Dame of the British Empire in 1979, the year of her death.

The secret of her popularity can be heard most clearly in the recordings of her live performances. She plays an audience, goading it into enjoyment, feeding it the kind of cheek that passes for affection, and appealing to a shared contempt for pretension. Even her own claims to be taken seriously as an 'artiste' are constantly undermined by physical and vocal clowning. In the films, she creates the same solidarity with her working-class audience but also functions as the bridge to a national community which crosses class boundaries. As 'consensus personified' (Jeffrey Richards' phrase), Gracie tends not to have a plot or a romance of her own but facilitates the plots and the romances of others, her own romantic inclinations only hinted at with a glance and quickly suppressed with a shrug or a funny face. In *Sing As We Go* (1934), probably her best film, it is she who mediates with management on behalf of the workers, and when her mediation fails (despite the benign good intentions of the managers) it is Gracie who leads the redundant workforce into a rousing chorus of 'Sing As We Go' as they march jauntily into unemployment, the Depression and the hunger marches. The films are sentimental and reassuring, but they also tap into real social anxieties, and the sentiment is sometimes laced with vinegar. As the 1930s progressed, the national interest asserted itself and the films, while retaining their class roots, increasingly served the needs of a cheerful patriotic consensus. JC

Bib: Jeffrey Richards, *The Age of the Dream Palace: Cinema and Society in Britain, 1930–1939* (1984).

Other Films: *Sally in Our Alley* (1931); *Looking on the Bright Side* (1932); *This Week of Grace* (1933); *Love, Life and Laughter* (1934); *Look Up and Laugh* (1935); *Queen of Hearts* (1936); *The Show Goes On* (1937); *We're Going to be Rich, Keep Smiling* (1938); *Shipyard Sally* (1939). **In the US**: *Stage Door Canteen* [cameo], *Holy Matrimony* (1943); *Molly and Me, Paris Underground* (1945).

FILM COMPANY OF IRELAND

Irish production company. The Film Company of Ireland was the most important Irish production company of the silent period. Between 1916 and 1920 it made more than twenty fiction films, including three features. Eight of the first year's nine short films were directed by the Abbey Theatre's J. M. Kerrigan, who later became a Hollywood character actor. The most important films were *Knocknagow* (1918), a landlord/tenant drama set in 1848 during the Great Famine, and *Willie Reilly and his Colleen Bawn* (1918), set in the 1740s and 1750s and centred on the relationship between a Catholic man and a Protestant woman. Other personnel associated with the company, especially producer James M. Sullivan, and director John MacDonagh, who had been sentenced to death for his role in the 1916 Rising, were closely associated with the radical nationalist movement and, as a result, were targeted by the British authorities. KR

Bib: Kevin Rockett, Luke Gibbons, John Hill, *Cinema and Ireland* (1988).

FILM INSTITUTE OF IRELAND

Irish organisation. Originally established in 1945 as the National Film Institute of Ireland, a Catholic propagandist organisation, it was taken over and secularised in the 1980s under the name Irish Film Institute. Following the establishment of the Irish Film Centre*, a project initiated by the Irish Film Institute, it was renamed again (as the Film Institute of Ireland), though its policies remain those of the IFI. These include the development of the Irish Film Archive, which houses the largest collection of Irish film material held anywhere, two successful art cinemas, the promotion of media education, and occasional publications. Its involvement in the European Union's* MEDIA programmes [> EUROPEAN COMMUNITY AND THE CINEMA] has included the establishment of Espace Vidéo Européen, which is housed at the Film Centre. KR

FILM SOCIETY, The

British institution, established by Ivor Montagu* and others to show artistic films which, because of censorship or lack of commercial appeal, would not be shown in other cinemas. The Society catered to the growing band of intellectuals who saw the cinema as a new art form, were attracted to modernist forms, and could afford the subscription. Early members included Roger Fry, Keynes, Shaw, Ellen Terry and H. G. Wells, and the first council included Montagu, Sidney Bernstein, Iris Barry, Thorold Dickinson* and Basil Wright*. The Film Society established the model for a number of regional film societies. It angered those on the left who resented socialist films being restricted to an elite, provoking the moves which led to the Federation of Workers' Film Societies. Iris Barry, film critic and early member of the Film Society council, emigrated to New York in 1931 and became the first film curator of the Museum of Modern Art. JC

Bib: Don Macpherson (ed.), *Traditions of Independence: British cinema in the 1930s* (1980).

FINNEY, Albert

Salford 1936

British actor. A leading member of the generation of northern actors which took the British theatre by storm in the mid-1950s, and gained prominence in cinema in the social realism of the British New Wave*. Finney made his film debut in 1960 in *The Entertainer*. It was, however, the other role he created that year – that of Arthur Seaton in *Saturday Night and Sunday Morning* (1960) – which stamped a new image on British cinema. A bookie's son from Salford, Finney's characterisation seemed to come from inside the new, young, dissatisfied working class, and with its insolent defiance, aggressive sexuality and self-absorbed cockiness dispelled the dreams of a decent and contented class community left over from Ealing. Finney's performance in the title role of *Tom Jones* (1963) carried some of the same class insolence and a lot of the sexuality, and the success of the film made him an international star. With hints of autobiography, in 1967 he directed and starred in

Charlie Bubbles, a film from a Shelagh Delaney script about the disenchantments of success. The loss of youth was also at the centre of Stanley Donen's *Two for the Road* (1967), in which he starred with Audrey Hepburn. His career did indeed stall after *Gumshoe* (1971), and films like *Murder on the Orient Express* (1974) added very little to his stature as an actor. In the 1980s and 1990s, however, he has re-emerged, often with a kind of dissipated grandeur, in *Shoot the Moon* (1982, US), *The Dresser* (1984), *Under the Volcano* (1984, US), and *Miller's Crossing* (1990, US). He continues to work in theatre and on television. JC

Other Films Include: *The Browning Version* (1994); *A Man of No Importance* (1994, UK/Ireland); *The Run of the Country* (1995, Ireland).

FISHER, Terence London 1904 – Twickenham 1980

British director, whose name is most closely associated with the series of horror films he made at Hammer*, beginning with *The Curse of Frankenstein* in 1957. Before Hammer, Fisher had been an editor since 1933, and a director since 1948, but it is in the relatively low-budget horror genre that he most clearly laid claim to the status of *auteur*, a claim which was honoured in France before it was considered seriously in Britain. Criticised by some British critics of the time for being 'disgusting' and by others for lacking the expressionist touches of European horror or the Universal cycle of the 1930s, Fisher's technique is, as Robert Murphy describes it, 'almost pedantically disciplined'. The camera follows the action with a realistic restraint which gives a cool objectivity to the sexual fantasies, body horrors and oedipal nightmares which are being enacted. Fisher left Hammer briefly in the early 1960s and made *Sherlock Holmes und das Halsband des Todes/Sherlock Holmes and the Deadly Necklace* (1962, Ger./It./Fr.) in Germany, before returning to home base to make such films as *The Gorgon* (1964), *Dracula – Prince of Darkness* (1965) and *Frankenstein Must be Destroyed* (1969). JC

Bib: David Pirie, *A Heritage of Horror* (1973).

Other Films Include: *The Astonished Heart* [co-dir.], *So Long at the Fair* [co-dir.] (1950); *Stolen Face* (1952); *Four-Sided Triangle* (1953); *Face the Music* (1954); *Dracula, The Revenge of Frankenstein* (1958); *The Hound of the Baskervilles, The Mummy* (1959); *The Brides of Dracula* (1960); *The Curse of the Werewolf* (1961); *The Phantom of the Opera* (1962); *Frankenstein Created Woman* (1967); *The Devil Rides Out* (1968); *Frankenstein and the Monster from Hell* (1974).

FITZGERALD, Barry

William Joseph Shields;
Dublin 1888–1961

Irish actor. While a civil servant, he played in amateur theatrical productions and changed his name to Barry Fitzgerald to avoid dismissal from employment (his brother, actor Arthur Shields, kept his name). Fitzgerald occasionally played at the Abbey Theatre from 1916 before becoming a full-time actor in 1929. His first film role was in the Irish-produced *Land of Her Fathers* (1924). He played the Orator in Alfred Hitchcock's* version of O'Casey's *Juno and the Paycock* (1929), while his stage role of Captain Boyle was given to the inexperienced British actor Edward Chapman. Contracted by RKO to play one of his most famous roles, that of Fluther Good in O'Casey's *The Plough and the Stars*, in John Ford's 1936 film version of the play, he thereafter worked mainly in Hollywood, where he won an Oscar for his role as Father Fitzgibbons in *Going My Way* (1944). He returned to Ireland frequently and played his most memorable role as the impish matchmaker in John Ford's *The Quiet Man* (1952). KR

Other Films Include: *The Long Voyage Home* (1940, US); *How Green Was My Valley* (1941, US); *Happy Ever After* (1954); *The Catered Affair* (1956, US); *Broth of a Boy* (1959).

FLAHERTY, Robert

Iron Mountain, Michigan
1884 – Dummerston, Vermont 1951

American director, who spent four years in Britain between 1933 and 1937 and played an important part in the development of the British Documentary Movement*. His reputation had been established with *Nanook of the North* (1922, US), *Moana* (1926, US) and *Tabu* (1931, US). In Britain, *Industrial Britain* (1933), made with John Grierson's* support, left behind a great deal of footage which was subsequently edited by, among others, Marion Grierson. He spent three years in the Aran Isles making *Man of Aran* (1934), and went to India with Zoltan Korda to make *Elephant Boy* (1937). Returning to the US, he received an International Prize from the Venice Festival for *Louisiana Story* (1948, US). Flaherty was a romantic rather than an ethnographer, but he set many of the problems of ethnographic film in motion. Grierson admired his lyrical poetry 'with its emphasis of man against the sky', but was inclined to add, 'I hope the neo-Rousseauism implicit in [his] work dies with his own exceptional self.' JC

Bib: Arthur Calder-Marshall, *The Innocent Eye: The Life of Robert J. Flaherty* (1963).

FORBES, Bryan   John Theobald Clarke; London 1926

British actor, writer, director and producer. Forbes began as a film actor in *The Small Back Room* (1949) and became a familiar figure in such male bonding films of the 1950s as *The Wooden Horse* (1950) and *The Colditz Story* (1955). Since the mid-1950s he has written a number of original screenplays, including *The League of Gentlemen* (1960), in which he also played a part, and *The Angry Silence* (1960), which he wrote for Beaver, the company he formed with Richard Attenborough* in 1959. His directorial debut was *Whistle Down the Wind* (1961), and he directed, wrote and often produced such well-known films of the 1960s as *The L-Shaped Room* (1962), *Seance on a Wet Afternoon* (1964) and *The Whisperers* (1966). In 1969 he was appointed head of production in EMI's attempt to crack the nut of British film production at Elstree, but despite commercial success with *The Railway Children* (1970) and critical success with Joseph Losey's* *The Go-Between* (1970), the attempt failed and he resigned in 1971. His subsequent career has included directing *The Stepford Wives* (1975, US) and co-scripting – with William Boyd and William Goldman – Attenborough's *Chaplin* (1992). JC

Bib: Bryan Forbes, *A Divided Life: Memoirs* (1992).

FORMBY, George   Wigan 1904 – Preston 1961

British actor. Coming from the northern music hall (his father George Formby Sr. was a music-hall favourite before him), and gaining a national audience through radio, Formby became the most popular male domestic star with British audiences in the late 1930s, alternating at the top of the polls with Gracie Fields*. While Hollywood attempted to woo most other British box-office favourites of the period, including both Fields and Jessie Matthews*, it is hard to imagine what they could have done with Formby. Like his French counterpart, Fernandel, with whom he was often compared, his particular appeal resisted translation. His characters are based on sexual innocence: romantically inept, they nevertheless aspire to the girls of their dreams. His songs, which he sang to a symbolically small ukulele, are based on a complicit game with the audience about how far you can take sexual innuendo: while Gracie could be coy, George could be smutty. But however smutty it got, it was safe. George was just being naughty, and the audience could permit itself the joke because, coming from George, it could never be seriously offensive or sexually threatening. The game is peculiarly English, drawing both from the seaside postcards of Donald McGill and from the northern music-hall tradition, and surfacing again in the *Carry On** films.

Formby made his most popular films under contract to Basil Dean* at Ealing, providing a voice of populist consensus immediately before the war and during its early years. He never recovered the popularity of those years, and when *George in Civvy Street* (1946) flopped, he returned to the music hall. JC

Bib: Jeffrey Richards, *The Age of the Dream Palace: Cinema and Society in Britain, 1930–1939* (1984).

Other Films: *By the Shortest of Heads* (1915); *Boots! Boots!* (1934); *Off the Dole, No Limit* (1935); *Keep Your Seats Please* (1936); *Keep Fit, Feather Your Nest* (1937); *It's in the Air, I See Ice!* (1938); *Trouble Brewing, Come On George!* (1939); *Let George Do It!, Spare a Copper* (1940); *South American George, Turned Out Nice Again* (1941); *Much Too Shy* (1942); *Get Cracking, Bell-Bottom George* (1943); *He Snoops to Conquer* (1944); *I Didn't Do It* (1945).

FORSYTH, Bill — Glasgow 1946

British director and writer, who spent fifteen years working in Scottish-sponsored documentaries before making *That Sinking Feeling* (1980). The film, a 'no-budget' comedy using members of the Glasgow Youth Theatre, was, he claims, the first fiction narrative feature to be made in Scotland by a native Scot living in Scotland. Its success at the Edinburgh Film Festival* led to funding for an earlier script for *Gregory's Girl* (1981), using many of the same actors for a comedy of teenage manners (and lack of them) in Cumbernauld New Town. *Local Hero*, made for Goldcrest* in 1982 (released 1983), was his entry into the Big Time. Set again in Scotland, but with Burt Lancaster adding star appeal, the film revisits some of the territory of Alexander Mackendrick's* *The Maggie* (1954), with the twist that the 'innocent' villagers are eager participants in their own sell-out to international capitalism. After *Comfort and Joy* (1984), Forsyth found it impossible during the rest of the 1980s to get the backing to make films in Scotland. His work in Hollywood has included one excellent and under-recognised film, *Housekeeping* (1987, US), adapted from Marilynne Robinson's novel, and *Breaking In* (1989, US), starring Burt Reynolds from a John Sayles script. Forsyth's skills are in localised, eccentric observation and idiosyncratic detail rather than in seamless narrative: skills which he struggles to maintain as the stars sparkle and the budgets rise. *Being Human* (1994), starring Robin Williams, with a budget of $20 million from Warner Bros, struggled under the weight of studio expectations, but may have convinced Forsyth that Hollywood is not the best place for a European eccentric. JC

Bib: Alan Hunter in Eddie Dick (ed.), *From Limelight to Satellite: A Scottish Movie Book* (1990).

FRANCIS, Freddie

London 1917

British cinematographer and director. After serving as a camera operator in the 1950s on a number of Powell* and Pressburger films, including *The Small Back Room* (1949), *Gone to Earth* (1950) and *The Tales of Hoffmann* (1951), and as second unit photographer on John Huston's *Moby Dick* (1956), Francis received his first cinematographer credit on *A Hill in Korea* (1956). He photographed *Room at the Top* (1959), *Saturday Night and Sunday Morning* (1960), and won an Oscar for *Sons and Lovers* (1960), directed by another cinematographer, Jack Cardiff*. He went to Hammer* Films in 1962, and somewhat reluctantly became a noted director of horror films such as *The Evil of Frankenstein* (1964), *The Skull* (1965) and *Dracula Has Risen from the Grave* (1968). He gave up directing in 1975 and returned to cinematography for David Lynch's *The Elephant Man* (1980, US/UK), working with Lynch again on *Dune* (1984, US). In 1991, he shot the remake of *Cape Fear* (US) for Martin Scorsese and in 1994, he was cinematographer for Michael Austin's *Princess Caraboo* (US). JC

FREARS, Stephen

Leicester 1941

British director, whose early film credits include assistant director on *Morgan a Suitable Case for Treatment* (1966), *If....* (1968) and *O Lucky Man!* (1973). He made his first feature film, *Gumshoe,* in 1971, but between 1971 and 1984, when he made *The Hit,* he worked in television drama. *My Beautiful Laundrette* (1985) was also made for television, but its surprise success earned it a cinema release in the United States and an Oscar nomination. This film and *Sammy and Rosie Get Laid* (1987), both made collaboratively with the writer Hanif Kureishi*, are key films of the 1980s, unpicking the social fabric of Thatcherism into its multicultural and multisexual threads. Since 1987, Frears has built up a successful Hollywood career with *Dangerous Liaisons* (1988, US), from a Christopher Hampton script; *The Grifters* (1990, US), produced by Martin Scorsese from a Jim Thompson novel; and *Hero/Accidental Hero* (1992, US). Described in a *Guardian* interview as neither a jobbing director nor an *auteur* (and despite his elevation to *auteur* status in France), Frears characterises himself as 'an old BBC drama department man', willing to implement the writer's intentions rather than to express his own personality. He very successfully directed the adaptation of Roddy Doyle's *The Snapper* (1993) for television and cinema release, but ran into trouble with Julia Roberts and the studio on *Mary Reilly* (release delayed to 1996). JC

Bib: Jonathan Hacker and David Price, *Take 10: Contemporary British Film Directors* (1991).

FREE CINEMA

British movement. Free Cinema consisted of six programmes of films shown at the National Film Theatre between 1956 and 1959. More broadly, it refers to a movement which linked the journal *Sequence** with the British New Wave*. What made the films 'free' was an attitude to 'the poetry of everyday life', an engagement (in the existentialist sense), and a free expression of personality which escaped the routines of commercial cinema or the standard British documentary. 'These films are free,' declared a programme leaflet, 'in the sense that their statements are entirely personal.' The programmes were assembled by a group which included Lindsay Anderson*, Karel Reisz*, John Fletcher and Walter Lassally, and included films – mainly documentaries, with a few animations – by Anderson: *O Dreamland* (1953), *The Wakefield Express* (1952), *Every Day Except Christmas* (1957); Reisz: *Momma Don't Allow* (1956), *We Are the Lambeth Boys* (1959); Tony Richardson*: *Momma Don't Allow* (1956); Norman McLaren*: *Neighbours* (1953); Georges Franju*: *Le Sang des bêtes* (1949); Jan Lenica* and Walerian Borowczyck*: *Once Upon a Time* (1957), *Dom* (1958); Roman Polanski*: *Two Men and a Wardrobe* (1958); Claude Goretta* and Alain Tanner*: *Nice Time* (1957); François Truffaut*: *Les Mistons* (1957); and Claude Chabrol*: *Le beau serge* (1957). Appearing in 1956, Free Cinema was the first expression in the cinema of the generational shift that was occurring in the Royal Court Theatre around *Look Back in Anger*. JC

Bib: Alan Lovell and Jim Hillier, *Studies in Documentary* (1972).

FRICKER, Brenda

Dublin 1944

Irish actress. Fricker has worked on stage and in television, including roles in the first Irish television soap in the 1960s, *Tolka Row*, the British television hospital series, *Casualty* (1986–90), and the *Brides of Christ* mini-series (1992). Her television films have included Pat O'Connor's* *The Ballroom of Romance* (1982), in which she played an unmarried woman in search of a husband in 1950s rural Ireland, and *Utz* (1991). She came to international prominence through winning an Oscar for her role as Christy Brown's mother in *My Left Foot* (1989). She continued to work with *My Left Foot* director Jim Sheridan* on *The Field* (1990, UK/Ir.), in which she again played a long-suffering woman, a characterisation which has become something of a trademark. KR

Other Films Include: *Deadly Advice* (1993, UK); *A Man of No Importance* (1994, UK/Ireland); *Angels* (1995, US).

G

GAINSBOROUGH MELODRAMA

British genre, which appeared at Gainsborough Studios during and immediately after World War II, offering an escape from the proprieties of wartime propaganda and realism. The series of films was ushered in with *The Man in Grey* (1943), released as part of the varied programme which Edward Black had been developing at the studio since 1931. The box-office success of this film, and of *Fanny by Gaslight* (1944), another costume melodrama, encouraged the more entrepreneurial Maurice Ostrer to give the audience the 'escape' it wanted, and, recognising where his wartime market lay, to concentrate on women's pictures. Predictably, the policy brought critical contempt hand-in-hand with huge commercial success, establishing James Mason*, Stewart Granger* and Margaret Lockwood* as top box-office stars. Recent feminist criticism has rediscovered the Gainsborough melodramas, in particular the costume films. The interest lies in their difference from the overwhelmingly masculine wartime and postwar cinema. They may not offer correct, positive heroines, but they leave space for female fantasy, with Margaret Lockwood masquerading as a highwayman in *The Wicked Lady* (1945) and offering a seductive alternative to the moral probity of Phyllis Calvert's* version of femininity in *The Man in Grey* – 'I don't care for sugary things,' she says. The wicked ladies are punished in the end, but not before they have left their mark and cut a dash through decency and emotional restraint. The brief cycle of Gainsborough melodramas offers feminist criticism one of the few examples of the woman's film as a genre in postwar British cinema. JC

Bib: Sue Aspinall and Robert Murphy (eds.), *Gainsborough Melodrama,* BFI Dossier 18 (1983).

GIELGUD, (Sir) John — London 1904

British actor. Of the leading trio of 'theatrical knights' – with Ralph Richardson* and Laurence Olivier* – Gielgud has remained most firmly wedded to theatre, seeming most at ease in direct stage adaptations such as Olivier's *Richard III* (1955) or Joseph Losey's* *Galileo* (1976). While his theatrically modulated delivery resists the naturalism of extended film characterisation, his cameo appearances are always a delight to watch. Although, like Olivier's, his later career has included some routine bread-and-butter work, since the 1930s he has also appeared in distinctive films by Victor Saville*, Alfred Hitchcock*,

Thorold Dickinson*, Otto Preminger, Orson Welles, Andrzej Wajda and David Lynch, and his is the unmistakable voice of Humphrey Jennings'* *A Diary for Timothy* (1945). More recently, he has given extended performances in Alain Resnais' *Providence* (1977) and Peter Greenaway's* *Prospero's Books* (1991). JC

Other Films Include: *The Good Companions* (1933); *Secret Agent* (1936); *The Prime Minister* (1941); *Julius Caesar* (1953, US); *The Barretts of Wimpole Street, Saint Joan* (1957); *Becket* (1964); *Campanadas a medianoche/Chimes at Midnight* (1966, Sp./Switz.); *The Charge of the Light Brigade* (1968); *Oh! What a Lovely War* (1969); *Dyrygent/The Conductor* [Pol.], *The Human Factor* (1979); *The Elephant Man* (1980, US/UK); *Arthur, Chariots of Fire* (1981, US); *Gandhi* (1982); *First Knight* (1995, US); *Haunted* (1995, US).

GILLIAM, Terry

Minneapolis, USA 1940

American/British director, who moved to Britain in 1967 and became part of the Monty Python's Flying Circus team, contributing a series of uncharacteristically bleak animation sequences to the television series. He directed *Monty Python and the Holy Grail* (1975) with the same team, and has subsequently established an independent existence as a director of eccentric and sometimes unsettling mythologies and fantasies, including the wonderfully dystopic *Brazil* (1985). Gilliam had a struggle to retain the dystopia in Hollywood, and *The Fisher King* (1991, US) returns to the Grail legend with a gentler ending. Responding to a Toronto Festival award for the film, Gilliam wrote, 'Thank you very much for justifying my decision to sell out.' *Twelve Monkeys* (1996), inspired by Chris Marker's *La Jetée* (1962), returns to unsettling, even apocalyptic, territory. JC

Other Films Include: *Jabberwocky* (1977); *Time Bandits* (1981); *The Adventures of Baron Munchausen* (1988, UK/Ger.).

GILLIAT, Sidney – see LAUNDER, Frank

GODFREY, Bob

West Maitland, Australia 1921

British animator, of Australian parentage, who attracted attention with *The Do-It-Yourself Cartoon Kit* (1961), and whose 30-minute film *Great* (1975), a comic musical treatment of Brunel, won an Academy Award. Godfrey's work, in films like *Polygamous Polonius* (1960), *Henry 9 Till 5* (1970) and *Kama Sutra Rides Again* (1971), is admired for its surreal visual imagination and is notorious for its sexism. He provided animation sequences for Roman Polanski's* *Dance of the*

Vampires (1967). He has recently begun a collaboration with the *Guardian* cartoonist Steve Bell. JC

GOLDCREST

British production company, which symbolised renaissance for the British film industry after *Chariots of Fire* in 1981, and despair following the failure of *Revolution* in 1985. Goldcrest was started by Jake Eberts in 1977 as a film development company. Following the international success of *Chariots of Fire* and *Gandhi* (1982), Goldcrest became an independent production company with David Puttnam* and Richard Attenborough* on the Board. It had an ambitious slate aimed at the American market with smaller budget productions for television and cable. Success and prestige continued with *Local Hero* (1983) and *The Killing Fields* (1984), and it seemed that Goldcrest could do no wrong. In 1985, James Lee, Chief Executive after Eberts left in 1983, declared, 'Hopefully, this will be the last year we find ourselves quite as vulnerable to one film.' The one film was the commercially disastrous *Revolution* (1985), with *Absolute Beginners* (1986) to follow. *A Room with a View* (1985) and *The Mission* (1986) continued to win Oscars for the company but could not save it, and it was sold in 1987. The ambitions of Goldcrest, and their failure, concentrated minds on the nature of a British national cinema. JC

Bib: Jake Eberts and Terry Ilott, *My Indecision is Final: The Rise and Fall of Goldcrest Films* (1990).

GRANGER, Stewart

James Leblache Stewart; London 1913 – Santa Monica, USA 1993

British actor, who, with James Mason*, was one of the top British box-office attractions as a romantic lead in the Gainsborough melodramas* of the 1940s. Less dangerous than Mason, in *The Man in Grey* (1943) and *Fanny by Gaslight* (1944) he played the chivalrous champion of damsels placed in distress by Mason's aristocratic villainy. In *Love Story* (1944), a contemporary melodrama, he played a gallant RAF pilot threatened by blindness, while in the exotic *Madonna of the Seven Moons* (1944) he was a gypsy brigand offering Phyllis Calvert* a romantic alternative to respectablity with a rich Italian banker. Outside the Gainsborough series, but still a romantic genre actor, he starred in Frank Launder's* *Captain Boycott* (1947) and Basil Dearden's* *Saraband for Dead Lovers* (1948), before moving to Hollywood in the 1950s for a series of swashbuckling adventurer roles under contract to MGM: *King Solomon's Mines* (1950), *Scaramouche* (1952), *The Prisoner of Zenda* (1952), *Beau Brummell* (1954),

Moonfleet (1955) and *Bhowani Junction* (1956) [all US]. In realistic vein, Sidney Gilliat cast him as a predatory spiv in *Waterloo Road* (1945) and Dearden exploited his moral ambiguity in *The Secret Partner* (1961). His film career declined in the 1970s, and he later worked mainly for American television. JC

GREENAWAY, Peter London 1942

British director, whose highly intellectual films, described by Chris Auty as 'beautiful butterflies trapped down by drawing pins', have moved from the seclusion of the avant-garde cinema of the 1970s to success with art-house audiences since *The Draughtsman's Contract* in 1982. A product of a 1960s art school training, influenced by John Cage and serialism, Greenaway is a neo-classical rather than a neo-romantic modernist, structuring his films around classificatory systems and numbers, splitting and doubling his characters, and distracting his narratives in red herrings, puns, non sequiturs and verbal disquisitions. Greenaway offers his art-house aficionados the pleasures of the puzzle rather than the satisfactions of resolution, and offers to more sceptical spectators a *mise-en-scène* of sumptuous cleverness which teeters on the brink of the ridiculous and lends itself easily to parody. The visual pastiche and narrative repetitions of the films are echoed in the tuneful minimalism of Michael Nyman's scores. 'At heart,' says Peter Wollen*, 'Greenaway, like R. B. Kitaj, is a collagist, juxtaposing images from some fantastic archive, tracing erudite coincidental narratives within his material, bringing together Balthus and Borges in a bizarre collocation of bizarre eroticism and trompe-l'oeil high modernism.' *The Baby of Mâcon* (1993), a co-production involving the UK, Netherlands, France and Germany, maintains the virtuosity, but suggests a director badly in need of a new idea. JC

Bib: Peter Wollen, 'The Last New Wave', in Lester Friedman (ed.), *British Cinema and Thatcherism* (1993).

Other Films Include: *Five Postcards from Capital Cities* (1967); *H is for House* (1973); *Dear Phone* (1977); *1–100, A Walk Through H, Vertical Features Remake* (1978); *The Falls* (1980); *Zandra Rhodes* (1981); *Four American Composers* (TV, 1983); *A Zed & Two Noughts* (1985); *The Belly of an Architect* (1987); *Drowning by Numbers* (1988); *The Cook the Thief His Wife & Her Lover* (1989); *A TV Dante – Cantos 1–8* [TV] (1990); *Prospero's Books* (1991).

GREENE, Graham

Berkhamsted 1904 – Vevey, Switzerland 1991

British novelist, scriptwriter and critic. Graham Greene is identified with the 'literary tradition' of British cinema, dealing in Paul Rotha's words with 'complex themes of great importance'. His early contact with cinema was as film critic for the *Spectator* from 1935 to 1940. His criticism was often caustic, but in his advocacy of a 'poetic cinema' he anticipated Lindsay Anderson* and the critics of *Sequence**. A collection of his film criticism, *The Pleasure Dome*, was published in 1972, and a Graham Greene Film Reader, *Mornings in the Dark*, in 1993. He is probably the most adapted of the major contemporary British novelists, with his novels or short stories forming the basis for Alberto Cavalcanti's* *Went the Day Well?* (1942), Fritz Lang's* *Ministry of Fear* (1944, US), John Ford's *The Fugitive* (1947, US) and George Cukor's *Travels with My Aunt* (1972, US), among others. His own experience of writing for the cinema has been uneven, and he writes of it with some scepticism. His collaboration with Carol Reed* did, however, produce three distinctive films: *The Fallen Idol* (1948), *The Third Man* (1949) and *Our Man in Havana* (1960); and for John Boulting* he adapted his own novel, *Brighton Rock* (1947). JC

Bib: *Mornings in the Dark: Graham Greene Film Reader* (1993).

Other Films As Scriptwriter Include: *La mano dello straniero/The Stranger's Hand* [from his own short story] (1954, It./UK); *Loser Takes All* [from his own novel] (1956); *Saint Joan* (1957); *The Comedians* [from his own novel] (1967).

GREENWOOD, Joan

London 1921–87

British actress, whose particular contribution to postwar cinema was to introduce a genteel eroticism to the English upper classes, playing off an unmistakable husky voice against 'English rose' respectability. In *Kind Hearts and Coronets* (1949) there is an unambiguous sexuality in her performance, suggesting a delight in adultery unexpected in an Ealing* comedy. Her performance as Gwendolen in *The Importance of Being Earnest* (1952) confirmed her strength in high theatrical comedy. Ealing was probably not the place to develop her particular erotic potential, though she played winsome leads for Alexander Mackendrick* in *Whisky Galore!* (1949) and *The Man in the White Suit* (1951), and the British cinema in general offered her very little after another sexy cameo in *Tom Jones* (1963). She continued to work in theatre, and returned to television in 1981 to play a wonderfully dotty, husky and still sexy aunt in Trevor Griffiths' *Country*. JC

GRIERSON, John

Deanston, Scotland 1898 – Bath 1972

British producer, director and critic, founder of the British Documentary Movement* and one of the most influential figures in the development of British film culture. Grierson was born near Stirling in Scotland and educated in Literature and Philosophy at the University of Glasgow. He travelled on a scholarship to the United States, where he studied mass communications and wrote on cinema. On his return to Britain, he joined the Empire Marketing Board (EMB) as Assistant Films Officer in 1927, and produced and directed *Drifters,* which was premiered at the London Film Society with *Battleship Potemkin* in 1929. He persuaded Stephen Tallents to form the EMB Film Unit, and began to assemble a team of young film-makers who formed the Documentary Movement, moving to the General Post Office (GPO) Film Unit when the EMB was disbanded in 1933. Grierson left the GPO in 1936, and was appointed Film Adviser to the Imperial Relations Trust and to the governments of Australia, New Zealand and Canada. In 1938 he formed Film Centre with Arthur Elton, Basil Wright* and Stuart Legg to explore the possibilities of the sponsored documentary independent of government, and became Production Adviser to Films of Scotland. He advised on the establishment of the National Film Board of Canada and became its first Commissioner in 1939. Similar Film Boards were established in New Zealand and Australia in the 1940s. In 1945, based in New York, he was investigated for Communist sympathies. Visiting Britain in 1947, he was refused a re-entry visa to the US, and worked for UNESCO in Paris. Returning to Britain, he was Controller of the Films Division of the Central Office of Information from 1948 until 1950, and from 1951 until 1954 he was Executive Producer of Group 3, a body established by the newly formed National Film Finance Corporation to produce feature films. In 1955 he joined Scottish Television (STV), producing and presenting *This Wonderful World*, a selection of international documentaries, until 1965.

The reach of Grierson's influence is less in the films he directed (which are uncertain as credits were a matter of little concern), or even produced, than in the institutions he established, the careers he began, the production opportunities he opened, the aesthetics he promoted, and the critical values he advocated. Taken together, these gave a material reality to the discourse of a cinema of public service, civic responsibility and the 'creative treatment of reality'. 'I regard cinema as a pulpit,' he famously declared, and the word which he preached has left an inheritance of social democratic values that still underpins many of the critical discourses which seek to define British cinema. JC

Bib: Ian Aitken, *Film and Reform: John Grierson and the Documentary Movement* (1990).

GUINNESS, (Sir) Alec

Alec Guinness de Cuffe;
London 1914

British actor, distinctive in his ability to combine the skills of character actor and realistic performance in the same role. Although he is identified with the school of acting which works from the outside in rather than from the inside out, accumulating external details rather than revealing inner truths, the virtuosity of his impersonations does not seem to damage the credibility of his characterisations. His Fagin in David Lean's* *Oliver Twist* (1948), though physically a caricature, is emotionally a character of some depth. In the Ealing comedies*, *Kind Hearts and Coronets* (1949), in which he plays all eight of the doomed d'Ascoynes, gives full scope to his playful virtuosity, while *The Man in the White Suit* (1951) gives him a role of appealing but dangerous innocence. Guinness won an Oscar, a New York Film Critics award and a British Academy award for his performance as the insanely uncompromising Captain Nicholson in Lean's *The Bridge on the River Kwai* (1957), a theme on which he played variations in *Tunes of Glory* (1960). Since the 1960s, his performances have been a little more predictable, though his role as Obi Wan Kenobi in the *Star Wars* series almost stole the movies from the action men. His most satisfying and complete characterisation in recent years was as George Smiley in the BBC television serialisations of John Le Carré's *Tinker, Tailor, Soldier, Spy* (1979) and *Smiley's People* (1982).

Knighted in 1959, he was given a Special Academy Award in 1979 for 'advancing the art of screen acting through a host of memorable and distinguished performances'. JC

Other Films Include: *Great Expectations* (1946); *The Mudlark* (1950); *The Lavender Hill Mob* (1951); *Father Brown* (1954); *The Ladykillers* (1955); *The Horse's Mouth* (1959); *Our Man in Havana* (1960); *Lawrence of Arabia* (1962); *Doctor Zhivago* (1965); *Fratello Sole, Sorella Luna/Brother Sun Sister Moon* (1973, It./UK); *Star Wars* (1977, US); *The Empire Strikes Back* (1980, US); *Return of the Jedi* (1983, US); *A Passage to India* (1985); *A Handful of Dust* (1987); *Kafka* (1991, US/Fr./UK); *Mute Witness* (1995, UK/Ger./Russia).

HALAS, John – see BATCHELOR, Joy

HAMER, Robert   Kidderminster 1911 – London 1963

British director, who, on the basis of three and a bit feature films at Ealing in the 1940s, has claims to being one of the distinctive *auteurs* of British postwar cinema. His signature, as Charles Barr has pointed out, is the mirror worlds played out in 'The Haunted Mirror' episode of *Dead of Night* (1945), in which a world of dull respectability is undermined by a world in which passion slips from control. In *Pink String and Sealing Wax* (1945) the world of the chemist shop is mirrored in reverse by the world of the public house. In *Kind Hearts and Coronets* (1949) the dignified restraint of Louis' commentary is in comic counterpoint to the lust and murder which he is commenting upon. *It Always Rains on Sunday* (1947) is almost an attack on Ealing itself, the world of the self-regulating community disintegrating in its conflict with a mirror world of criminality and repressed sexual desire. Hamer has a reputation as a 'woman's director' and indeed, unusually for Ealing, strong women are at the centre of each of the films: most characteristically, Googie Withers*. But the women pay for their strength, and there is something at least ambivalent if not sadistic in the way female desire is punished.

Hamer fought a losing battle with alcoholism, and died at the age of 52. JC

Bib: Charles Barr, *Ealing Studios* (1977).

Other Films Include: **As Editor** – *Jamaica Inn* (1939); *The Foreman Went to France* (1942). **As Director** – *The Loves of Joanna Godden* [Hamer directed some sections while Charles Frend was ill] (1947); *Father Brown* (1954); *School for Scoundrels* (1960).

HAMMER HORROR

British genre, developed by Sir James Carreras' Hammer Films between 1954 and 1968 at Bray Studios. Hammer went into production in 1948, taking over a large country house at Bray, west of London, as its studio. Carreras was unashamedly commercial, working in 'B' features with tightly controlled budgets and going wherever public taste took him. In 1955, he exploited the success of the BBC serialisation of *The Quatermass Experiment* (1953) and produced *The Quatermass Xperiment* (1955) with the emphasis on the X. Its success encouraged him to pursue the horror genre, and in 1957 he released *The Curse of Frankenstein*, which was made for £65,000 and grossed around £2 million, with £1 million coming from America. The horror films which followed continued the box-office success, particularly in the overseas market, earning Carreras the contempt of British quality critics and a 1968 Queen's Award for Industry.

Dave Pirie suggests that the horror genre 'remains the only staple cinematic myth which Britain can claim as its own and which relates to it in the same way as the Western relates to America.' At its best, Hammer horror, like Gainsborough melodrama* before it, brought to the genre a stylistic approach which played off the restraint characteristic of British cinema against the excess of the conventions, the decency of Peter Cushing against the monstrous sexuality of Christopher Lee, exposing the familiar myths of class and sexuality to the uncanny and the undead. JC

Bib: Dave Pirie, *Hammer: A Cinema Case Study* (1980).

HARRIS, Richard — Limerick 1933

Irish/British actor. Trained at the London Academy of Music and Dramatic Art, and a graduate of Joan Littlewood's Theatre Workshop, Harris appeared in a number of British films in the late 1950s (often associated with Ireland). His performance as Frank Machin in *This Sporting Life* (1963) gave him international recognition, a Best Actor award from Cannes and an Oscar nomination. A landmark performance in the British New Wave*, his representation of masculinity owes more to the individualism of the American Method school than to the social naturalism of Albert Finney*, with Marlon Brando lurking behind Machin's inarticulate physicality. It was a level of performance he did not repeat, though it revealed a current of masochism in Harris' career (and his life) which he drew on more graphically in *A Man Called Horse* (1970, US). His career in the 1970s and 1980s was more marked for its boozy scandals than for his acting. Since his recent return to Ireland, however, he has won an Oscar nomination for his part in Jim Sheridan's* *The Field* (1990, UK/Ireland), was memorably masochistic in Clint Eastwood's *Unforgiven* (1992, US), and has been praised for his West End stage performance in the title role of Pirandello's *Henry IV* (1992). JC

Other Films Include: *Shake Hands with the Devil* (1959); *A Terrible Beauty* (1960); *The Guns of Navarone, Mutiny on the Bounty* (1962); *Il Deserto rosso/The Red Desert* (1964, It.); *Major Dundee* (1965, US); *Camelot* (1967, US); *The Molly Maguires* (1970, US); *Robin and Marian, The Return of a Man Called Horse* (1976, both US); *El triunfo de un hombre llamado Caballo/Triumphs of a Man Called Horse* (1982, US).

HARRISON, (Sir) Rex

Huyton, Lancashire 1908 – New York, USA 1990

British actor. Never an actor of hidden profundities, Harrison's natural environment was theatrical light comedy in which elegance was preferred to depth, and urbanity to rough edges. Though, in keeping with the mood of the late 1930s, he plays an idealistic reporter in Victor Saville* and Ian Dalrymple's* *Storm in a Teacup* (1937) and appears in King Vidor's socially conscious *The Citadel* (1938), he seems more at home in Herbert Wilcox's* *I Live in Grosvenor Square*, David Lean's* *Blithe Spirit*, or Sidney Gilliat's* *The Rake's Progress* (all made in 1945). His career on stage was as successful as his career in film, and the two came together in his performance as Professor Higgins in *My Fair Lady* on Broadway (1956–8) and in George Cukor's film adaptation (1964, US), for which he won an Oscar. It was one of those parts in which character and actor come to define each other, and though Harrison continued to give good performances (in, for example, *The Yellow Rolls-Royce*, 1964; and in the US: *The Agony and the Ecstasy*, 1965, *Doctor Dolittle*, 1967, and *Staircase*, 1969), they tended to live under the shadow of Henry Higgins. JC

HAWKINS, Jack

London 1910–73

British actor, whose distinctive persona seemed to remain constant across a range of parts and genres. A child actor from the age of thirteen, he made his film debut in 1930 in Basil Dean's* *Birds of Prey*. He appeared mainly in supporting roles in the 1930s and early 1940s when his first love was still theatre, but came into prominence in the postwar cinema as one of the stalwarts of well-bred and stiffly backboned English middle-class manhood. His role as the Captain in *The Cruel Sea* (1953) called upon his qualities of decent concern and moral decisiveness, while *Mandy* (1952) offered him a sensitive and caring role as a teacher of deaf children. During the 1950s he became the acceptable image of the British police in, for example, *Home at Seven* (1952), *The Long Arm* (1956) and John Ford's *Gideon's Day* (1958), while simultaneously playing lead roles, somewhat surprisingly, in such Hollywood epics as Howard Hawks' *Land of the Pharaohs* (1955, US) and William Wyler's *Ben-Hur* (1959, US). Always in demand, he continued to act, with dubbing, after an operation for cancer of the larynx in 1966. JC

Other Films Include: *The Good Companions* (1933); *The Next of Kin* (1942); *The Fallen Idol, The Small Back Room* (1949); *The Elusive Pimpernel* (1950); *Fortune is a Woman, The Bridge on the River Kwai* (1957); *The League of Gentlemen* (1960); *Lawrence of Arabia* (1962); *Zulu* (1963); *Guns at Batasi* (1964); *Lord Jim* (1965); *Shalako* (1968);

Oh! What a Lovely War (1969); *The Adventures of Gerard, Waterloo* [It./USSR] (1970); *Nicholas and Alexandra (*1971, US); *Kidnapped, Young Winston* (1972).

HAY, Will Stockton-on-Tees 1888 – London 1949

British actor, who was one of the northern music-hall performers popular in Britain between 1936 and 1940. Like Gracie Fields* and George Formby*, his performances adapted his music-hall style to film rather than simply transferring stage routines. His screen character developed around the theme of incompetence rewarded and official pomposity overthrown. With his pince-nez as his standard prop, his most familiar role was as the schoolmaster desperately trying to cover up his own incompetence with verbal pretentiousness, inconsequentiality, and a bemused double take which was all his own. Like Karl Valentin or W. C. Fields, he did not share in the joke, nor was he romantically inclined – in *Where There's a Will* (1937) he almost puts his hand on a young woman's knee, but it is absent-mindedness rather than lechery and he thinks better of it. Hay made a series of comedies with Gainsborough before moving to Ealing. He was directed by Marcel Varnel between 1937 and 1941, and co-directed three films with Basil Dearden*: *The Black Sheep of Whitehall* (1941), *The Goose Steps Out* (1942) and *My Learned Friend* (1943). JC

Other Films Include: *Those Were the Days* (1934); *Boys Will Be Boys* (1935); *Good Morning, Boys, Oh, Mr Porter!* (1937); *Convict 99* (1938); *Ask a Policeman* (1939); *The Ghost of St Michael's* (1941); *The Big Blockade* (1941).

HEPWORTH, Cecil London 1874–1953

British director and producer, who formed the Hepworth Manufacturing Company at the Walton-on-Thames Studios in 1904 and went on to become the most important film producer in the early history of British cinema. 'Throughout its quarter century of existence,' says Rachael Low, the Hepworth Manufacturing Company 'gave the British film industry its greatest and sometimes its only source of pride.' Hepworth entered the film industry with a patented electric arc lamp in 1896, and by 1897 had published the first handbook on cinematography, *Animated Photography: The ABC of the Cinematograph*. For the first decade of the century, he produced, directed and photographed short subjects, both factual and fictional, most notably *Rescued by Rover* (1905) and *John Gilpin's Ride* (1908). He then concentrated on producing and building up a stable of successful contract stars, including Chrissie White, Alma Taylor and Stewart Rome. In 1910 he patented a primitive sound system,

Vivaphone. By 1911 the Hepworth Company was producing longer features, and Hepworth returned to directing in 1914, releasing his two best-known films, *Annie Laurie* and *Comin' Thro' the Rye* in 1916, with Chrissie White. *Comin' Thro' the Rye* was remade in 1923. He was a meticulous craftsman with a feel for natural setting, but his conservativeness became apparent in the 1920s when he failed to keep up with the way cinema was developing. His company went into bankruptcy in 1924, and he released only one more feature, *The House of Marney* (1926) with Alma Taylor. He published his autobiography in 1951. JC

Bib: Cecil Hepworth, *Came the Dawn: Memories of a Film Pioneer* (1951).

HICKEY, Kieran [?]1936 – Dublin 1993

Irish director and writer. Hickey was one of only a few Irish film-makers of his generation to study film formally. He began his career as a director of documentaries with his partners, cameraman Sean Corcoran and editor Pat Duffner. They made sponsored documentaries for state agencies, while also producing films on writers Jonathan Swift and James Joyce. In the 1970s Hickey was one of the first film-makers, along with Bob Quinn*, to help carve out an indigenous Irish cinema. His film *Exposure* (1978), about the suppressed sexuality of three male surveyors who come into contact with a foreign woman, identified an interest in the middle class. This concern was pursued in *Criminal Conversation* (1980), written, like *Exposure*, in collaboration with Philip Davison, which explores the world of Dublin's nouveaux riches. KR

Other Films Include: *A Child's Voice* (1978); *Attracta* (1983); *Short Story: Irish Cinema 1945–1958* (1986); *The Rockingham Shoot* (TV, 1987).

HILLER, (Dame) Wendy Bramshall, Cheshire 1912

British actress. A bright shining star of British cinema, Wendy Hiller has made only around twenty films since her debut in the 1937 quota quickie *Lancashire Lass*, and the particular affection which she seems to inspire can be laid at the door of only three of these twenty: Anthony Asquith's* *Pygmalion* (1938), Gabriel Pascal's *Major Barbara* (1941), and *I Know Where I'm Going!* (1945), directed by Michael Powell* and Emeric Pressburger. What inspires the affection is an unmannered directness, a shyness, an aloofness from seduction, and an economy of performance which makes restraint seem like a positive value rather than an absence of passion. Her alert intelligence in *I Know Where I'm Going!* may be blown a little off course by romance, but she falls in love with dignity and retains a sense of herself. After 1945 much of her work was in theatre, and though she won an Oscar for her supporting role in *Separate Tables* (1958), and was memorable as Gertrude Morel opposite Trevor Howard* in *Sons and Lovers* (1960), her appearances in film were intermittent and succumbed to the 'British disease' of anthology casting: *Murder on the Orient Express* (1974), *Voyage of the Damned* (1976). *The Elephant Man* (1980, US, UK) and *The Lonely Passion of Judith Hearne* (1987) offered her small but rewarding parts, and television gave her some excellent roles – perhaps most notably as the steely matriarch of Trevor Griffiths' *Country* (1981). JC

Other Films Include: *To Be a Woman* [co-narrator] (1951, dir. Jill Craigie); *An Outcast of the Islands* (1952); *Single-handed* (1953); *Something of Value* (1957, US); *Toys in the Attic* (1963, US); *A Man for All Seasons* (1966); *David Copperfield* (1970); *Making Love* (1982, US).

HITCHCOCK, (Sir) Alfred — London 1899 – Los Angeles, California 1980

British director. Hitchcock's contribution to British cinema in the 1920s and 1930s is well documented. Starting as a title card designer with Famous Players–Lasky at Islington Studio, he served as scriptwriter, assistant director and art director to Graham Cutts* on such films as *The Prude's Fall* and *The Passionate Adventure* (both 1924). In 1926, he directed his first two features for Michael Balcon* in Germany, *The Pleasure Garden/Irrgarten der Leidenschaft* and *The Mountain Eagle/Der Bergadler*, absorbing influences from German Expressionism and Soviet montage which would inform his later style. After *The Lodger* (1926), he was one of Britain's most commercially successful directors, and *Blackmail* (1929), though shot silent, was released as Britain's first synchronous sound feature. Its creative and expressive use of sound was greeted in the avant-garde journal *Close Up** as a welcome departure from the 'photographs of people talking' of early sound cinema. In general, Hitchcock's British films, while remaining firmly within a popular tradition of film narrative, show the more diverse and experimental influences of a European art cinema in relation to visual style. After the success of *The Man Who Knew Too Much* (1934) and *The 39 Steps* (1935), however, it was apparent that the future lay in Hollywood. Hitchcock was signed to Selznick in 1938, and moved to America to make *Rebecca* (1940), which won Best Picture and Best Director Academy Awards. It is worth quoting at length the editorial of *Film Weekly* for 16 July 1937, both to indicate the standing which Hitchcock had in Britain, and to show a level of awareness in the trade press which was missing from most other areas of film criticism until the 1960s:

> So Alfred Hitchcock has decided to make a film in Hollywood after all [. . .]. I do not always applaud these Hollywood captures; but in Hitchcock's case I am sure experience of Hollywood's mass-production methods will improve his work. Hitchcock, still probably Britain's most talented director, certainly the most individualistic, has suffered for too long from being unchallenged in his own field and from being allowed to make his pictures almost exactly as he pleases.
>
> There is a strain of wilfulness in Hitchcock which has become more and more apparent with every picture he has made. He is a man with a cold and sardonic eye. He sees the grotesque side of his fellow men. And he is always more than ready to include one scarifying, impish touch even at the risk of sacrificing the mood of a scene or a whole picture. He pleases himself.
>
> Hitchcock is an individualist. Most of us believe him to be a genius in his own line. But he has always lacked restraint. In America he will come in contact with the producer system – the firm guiding hand that has seldom been felt in British studios. That system should curb his waywardness, and give his peculiar talent a more universal feel.

The possibility that Hitchcock might remain in Britain and become a great European director was beyond contemplation. Hitchcock returned to Britain to make two Ministry of Information shorts during the war, *Aventure Malgache* and *Bon Voyage* (both 1944); he supervised the editing of Harry Watt's* *Target for To-night* (1941) for American release, and was supervising director of the first documentary on the opening of the concentration camps, *Memories of the Camps* (1945). He made *Under Capricorn* in Britain in 1949, and returned in 1972 for *Frenzy*.

He was knighted in 1980. JC

Bib: Tom Ryall, *Alfred Hitchcock and the British Cinema* (1986).

Other British Films: *Number Thirteen* [uncompleted] (1922); *Always Tell Your Wife* [dir. Croise; completed direction] (1923); *Downhill, Easy Virtue, The Ring* (1927); *The Farmer's Wife, Champagne* (1928); *The Manxman, Juno and the Paycock* (1929); *Elstree Calling* (dir. Brunel; completed direction], *Murder, An Elastic Affair* [short] (1930); *The Skin Game, Rich and Strange* (1931); *Number Seventeen* (1932); *Waltzes from Vienna* (1934); *Secret Agent, Sabotage* (1936); *Young and Innocent* (1937); *The Lady Vanishes* (1938); *Jamaica Inn* (1939).

HOPKINS, (Sir) Anthony — Port Talbot, Wales 1937

British actor, who achieved international recognition for strong dramatic acting in the 1970s and 1980s, and notoriety for the monstrous credibility of his Hannibal Lecter in *Silence of the Lambs* (1990, US). A respected theatre and television actor, his best film performances are those which allow him a little scope for theatricality. His Captain Bligh in the 1984 version of *The Bounty* rivalled Charles Laughton's*; Richard Attenborough* discovered his sinister qualities in *Magic* (1978, US); and David Lynch cast him effectively as Dr Treves in *The Elephant Man* (1980, US/UK). His more subdued acting skills are evident in *84 Charing Cross Road* (1986), which began life as a BBC television play. More recently, he has taken out a patent on the emotional reticence of the middle-aged English male with a restrained performance as a repressed Edwardian patriarch in *Howards End* (1991), as a butler struggling with feelings while the world turns in *Remains of the Day* (1993), and as the writer C. S. Lewis in *Shadowlands* (1993). More irrepressibly, he has punctuated this streak of constricted Englishness with a wonderfully over-the-top performance as the Dutchman Van Helsing in *Bram Stoker's Dracula* (1992, US).

He was knighted in 1993. His recent films include John Schlesinger's* *The Innocent* (1993, UK/Ger.), and the epically melodramatic *Legends of the Fall* (1994, US). He plays the title role in Oliver Stone's *Nixon* (1995, US). JC

HOSKINS, Bob — Bury St Edmunds 1942

British actor, who received international recognition for his performance as an old-fashioned London gangster out of his depth against new Britons, new sexualities and new criminal forces in Neil Jordan's* *Mona Lisa* (1986). Hoskins received Best Actor awards from Cannes, the New York Film Critics, the Los Angeles Film Critics, and BAFTA. Short, stocky and balding, but nonetheless a romantic, Hoskins' ability to play the bewilderment of the common man had first emerged in Dennis Potter's BBC six-part serial, *Pennies from Heaven* (1978), and was developed in *The Lonely Passion of Judith Hearne* (1987). His tendency to express his bewilderment through violence had appeared in John MacKenzie's *The Long Good Friday* (1981). He plays J. Edgar Hoover in Oliver Stone's *Nixon* (1995, US). JC

Other Films Include: **As Actor** – *The National Health* (1973); *Pink Floyd The Wall* (1982); *The Honorary Consul* (1983); *The Cotton Club* (1984, US); *Brazil* (1985); *Who Framed Roger Rabbit* (1988, US). **As Director** – *The Raggedy Rawney* (1987).

HOWARD, Leslie

Leslie Howard Stainer; London 1893 – shot down over France 1943

British actor, who as a Hollywood and Broadway star in the 1930s represented the best of Englishness for Americans, and on his return to Britain came to represent England's ideals for the English. Jeffrey Richards identifies three components in Howard's Englishness: 'the mystic, the intellectual, and the gentleman amateur'. The three qualities come together in *'Pimpernel' Smith* (1941), which he also produced and directed. A Cambridge professor who uses archaeology as a cover for rescuing intellectuals and artists from Nazi Germany, Smith (Howard) evades his captors at the end by vanishing, quite literally, in a cloud of smoke. There is much in the film which suggests that Howard's identification with the struggle against fascism was idealistic rather than political, and when asked by an American student how he got into the racket Smith responds, 'When a man holds the view that progress and civilisation depend in every age upon the hands and brains of a few exceptional spirits it's rather hard to stand by and see them destroyed.' The film also throws light on Howard's platonic attractiveness: Smith's only love is for 'the one sublime woman', a Greek marble of Aphrodite. That he had a great deal of respect for real women, however, is demonstrated by his last film as a director, *The Gentle Sex* (1943, co-dir. Maurice Elvey), which centres on women's contribution to the war effort.

Howard's best known part may be as Ashley in *Gone With the Wind* (1939, US), but he was best loved as the ideal Englishman: patriotism with a light touch, often whimsical, sometimes comic, never too serious to be jingoistic. When he died in 1943 after his plane was shot down by the Luftwaffe, C. A. Lejeune* wrote, 'Howard was more than just a popular actor. Since the war he has become something of a symbol to the British people.' JC

Bib: Jeffrey Richards, *The Age of the Dream Palace: Cinema and Society in Britain, 1930–1939* (1984).

Other Films Include: *The Heroine of Mons* [short] (1914); *The Happy Warrior* (1917); *The Lackey and the Lady* (1919); *Outward Bound* (1930, US); *Service for Ladies, The Animal Kingdom* (1932, US); *Secrets, Berkeley Square* (1933, US); *Of Human Bondage, British Agent* (1934, US); *The Scarlet Pimpernel* (1935); *The Petrified Forest, Romeo and Juliet* (1936, US); *Pygmalion* [co-dir. Asquith] (1938); *Intermezzo: A Love Story* (1939, US); *49th Parallel, From the Four Corners* [short] (1941); *The First of the Few* [also dir.] (1942); *The Lamp Still Burns* [prod. only] (1943).

HOWARD, Trevor

Cliftonville 1916 – Bushey 1988

British actor, who worked in the theatre for ten years before making his film debut in 1944 in Carol Reed's* *The Way Ahead*. This was followed in 1945 with a role in Anthony Asquith's* *The Way to the Stars*, and with the part for which he is perhaps best remembered, that of the doctor in David Lean's* *Brief Encounter*. British cinema after the war generated a club of typical English men, of which Howard was one, his particular strength being to make English dullness interesting. His characters were typically restrained, but the restraint covered complex emotions and the typicality was finely nuanced. His success in films like Alberto Cavalcanti's* *They Made Me a Fugitive* (1947), David Lean's* *The Passionate Friends* (1949) and Reed's *The Third Man* (1949) made him one of the key actors of the postwar period, and he continued to deliver well-judged character parts for the next three decades. JC

Other Films Include: *I See a Dark Stranger, Green for Danger* (1946); *Odette* (1950); *Lady Godiva Rides Again, Outcast of the Islands* (1951); *The Heart of the Matter* (1953); *The Cockleshell Heroes* (1955); *The Key* (1958); *Sons and Lovers* (1960); *Mutiny on the Bounty* (1962); *Von Ryan's Express* (1965, US); *The Charge of the Light Brigade* (1968); *Ryan's Daughter* (1970); *Ludwig* [It./Fr./Ger.], *A Doll's House* [UK/Fr.] (1973); *Conduct Unbecoming* (1976); *Sir Henry at Rawlinson End* (1980); *Gandhi* (1982); *White Mischief* (1987).

HURST, Brian Desmond

Castle Reagh 1900 – London 1986

Irish director. In 1925 Hurst went to Hollywood, where he worked as an assistant to John Ford, but he returned to England in 1934 and began directing films. One of his first films was *Irish Hearts* (1934), and though he made a number of other Irish-subject films during his career, including *Riders to the Sea* (1935), *Ourselves Alone* (1936), *Hungry Hill* (1946) and *The Playboy of the Western World* (1962), they are not among his best work. Working in a number of genres, including crime, musical, war, comedy, historical romance, and horror, Hurst's career was punctuated by hits and misses, mostly the latter. KR

Other Films Include: *Dangerous Moonlight* (1941); *Scrooge* (1951).

HURT, John Chesterfield 1940

British actor. His career as leading victim of the British cinema was established with a brilliant characterisation of Timothy Evans, hanged in 1944 for crimes he did not commit, in Richard Fleischer's *10 Rillington Place* (1970). Hurt's image projects pain and vulnerability, and his distinctive voice quavers with sensitivity. Regularly cast for type, his performances have a strength which his characters may lack. He won a British Academy Best Supporting Actor award for his role in Alan Parker's* *Midnight Express* (1978) and a Best Actor award for his unsentimental performance in the title role of David Lynch's *The Elephant Man* (1980, UK/US). One of his most distinctive achievements was on television in *The Naked Civil Servant* (1975), where his Quentin Crisp responds to his victimisation with flamboyant eccentricity. His appearance in *Alien* (1979, US) is brief, but to the point; he gives a near definitive performance as Winston Smith in Mike Radford's *Nineteen Eighty-Four* (1984); and his performance in *The Field* (1990, UK/Ir.) is as grotesque and excessive as the character demands. More recently he has had supporting roles in Chris Menges' *Second Best* (1993, US), Gus Van Saut's *Even Cowgirls Get the Blues* (1993, US), and as the very wicked Tim Roth's moderately wicked patron in *Rob Roy* (1995, US). JC

I

IRELAND AND OTHER CINEMAS

Since regular indigenous Irish fiction film production only developed in the late 1970s, most films about the Irish have been produced by British and American film-makers. American cinema has largely constructed Ireland as a bucolic haven free from the rigours of American competitiveness and its capitalist ethos, with a particular celebration of the pre-modern virtues of the West of Ireland, as in *The Quiet Man* (1952). In these films, the work-shy, carefree Irish 'peasants' with their fondness for drink and sport are endorsed. By contrast, British cinema, when not imposing its particular form of racist humour on the Irish, has concerned itself with Irish history (*Captain Boycott*, 1947) or political violence in partitioned Ireland. The latter group of films, such as *The Gentle Gunman* (1952) and *A Prayer for the Dying* (1987), have tended to construct a view of the Irish where historical and political events are dehistoricised and desocialised. To this end, characters such as those played by John Mills* in *The Gentle Gunman* or Stephen

Rea* in *The Crying Game* (1992) are endorsed, since their humanistic concerns lead them to a rejection of the increasingly irrational violence represented by Dirk Bogarde* in *The Gentle Gunman* and Miranda Richardson in *The Crying Game*. It has been argued by John Hill that Irish film-makers, in particular Pat O'Connor* in *Cal* (1984) and Neil Jordan* in *Angel* (1982), carry this British tradition into contemporary Irish cinema. KR

Bib: Kevin Rockett, 'The Irish Migrant and Film', in Patrick O'Sullivan (ed.), *The Creative Migrant* (1994).

IRISH FILM BOARD – see BORD SCANNAN NA hEIREANN

IRISH-LANGUAGE FILM-MAKING

The first Irish-language sound film was a short, *Oidhche Sheanchais/Storyteller's Night* (1935), made by American-born Robert Flaherty* shortly after his *Man of Aran* (1934). It was not until the late 1940s, however, that Irish-language film-making became more frequent. Government-sponsored information films began to be produced in both Irish and English versions, while the Irish-language organisation, Gael Linn, pioneered an Irish-language newsreel, *Amharc Eireann* (A View of Ireland), which was shown in Irish cinemas from 1956 until 1964. Gael Linn made a number of documentaries, the most notable being two directed by George Morrison* which remain key texts for their use of actuality footage and for historical exploration. Gael Linn continued producing documentaries until the early 1970s. These were usually directed by the prolific producer Louis Marcus. By then, the Irish public service broadcasting service, Radio Telefis Eireann* (RTE), had taken on this role, and in 1993 the government announced the establishment of Telefis na Gaeilge, a separate Irish-language television channel, which is due to begin broadcasting in 1995. KR

IRONS, Jeremy Cowes 1948

British actor, a leading member of the generation of British film actors who emerged in the 1980s. With a distinguished stage career at the Royal Shakespeare Company in the 1970s, Irons first appeared as a star in 1981: on television in the international hit, *Brideshead Revisited*, and on film in Karel Reisz's* *The French Lieutenant's Woman*. A distinctly cool actor (with a chilly sexuality) who tends to work in flickers of expression and eloquent silences, he is quoted as saying, 'I dislike the vulgarity of excessive effort.' His most complex performance is as the psychologically indivisible twins in David Cronenberg's *Dead Ringers* (1988, Canada), for which he won a New York Film Critics award. Constantly in demand since his Oscar for *Reversal of Fortune* (1990, US), and increasingly threatened by type-casting, his acting – in, for example, Louis Malle's* *Fatale/Damage* (1992) – seems to depend more and more on a weak lower lip and an intense all-purpose gaze. JC

Other Films Include: *Nijinsky* (1980, US); *Moonlighting* (1982); *Betrayal, The Wild Duck* [Australia] (1983); *Un amour de Swann/ Swann in Love* (1984, Fr./Ger.); *The Mission* (1986); *A Chorus of Disapproval, Danny the Champion of the World* (1989); *Kafka* (1991, US/Fr./UK); *Waterland* (1992); *The House of the Spirits* [Ger./Den./ Port.], *M. Butterfly* [US] (1993); *Die Hard with a Vengeance* (1995, US).

IVORY, James – see MERCHANT-IVORY

J

JACKSON, Glenda

Hoylake 1936

British actress, who gained critical attention through her highly adventurous work with the Royal Shakespeare Company in Peter Brook's Artaud-inspired Theatre of Cruelty season in the 1960s. Her performance as Charlotte Cordier in Peter Weiss' *Marat/Sade* was translated to the screen in 1967, and the improvisatory Brook production on Vietnam, *U.S.*, was adapted as *Tell Me Lies* (1968). As in her theatre work, her work in the cinema has a thread of the dangerous running through it. Her career has been closely linked to Ken Russell's*, with an Oscar-winning performance in *Women in Love* (1969), and roles in *The Music Lovers* (1970), *The Boy Friend* (1972), *Salome's Last Dance* (1987) and *The Rainbow* (1988). A strong dramatic actress with an ability to play strong women, she received a British Academy Award for her performance in *Sunday Bloody Sunday* (1971), but showed herself adept at light comedy by winning a second Oscar for *A Touch of Class* (1973). In 1987, she appeared in Lezli-An Barrett's *Business as Usual*, one of the few British feature films directed by a woman. She became a Labour Member of Parliament in the 1992 election. JC

Other Films Include: *Mary Queen of Scots* [as Queen Elizabeth I] (1972); *Bequest to the Nation* (1973); *The Maids* (1976); *The Romantic Englishwoman/Une Anglaise romantique* (1975, UK/Fr.); *The Incredible Sarah* [as Sarah Bernhardt] (1976); *Hedda* (1977); *Stevie* [as Stevie Smith] (1978); *Hopscotch* (1980); *Strange Interlude* (TV, 1988); *A Murder of Quality* (TV, 1991).

JARMAN, Derek   Northwood 1942 – London 1994

British director. Coming out of art school in the 1960s, set designer for ballet and opera and for Ken Russell*, working with Super 8mm and video on lower than low budgets, Jarman has often been placed unproblematically by both critics and admirers in the gay avant-garde, radically and scandalously 'other' to the traditions of British cinema. Certainly, his work with cheap, accessible technologies, though it may not have been of his own choosing, has added new and distinctive formal possibilities to British cinema, and films like *Jubilee* (1978), *The Tempest* (1980) and *Edward II* (1991) offer a political attack on the state of England. By his own account, however, he is a traditionalist, consigned to the margins rather than choosing to work there: 'The one thing I really regret about my career was that I was put into the position of being anything but the most traditional film-maker of my generation.' The tradition to which he belongs might be that of Humphrey Jennings*: the same romanticism, the same love of style, of landscape and of Englishness. Both men were painters who began their careers as set designers; both have a connection to surrealist observation. But there is something disingenuous about Jarman's appeal to the English tradition, and it is tradition refracted through the more camp sensibility of Andy Warhol, Kenneth Anger and David Hockney. The films play out a tension between an elegiac traditionalism which continually returns to lost Golden Ages – Shakespeare, Marlowe, Caravaggio – and a gay, pop sensibility on which traditions founder. Jarman's emblematic image is the garden which he created at Dungeness and memorialised in *The Garden* (1990) – an exquisite, miniature English garden on an extremely stony soil.

His last film *Blue* (1993), a sound track against a blue screen, reflected on his experience of Aids and remembered the friends who had died of it, but refused what he called 'the pandemonium of images'. He died of Aids-related illness in 1994. JC

Bib: Jonathan Hacker and David Price, *Take 10: Contemporary British Film Directors* (1991).

Other Feature Films Include: *Sebastiane* [16mm; in Latin with subtitles] (1976); *The Angelic Conversation* [Super 8mm] (1985); *Caravaggio* [35mm] (1986); *Aria* ['Depuis le jour' ep.; Super 8mm and 35mm], *The Last of England* [Super 8mm] (1987); *War Requiem*

[35mm and Super 8mm] (1988); *Wittgenstein* [Super 8mm and 35mm] (1993).

JENNINGS, Humphrey

Walberswick, 1907 – Poros, Greece 1950

British director. 'Humphrey Jennings,' wrote Lindsay Anderson* in 1954, 'is the only real poet the British cinema has yet produced.' An intellectual and artist of enormous range, Jennings was a theatre set designer, poet and painter; he was a member, with Herbert Read, Roland Penrose and André Breton, of the Organising Committee of the International Surrealist Exhibition held in London in 1936; with Tom Harrisson and Charles Madge he was one of the initiators of Mass Observation, a project whose observations of the everyday were not so far removed from surrealism as one might suppose; and his uncompleted book, *Pandaemonium*, attempts an archaeology of discourses before Michel Foucault had invented the discipline. Jennings joined the GPO Film Unit in 1934, where he directed, worked with Len Lye* on his early animations, and designed for Alberto Cavalcanti*. Jennings was at the centre of English modernism throughout the 1930s, an avant-gardism and 'artiness' which reputedly was met with some suspicion by John Grierson*. The war, however, and the intense, romantic patriotism which it evoked, made him a lyrical rather than a critical modernist. His greatest achievement is represented by the group of films he made during the war: in particular, *Words for Battle* (1941), *Listen to Britain* (1942), made with Stewart McAllister, *Fires Were Started* (1943), and *A Diary for Timothy* (1945).

Jennings died in 1950 at the age of 43, falling from the rocks of the Greek island of Poros while scouting locations. JC

Bib: David Parkinson (ed.), *The Humphrey Jennings Film Reader* (1993).

Other Films Include: *Post-Haste, The Story of the Wheel* (1934); *Spare Time, The First Days* [with Harry Watt and Pat Jackson] (1939); *Spring Offensive, London Can Take It!* [with Harry Watt] (1940); *Heart of Britain* (1941); *The Silent Village* (1943); *The True Story of Lili Marlene* (1944); *A Defeated People* (1946); *The Cumberland Story* (1947); *Dim Little Island* (1949); *Family Portrait* (1950).

JHABVALA, Ruth Prawer – see MERCHANT-IVORY

JOHNSON, (Dame) Celia

Richmond, Surrey
1908 – Nettlebed, Oxfordshire 1982

British actress. Celia Johnson has become so inextricably linked to the part of Laura in *Brief Encounter* (1945) that it is sometimes surprising to see her in other roles. Much of her career was in theatre, and since her acting is in any case quietly self-effacing she seems to invite her own invisibility. One only has to compare her role as the English suburban rose in *Brief Encounter*, however, with that of the respectable working-class mam in *This Happy Breed* (1944), made the year before, to recognise the skill and range she brought to her film performances. The British cinema of the 1960s and 1970s had little to offer her, other than a good supporting role in *The Prime of Miss Jean Brodie* (1969). In 1980 she partnered Trevor Howard* again, with passion spent but skill undiminished, in the BBC television adaptation of Paul Scott's *Staying On*. JC

JORDAN, Neil

Sligo 1950

Irish director and writer. Jordan was an established short story writer (*Night in Tunisia and Other Stories*, 1978) and novelist (*The Past*, 1980) before he made his first film, a documentary on the making of John Boorman's* *Excalibur* (1981). His first feature, *Angel* (1982), was funded by the Irish Film Board* and Channel 4* but since then, though continuing to live in Ireland, he has most frequently made films in Britain – *The Company of Wolves* (1984), *Mona Lisa* (1986) and *High Spirits* (1988) – and America – *We're No Angels* (1989). Despite using unconventional material, Jordan established himself as a commercial director with *The Crying Game* (1992), the most successful non-American film ever released in the USA, with cinema box-office takings alone in excess of $60 million. Building on this success, *Interview with the Vampire: the Vampire Chronicles* (1994, US) gave him a large canvas, a star cast (Tom Cruise and Brad Pitt), and a cult book (by Ann Rice). He handed the material with a sensuous decadence almost wearying in its relentlessness.

The Irish themes in Jordan's work include a concern with the metaphysics of political violence, focusing on individuals involved with Northern Ireland's paramilitary organisations and their attempts to start a new life (*Angel*, *The Crying Game*). The legitimacy of the state is rarely questioned, and it has been argued that the representation of Ireland in these films is a continuation of a British tradition of dehistoricising and desocialising Irish political violence. The modest scale of *The Miracle* (1991) brought Jordan back to his Irish roots with a low-key but effective exploration of an American woman's rediscovery of her Irish son after a long absence. KR

Bib: Kevin Rockett, Luke Gibbons, John Hill, *Cinema and Ireland* (1987).

JULIEN, Isaac

London 1961

British director, the first of the new wave of Black British independent film-makers to score at least a critical success with a feature film. *Young Soul Rebels* (1991), made through the BFI* Production Board with a budget of £1.2 million, won the Critics' Prize at the 1991 Cannes Festival. Set in 1977, the film uses the Queen's Silver Jubilee, the musical subcultures around punk, soul, disco and Rock against Racism, and the realignments in youth culture around anti-fascism, anti-racism and the gay movement, to explore a politics and a sensibility of racial and sexual difference and identity. Julien was a founder member of the Black Workshop, Sankofa. He co-directed with Maureen Blackwood *The Passion of Remembrance* (1986), and directed *This is Not an AIDS Ad* (1987) and *Looking for Langston* (1989), a visually stunning evocation of Langston Hughes, the gay Afro-American poet of the Harlem Renaissance. JC

Bib: Isaac Julien and Colin MacCabe, *Diary of a Young Soul Rebel* (1991).

KERR, Deborah

Deborah Jane Kerr-Trimmer; Helensburgh, Scotland 1921

British actress, with a distinguished record in some of the most vivid British films of the 1940s and some of the most memorable Hollywood melodramas of the 1950s and 1960s. Her role as the governess in *The King and I* (1956, US) is almost a parody of the qualities she brought to other dramatic roles: the spirited, independent woman, a little constrained by good breeding, up against a masculine force she had to bring under control. The 'breeding' was not always her hallmark. In her second film, John Baxter's* tough tragedy of the Depression, *Love on the Dole* (1941), she plays the working-class daughter who cynically sells herself to a rich spiv after the man she loved is killed in a demonstration. There were few parts for independent women in the patriotic films made during and after the war, and it was Michael Powell* and Emeric Pressburger* who offered Kerr her best parts, with striking roles in *The Life and Death of Colonel Blimp* (1943) and *Black Narcissus* (1947). She won a Best Actress Award from the New York Critics in 1947 for *Black Narcissus* and for Frank Launder* and Sidney Gilliat's* *I See a Dark Stranger* (1946). Offered a contract by MGM, she moved to Hollywood in 1949. She was nominated for the Best Actress Oscar for *Edward My Son* (1949), *From Here to Eternity* (1953, US), *The King and I*, *Heaven Knows, Mr Allison* (1957), *Separate Tables* (1958, US) and *The Sundowners* (1961, US/Australia). She was made a Fellow of the British Film Institute* in 1986. JC

Other Films Include: *Perfect Strangers* (1945); *King Solomon's Mines* (1950, US); *Quo Vadis* (1951, US); *Tea and Sympathy* (1956, US); *An Affair to Remember* (1957, US); *Bonjour Tristesse* (1958); *Beloved Infidel* (1959, US); *The Innocents* (1961); *The Night of the Iguana* (1964, US); *The Arrangement* (1969, US); *The Assam Garden* (1985).

KILLANIN, (Lord) Michael

Born 1914

Irish film producer. Though Lord Killanin's career covers an exceptionally broad range of activities, from journalist in China in the 1930s to President of the International Olympic Commission during one of its most turbulent times, the Moscow Olympics, his role as go-between and producer with John Ford in particular is of considerable importance. Befriending Ford in Hollywood in the 1930s, in part because he was from the same area of County Galway as Ford's ancestors, he acted as local liaison in Ireland during the making of *The Quiet Man* (1952). Killanin, with Ford and Tyrone Power, formed Four Provinces Films, with the intention of producing films in Ireland. Their first project was Ford's *The Rising of the Moon* (1957), but Power died shortly after its completion, thus effectively ending the partnership, though Killanin produced Ford's *Gideon's Day* (1958), a Scotland Yard story. He was also associate producer on *Young Cassidy* (1964), part of which was directed by Ford, and was co-producer of Brian Desmond Hurst's* *The Playboy of the Western World* (1962). Killanin's son, Redmond Morris, also works in film, having been associate producer of Thaddeus O'Sullivan's* *December Bride* (1990) and co-producer of Neil Jordan's* *The Miracle* (1991). KR

KORDA, (Sir) Alexander

Sándor László Kellner; Puszta Turpósztó, Hungary 1893 – London 1956

British producer and director of Hungarian origin. Korda entered the film industry in his native Hungary, where he directed his first film in 1914. After arrest under the Horthy regime, he fled to Vienna in 1919.

He continued producing in Austria and Germany and spent three undistinguished years in Hollywood, before moving to Paramount's subsidiary in Paris in 1930, where he notably directed the classic *Marius* for Marcel Pagnol. In 1932, he arrived in Britain, where he founded London Films, and worked with his brothers, Zoltan and Vincent*.

London Films' first features were 'quota quickies', but in 1933 Korda himself directed the hugely successful *The Private Life of Henry VIII*. The film cost £60,000 to make and grossed £500,000 in its first international run. In the US it broke box-office records for first-day admissions at Radio City Music-hall. This set Korda's course, a course which was decidedly bumpy in financial terms but pre-eminent in influence. He built Denham Studios near London in 1935 (though he was forced to sell in 1938). The same year he was made a partner, with Chaplin, Pickford and Fairbanks, in United Artists. During the war, he shuttled between Britain and America. Karol Kulik, in her biography of Korda, suggests that he may have been acting as a special envoy for his friend Winston Churchill, a task for which his knighthood in 1942 may have been the reward. He resumed directing briefly after the war, revamped London Films, which was responsible for such films as *The Third Man* (1949), *The Tales of Hoffmann* (1951), *Hobson's Choice* (1954) and *Richard III* (1955), took a controlling interest in British Lion in 1946 until it went into receivership in 1954, and founded the British Film Academy in 1947.

Like John Grierson*, Korda is less important for the individual films he directed or produced than for the influence he exerted and the context he framed. Like Grierson also, the influence is open to debate. Korda was determined that the British cinema should be an international cinema, and to be international it had to compete with Hollywood. Hence the rocky financial road. At the same time, he recognised that 'to be truly international a film must first of all be truly and intensely national', and hence the important careers which he encouraged, the projects he initiated, and the opportunities which he created. JC

Bib: Karol Kulik, *Alexander Korda: The Man Who Could Work Miracles* (1975).

Other Films Include: **As Director** (UK unless indicated) – *Tutyu és Totyo* (1914, Hung.); *Eine Dubarry von heute/A Modern Dubarry* (1927, Ger.); *The Private Life of Helen of Troy* (1927, US); *Service for Ladies, Wedding Rehearsal* (1932); *The Private Life of Don Juan* (1934); *Rembrandt* (1936); *That Hamilton Woman/Lady Hamilton* (1941, US); *Perfect Strangers* (1945); *An Ideal Husband* (1948). **As Producer –** *Catherine the Great* (1934); *The Scarlet Pimpernel* (1935); *Sanders of the River, The Ghost Goes West, Things to Come, The Man Who Could Work Miracles* (1936); *I, Claudius* [uncompleted], *Elephant Boy, Knight Without Armour* (1937); *The Divorce of Lady X,*

The Drum (1938); *The Four Feathers, The Lion Has Wings* (1939); *Conquest of the Air* (1936–40), *The Thief of Bagdad* (1940); *Jungle Book* (1942, US); *Anna Karenina* (1948).

KORDA, Vincent

Puszta Turpósztó, Hungary 1897 – London 1979

British art director of Hungarian origin, who was an accomplished painter, studying in Budapest and Paris, before being brought to Denham Studios by his older brother, Alexander. He designed most of the memorable Korda productions of the 1930s, including *The Private Life of Henry VIII* (1933), *Things to Come* (1936) and, his masterpiece, *Rembrandt* (1936). He worked with Zoltan Korda on *Sanders of the River* (1935), *Elephant Boy* (1937) and *The Drum* (1938), and won an Oscar for *The Thief of Bagdad* (1940). Korda's designs are never simply backgrounds, and particularly in *Things to Come* and *The Third Man* (1949) they show the influence of his painterly training and of his interest in European modernism, expressionism and art deco. JC

Other Films Include: *Marius* (1931, Fr.); *The Girl from Maxim's* (1933); *Catherine the Great, The Private Life of Don Juan* (1934); *The Scarlet Pimpernel, Moscow Nights* (1935); *The Ghost Goes West, The Man Who Could Work Miracles* (1936); *The Spy in Black, The Lion Has Wings* (1939); *Lady Hamilton* (1941); *To Be or Not to Be, Jungle Book* (1942, both US); *Perfect Strangers* (1945); *An Ideal Husband, The Fallen Idol* (1948); *Outcast of the Islands* (1951); *The Sound Barrier* (1952); *Summer Madness, The Deep Blue Sea* (1955); *The Yellow Rolls-Royce* (1964).

KUBRICK, Stanley

New York 1928

American director, who has made films in both Britain and America since the early 1960s, moving to England in 1974. The move was precipitated by a mixture of anglophilia and a desire for greater creative freedom, but unlike his compatriot Joseph Losey*, Kubrick has remained an American director in exile rather than a British or European director. *Lolita* (1962) and *2001: A Space Odyssey* (1968), though technically British films, are American in their conception; and *Barry Lyndon* (1975), based on a Thackeray novel, loses the sense of Thackeray's Englishness in an overlush visual style. Only the brilliant *A Clockwork Orange* (1972), from an Anthony Burgess novel, has a great deal to say about Englishness, projecting it to a futuristic decadence with a glossy, hard-edged violence which provoked the anxiety of the British Board of Film Censors*. JC

KUREISHI, Hanif

London 1954

British writer and director, who scripted two of the most successful Channel 4* films of the 1980s: *My Beautiful Laundrette* (1985) and *Sammy and Rosie Get Laid* (1987), both directed by Stephen Frears*. *My Beautiful Laundrette* was a surprise success in both Britain and America, winning Kureishi an Oscar nomination for Best Screenplay. Centring on a mixed-race gay relationship in a Pakistani-owned laundrette, it ironically dissects the multicultural structure of Thatcherite London. *Sammy and Rosie,* less admired by the critics, offers a bleaker account of Britain in the context of the Brixton riots. In 1991, Kureishi directed *London Kills Me* (1991), a Dickensian fable of London street life and drug-dealing, from his own screenplay. His novel *The Buddha of Suburbia* (1990) has been dramatised by the BBC (first shown 1993). JC

L

LAUGHTON, Charles

Scarborough 1899 –
Hollywood, California 1962

British actor, who became one of the most popular stars of the 1930s after his rumbustious, Oscar-winning performance in the title role of Alexander Korda's* *The Private Life of Henry VIII* (1933). He began on the stage, appearing with his wife, Elsa Lanchester, in London and on Broadway. In 1928 he made his film debut in two shorts, *Daydreams* and *Bluebottles*, directed by Ivor Montagu*. Following Broadway success in 1931, he was contracted to Paramount and throughout the 1930s he commuted between Britain and Hollywood, a star on both sides of the Atlantic. By 1939 he had taken up residence in Hollywood and became an American citizen in 1950.

A large actor in every sense, Laughton's appearance barred him from romantic leads, but the scale of his performance in character leads like Bligh in *Mutiny on the Bounty* (1935, US) or Ruggles in *Ruggles of Red Gap* (1935, US) left very little room on the screen for anyone else. Laughton's performance in *Henry VIII* (which had been conceived by Korda as a vehicle for Laughton and Lanchester) has been noted for the sexual innocence of its raunchiness, which John Grierson* attributed to the vitality and vulgarity of the music-hall tradition. The association with Korda continued in 1936 with *Rembrandt*, possibly a better film though a box-office failure, and with the ill-fated *I, Claudius* (1937), directed by Josef von Sternberg but unfinished.

Laughton returned to Britain in 1954 to make *Hobson's Choice* with David Lean*.

Laughton continued his theatrical career throughout his life, collaborating for three years with Bertolt Brecht in the first production of *Galileo*, directed in 1947 by Joseph Losey*. He directed and co-scripted one film, which has acquired cult status, *The Night of the Hunter* (1955, US), a baroque and tense thriller starring Robert Mitchum. JC

Bib: Simon Callow, *Charles Laughton: A Difficult Actor* (1987).

Other Films Include (US unless stated): *The Sign of the Cross* (1932); *The Barretts of Wimpole Street* (1934); *Les Misérables* (1935); *Vessel of Wrath* [UK], *St. Martin's Lane* [UK] (1938); *Jamaica Inn* [UK], *The Hunchback of Notre Dame* (1939); *The Tuttles of Tahiti* (1942); *This Land is Mine* [dir. Renoir] (1943); *The Canterville Ghost* (1944); *The Paradine Case, The Big Clock* (1948); *The Man on the Eiffel Tower/ L'Homme de la Tour Eiffel* [as Inspector Maigret] (1950, US/Fr.); *Young Bess* [as Henry VIII] (1953); *Witness for the Prosecution* (1958); *Spartacus* (1960); *Advise and Consent* (1962).

LAUNDER, Frank — Hitchin, 1906
and
GILLIAT, Sidney — Edgely 1908–1994

British directors, producers and writers. Their collaboration as screenwriters began in 1935, and included such films as *The Lady Vanishes* (1938) for Alfred Hitchcock* and *Night Train to Munich* (1940) and *The Young Mr Pitt* (1942) for Carol Reed*. Their first directorial credit was for *Millions Like Us* (1943), a documentary-style feature film on women factory workers during the war, which was followed in 1944 by *Two Thousand Women* (dir. Launder). Their collaboration continued until *The Great St Trinian's Train Robbery* in 1966. While they wrote together, they alternated between directing and producing, with Launder showing a tendency towards the eccentric farce of *The Happiest Days of Your Life* (1950) and the 'St Trinian's' series which followed it, and Gilliat favouring social comedies like *The Rake's Progress* (1945) and *Left, Right and Centre* (1959), with occasional black comedies like *London Belongs to Me* (1948). In the 1940s, both produced and directed effective and intricate thrillers such as *Green for Danger* (Gilliat, 1946) and *I See a Dark Stranger* (Launder, 1946), but in the 1950s and 1960s they specialised more in distinctively British comedy, based on literate scripts, eccentric characters, and a mildly caustic glance. JC

Bib: Geoff Brown, *Launder and Gilliat* (1977).

Other Films (All Written Together) Include: **Director Launder, Producer Gilliat** – *Captain Boycott* (1947); *The Blue Lagoon* (1949); *Lady Godiva Rides Again* (1951); *Folly to be Wise* (1952); *The Belles of St Trinian's* (1954); *Geordie* (1955); *Blue Murder at St Trinian's* (1957); *The Bridal Path* (1959); *The Pure Hell of St Trinian's* (1960); *Joey Boy* (1965). **Director Gilliat, Producer Launder** – *State Secret* (1950); *The Story of Gilbert and Sullivan* (1953); *The Constant Husband* (1955); *Fortune is a Woman* (1957); *Only Two Can Play* (1962).

LEAN, (Sir) David — Croydon 1908 – London 1991

British director. Lean began his long film career as a clapper boy with Maurice Elvey* in 1926. From 1930 he was an editor for Gaumont-British News, British Movietone News and British Paramount, editing such feature films as *Pygmalion* (1938) and *49th Parallel* (1941): 'the best editor I ever worked with,' says Michael Powell*, 'or should I say worked for.' His first film as a director, *In Which We Serve* (1942), was co-directed with Noël Coward*, and initiated a partnership which resulted in three more films from Coward scripts: *This Happy Breed* (1944), *Blithe Spirit* (1945) and *Brief Encounter* (1945). The next phase of his career, from 1946 to 1956, seems inflected by his encounter with Dickens – in the Dickensian atmosphere of *Hobson's Choice* (1954) as much as in the atmospheric adaptations of *Great Expectations* (1946) and *Oliver Twist* (1948). And the final phase, opened by *The Bridge on the River Kwai* (1957), is dominated by the wide-screen, 'big' theme, Oscar-winning epic – *Lawrence of Arabia* (1962), *Doctor Zhivago* (1965), *Ryan's Daughter* (1970) and, after a fourteen-year gap, *A Passage to India* (1985). The disparities of scale, from intimacy to epic distance, conceal any authorial consistency. There is a constant return from *Brief Encounter*, through *The Passionate Friends* (1949) and *Summer Madness* (1955), all the way to *A Passage to India*, of repressed passions and forfeited love, but the passions recede as the actors disappear into beautifully photographed landscapes. Roy Armes, discussing Lean, quotes John Grierson*: 'When a director dies, he becomes a photographer.'

Lean was knighted in 1984. JC

Bib: Gerald Pratley, *The Cinema of David Lean* (1974).

LEIGH, Mike — Salford 1943

British director, most of whose work has been in theatre and television drama since the 1970s, with only four feature films to his credit, and a seventeen-year gap between his first feature film, *Bleak Moments* (1971), and his next, *High Hopes* (1988), which won the Critics' Award at Cannes. Since 1988, his films have attracted increasing international attention. His extensive work in theatre and television established a highly individual working method in which scripts were developed out of improvisation, the director/writer's role being to 'sculpt' characters and situations out of the material which the actors threw up. The detailed observation is often astonishing, but his aesthetic owes more to the *Carry On** tradition than to the critical realist tradition, a comedy of character which ruthlessly exposes vulnerability and social pretension but ends up assuring the audience of its own superiority. In his third feature film, *Life is Sweet* (1990), the revelation that people without taste are not necessarily people without feeling seems patronising and predictable, while in *Naked* (1993), which brings a new level of intensity to its performances, the lingering question of whether Leigh's misogyny is a thing in itself or just an aspect of misanthropy seems to be resolved on the side of misogyny. JC

Bib: Andy Medhurst, 'Mike Leigh: beyond embarrassment', *Sight and Sound* (November 1993).

LEIGH, Vivien

Vivien Mary Hartley, Darjeeling, India 1913 – London 1967

British actress, written of as the fragile 'Dresden shepherdess' of English acting until she snatched the part of Scarlett O'Hara in *Gone With the Wind* (1939, US) from under the noses of a number of American hopefuls. She received an Oscar for her performance. She made her film debut in 1934, and was placed under contract by Alexander Korda* in 1935. A well-publicised extra-marital affair with Laurence Olivier* after their appearance together in *Fire Over England* (1937) gave her the other ingredient of international stardom – romantic scandal. Always a delicate and graceful actress, in her British films she seemed exquisitely English, though when her Englishness was set against the grosser, un-English masculinity of Clark Gable or Marlon Brando, the steel within the delicacy became apparent. She won an Oscar and Best Actress awards from the New York Film Critics, the Venice Festival and the British Film Academy for her performance as Blanche du Bois in *A Streetcar Named Desire* (1952, US). Her delicacy extended to her health, and she suffered from tuberculosis through much of her career. JC

Other Films Include: *Things Are Looking Up, Gentleman's Agreement, Look Up and Laugh* [with Gracie Fields] (1935); *Dark Journey, Storm in a Teacup* (1937); *A Yank at Oxford, St. Martin's Lane* (1938); *Waterloo Bridge* (1940, US); *That Hamilton Woman/ Lady Hamilton* [title role] (1941, US); *Caesar and Cleopatra* [title role]

(1946); *Anna Karenina* [title role] (1948); *The Deep Blue Sea* (1955); *The Roman Spring of Mrs Stone* (1961); *Ship of Fools* (1965, US).

LEJEUNE, C. A. Manchester 1897 – Pinner Hill 1973

British film critic, who wrote on cinema for almost forty years, in the *Manchester Guardian* from 1922 to 1928 and in the *Observer* from 1928 to 1960. She was also a regular broadcaster. Lejeune was a passionate advocate of a British cinema which celebrated British values. 'It is time,' she declared in 1931, 'that we began to be country-proud and empire-proud in the cinema, to boast a bit, to be a little swaggering for once. God knows, we have plenty to swagger about' – and she was clear that a British cinema of quality was a cinema of emotional restraint: Anthony Asquith's* *The Way to the Stars* (1945) had 'the great merit, rare in Hollywood pictures these days, of emotional restraint. [. . .] Again and again the audience is left to resolve its own tensions: an operation that is painful, unusual, and good for the soul.' Though she valued cinema's entertainment values – she enthused over Jessie Matthews*, for instance – she had little time for the bizarre or the excessive and no taste for the seamy. Strongly and conservatively moral, she retired because she did not approve of the growing trend of 'sex and savagery' in the cinema of the late 1950s and early 1960s.

Though no one would claim it as a victory for feminism, it is worth noting that there was a period in the 1950s when British film criticism was dominated by three women: C. A. Lejeune at the *Observer*, Dilys Powell* at the *Sunday Times*, and Penelope Houston, editor of *Sight and Sound**. JC

Bib: Anthony Lejeune, *The C. A. Lejeune Reader* (1991).

LESTER, Richard Philadelphia, USA 1932

American/British director, who has worked mainly in Britain since 1955. Coming out of music composition, television, and TV commercials, and passing through an association with Spike Milligan and Peter Sellers* on a television Goon Show spin-off called *A Show Called Fred* (1956), Lester brought a zany, pop sensibility to the cinema of the 1960s which set the style for the Beatles' first incursions into film, *A Hard Day's Night* (1964) and *Help!* (1965). In these films, and in his first feature, *It's Trad, Dad!* (1962) – starring Helen Shapiro – he brought the pacy editing and visual punch of television commercials to film, coining the vocabulary of early music video and catching the mood of the new music. *The Knack ... and How to Get It* (1965) anticipated the more cynical *Alfie* (Lewis Gilbert, 1966), and *The Bed Sitting Room* (1969) links the Goons and Monty Python. Some of the pop sensibility can still be glimpsed in Lester's contribution to the sagas of *Superman II* and *III* (1981 and 1983) and *The Three* (and *Four*) *Musketeers* (1974 and 1975), but the exuberant flair began to show its age and many of the later films could have been made by someone else. JC

LOACH, Ken

Nuneaton 1937

British director, whose work in political cinema and television over the past three decades has fuelled debate both about the content of political film and about its form. A former President of the Oxford University Dramatic Society, Loach joined the BBC in 1962. He directed early episodes of *Z Cars* (1962–), and the television play, *Up the Junction* (1965). In 1966, with producer Tony Garnett, he directed *Cathy Come Home* (1966), a documentary drama on the scandal of homelessness. 'Loach/Garnett' became a generic term for some of the best television drama of the 1960s and 1970s, raising debates on the left about the possibilities of 'progressive realism' and outrage on the right about the blurring of fact and fiction. Loach and Garnett adapted their approach to cinema in films such as *Kes* (1969) and *Family Life* (1971), concentrating on the apparent spontaneity of the actors (and non-actors) and a documentary camera style to create the effect of unrehearsed reality. Since 1981, Loach has worked independently of both Garnett and the BBC, though much of his work still retains a television involvement through Channel 4*. His film on the security forces in Northern Ireland, *Hidden Agenda,* won him a Special Jury Prize at the Cannes film festival in 1990, an award which he repeated in 1993 with *Raining Stones*. JC

Bib: Jonathan Hacker and David Price, *Take 10: Contemporary British Film Directors* (1991).

Other Films Include: *Poor Cow* (1967); *Black Jack* (1980); *Looks and Smiles* (1981); *Fatherland* (1986); *Riff-Raff* (1990); *Ladybird, Ladybird* (1993); *Land and Freedom* (1995).

LOCKWOOD, Margaret

Margaret Day; Karachi, India 1916 – London 1990

British actress. Margaret Lockwood had appeared in around thirty films by 1943, many of them 'quota quickies', but the list includes a number of roles for Michael Powell* and Carol Reed*, the lead role in Alfred Hitchcock's* *The Lady Vanishes* (1939) and a role as the idealistic Michael Redgrave's* scheming wife in *The Stars Look Down* (1939). From 1965 she had a second career on television in the popular soap opera, *The Flying Swan*. But it was the period from 1943 to

1947, from *The Man in Grey* (1943) to *Jassy* (1947), which defined her image as the wicked lady of the Gainsborough melodramas, offering to postwar women an alternative image of womanhood. Rather than the proper and moving denial of desire of *Brief Encounter* (1945), the Lockwood character wanted it all and wanted it now. Her exchanges with James Mason* in *The Wicked Lady* (1945) make it unambiguous that her body has a market value, to be bargained for rather than innocently wooed with romantic love. Of course, she is punished in the end, but not before she has established that conquest and desire are not exclusively male pursuits. The popularity, particularly among women, of the melodramatic extravagance of the Lockwood character suggests an undercurrent to the restraint of British realism which recent feminist criticism has begun to recognise. JC

Bib: Sue Aspinall and Robert Murphy (eds.), *Gainsborough Melodrama*, BFI Dossier 18 (1983).

Other Films Include: *Lorna Doone*, *Midshipman Easy* (1935); *Melody and Romance* (1937); *Owd Bob*, *Bank Holiday* (1938); *Rulers of the Sea* [US], *Susannah of the Mounties* [US], *A Girl Must Live* (1939); *Night Train to Munich*, *The Girl in the News* (1940); *Quiet Wedding* (1941); *Dear Octopus* (1943); *Give Us the Moon*, *Love Story* (1944); *A Place of One's Own*, *I'll Be Your Sweetheart* (1945); *Bedelia* (1946); *Cardboard Cavalier* (1949); *Highly Dangerous* (1950); *Trouble in the Glen* (1954); *Cast a Dark Shadow* (1955); *The Slipper and the Rose* (1976).

LONDON FILM-MAKERS CO-OP

British institution, which was established in 1966 on the model of the New York Film-makers' Co-op organised by Jonas Mekas in 1962. Its function was (and is) not simply to support the production of avant-garde film, but to set up mechanisms for distribution and exhibition and to provide a focus for theoretical debate. There has been no continuous avant-garde tradition in Britain, and the Co-op saw itself as part of an international movement. It did, however, develop a distinct national identity around 'structural film'. In the distinction which Peter Wollen* makes in his influential essay 'The Two Avant Gardes', the Co-op belongs to the painterly avant-garde deriving from explorations of the means of expression (time, repetition, space, duration) rather than from the more political traditions associated with Soviet cinema and Jean-Luc Godard*. The two traditions, of course, were never completely separate. The work of the Co-op, particularly through film-makers and writers like Malcolm Le Grice and Peter Gidal, is less a means of expression than a means of theoretical investigation through film of representation, meaning and film itself. JC

Bib: Peter Gidal, *Materialist Film* (1989).

LOSEY, Joseph

La Crosse, Wisconsin 1909 – London 1984

American/British director, who was blacklisted after his failure to attend the House Un-American Activities Committee in 1951, and moved to Britain where he established himself in the first rank of British and European directors. Losey's early career was in theatre, where he directed the Charles Laughton*/Bertolt Brecht collaboration on *Galileo* in 1947. He had attended film classes with Eisenstein in Moscow in the 1930s, and in Hollywood, in the 1940s, he had established a reputation as a director of tight *noir* thrillers. His early work in Britain, much of it directed under pseudonyms to conceal his participation from American exhibitors, followed in the same line with such films as *The Sleeping Tiger* (1954), directed as 'Victor Hanbury', *Blind Date* (1959) and *The Criminal* (1960). The European influence remained strong, however, and it emerged in an anglicised form in the collaboration he formed with Harold Pinter* for *The Servant* (1963), *Accident* (1967) and *The Go-Between* (1970). In the two films he made with Elizabeth Taylor, *Boom* (1968), which also had Richard Burton*, and *Secret Ceremony* (1968), also with Mia Farrow and Robert Mitchum, he tried, and failed, to bring the star system to the art cinema – 'I was the first person to make a picture with the Burtons that lost money' – and in *Modesty Blaise* (1966) he created a pop art version of a Bond* film. Losey, much more than Stanley Kubrick* or even Richard Lester*, brought to British cinema the eccentric sensibility of the exile, belonging neither to America, Britain or Europe, a cineaste still loyal to theatre, creating an art cinema of refracted perspectives. JC

Bib: Michel Ciment, *Conversations with Losey* (1985).

Other Films Include: *The Boy with Green Hair* (1949, US); *The Prowler, M* (1951, both US); *Eva/Eve* (1962); *The Damned* (1962); *King & Country* (1964); *Figures in a Landscape* (1970); *L'Assassinat de Trotsky/The Assassination of Trotsky* (1972, Fr./It./UK); *A Doll's House* (1973, UK/Fr.); *The Romantic Englishwoman/Une Anglaise romantique* (1975, UK/Fr.); *Galileo* (1976, UK/Canada); *Mr Klein* (1977, Fr./It.); *Don Giovanni* (1979, It./Fr./Ger.); *Steaming* (1985).

LUCAN, Arthur

Arthur Towle; Boston, Lincolnshire 1887 – Hull 1954

British actor and cross-dresser, who as Old Mother Riley made fourteen films between 1937 and 1952. A caricatural Irish 'washerwoman' in the tradition of British music hall, Mother Riley in the 1930s was the vituperative and populist scourge of capitalist enterprise, championing the working class, fulminating with malapropisms and maledictions against pretension and injustice, and transgressing all social niceties either by accident or design. 'Hers,' says Jeffrey Richards, 'is truly a case of body-language gone berserk, but it is an outward and visible sign of her refusal to be cowed or to conform.' During the war the character was taken over by the war effort, and spies and Nazis replaced the middle class as her/his adversaries. JC

Bib: Jeffrey Richards, *The Age of the Dream Palace: Cinema and Society in Britain, 1930–1939* (1984).

Films Include: *Old Mother Riley* (1937); *Old Mother Riley MP* (1939); *Old Mother Riley in Society, Old Mother Riley in Business* [both directed by John Baxter] (1940); *Old Mother Riley's Ghosts* (1941).

LYE, Len

Christchurch, New Zealand 1901 – Rhode Island, USA 1980

British animator. Born in New Zealand, arrived in Britain in the 1920s, and emigrated to the US in 1944. Lye's animation work is chiefly associated with the British Documentary Movement* in the 1930s and early 1940s. He is remembered as an experimentalist in both form and technique, inventing a system of painting directly onto film which was used in the award-winning *Colour Box* (1935). The technique was later adopted by Norman McLaren*. Lye's career did not progress in America, and he left film-making for painting and sculpture in the late 1950s. JC

Other Films Include: *Tusalava* (1928); *Birth of a Robot* (1935); *Rainbow Dance* (1936); *The Lambeth Walk* (1941); *Kill or be Killed* (1942); *Color Cry* (1955, US); *Rhythm* (1957, US).

McANALLY, Ray

Buncrana 1926 – Dublin 1989

Irish actor. Though McAnally began his theatrical career at a young age he did not come to international prominence until the 1980s, when he played the papal envoy in *The Mission* (1986) and Christy Brown's father in the Oscar-winning *My Left Foot* (1989). His work on television brought him an even wider audience. A much admired actor, he died just as his career was leading him to more prominent film and television roles. KR

Other Films Include: *Shake Hands With the Devil* (1959); *Billy Budd* (1962); *The Looking Glass War* (1969); *Fear is the Key* (1972); *Angel* (1982); *Cal* (1984); *Empire State* (1987); *The Fourth Protocol* (1987); *The Sicilian* [US], *Taffin, White Mischief* (1987); *High Spirits* (1988); *We're No Angels* (1989, US).

McDOWELL, Malcolm

Leeds 1943

British actor, who made his film debut in Ken Loach's* *Poor Cow* (1967), and became one of the representative figures of the 1970s through his roles in Lindsay Anderson's* Mick Travis trilogy, *If....* (1968), *O Lucky Man!* (1973) and *Britannia Hospital* (1982), and in Stanley Kubrick's* *A Clockwork Orange* (1972). McDowell brings a kind of innocent insolence to Mick Travis, a naivety which allows him to register experience while maintaining a critical distanciation in Anderson's mappings of the nation. Similarly, Kubrick's highly stylised Alex in *A Clockwork Orange*, though pathologically violent, allows McDowell to perform the character without becoming him. Apart from Schrader's *Cat People* in 1981, McDowell has not in recent years found films of similar interest. JC

Other Films Include: *Figures in a Landscape*, *The Raging Moon* (1970); *Royal Flash* (1975); *Voyage of the Damned* (1977); *Caligula* [title role] (1980, US/It.); *Blue Thunder* (1983, US); *Milk Money* (1994, US).

MACKENDRICK, Alexander

Boston, USA 1912 – California, 1993

British director. Born in Boston of Scottish parents, educated at Glasgow School of Art, Mackendrick joined Ealing* as a scriptwriter in 1946, having previously scripted a number of films for the Ministry of Information, including the Halas-Batchelor* '*Abu*' animation series. He began directing at Ealing* with *Whisky Galore!* (1949). The interest of his films lies in the tension between Michael Balcon's* gentle smile at the English ('We had great affection for British institutions: the comedies were done with affection'), and Mackendrick's more caustic, destructive (and Scottish?) laughter ('Personally, I am very attracted by comedy ... It lets you do things that are too dangerous'). Behind his version of the Ealing whimsy there are sharp edges, and anyone who is surprised by the venom of his first Hollywood movie, *Sweet Smell of Success* (1957, US), has missed the hardness of the Scottish comedies – the humiliating laughter at the end of *Whisky Galore!* or the relentless bewildering of the American in *The Maggie* (1954). Mackendrick is more interested in generational disorder than in sexual disorder, and children figure importantly in his work. *Mandy* (1952), his only non-comedy at Ealing, is, as Charles Barr argues, both 'one of the most affecting of all British films' and one of the least sentimental about children, playing out the child's struggle to enter language, the family and society with an ending which is both positive and provisional. It is precisely the ambivalence of Mackendrick's vision that makes him the least dated of Ealing directors.

With the exception of *Sweet Smell of Success*, his directing career in Hollywood failed to ignite. In 1969, he became Dean of the Film Department at the California Institute of the Arts. JC

Bib: Philip Kemp, *Lethal Innocence: The Cinema of Alexander Mackendrick* (1991).

Other Films Include: *The Man in the White Suit* (1951); *The Ladykillers* (1955); *Sammy Going South* (1963); *A High Wind in Jamaica* (1965); *Don't Make Waves* (1967, US).

McKENNA, Siobhan

Belfast 1923 – Dublin 1986

Irish actress. Best known as a versatile and talented stage actress from 1940, she worked in both Irish and English-language theatre. She made her film debut in Brian Desmond Hurst's* Irish historical drama *Hungry Hill* (1947), then played a murderous Irish servant girl in a melodrama, *Daughter of Darkness* (1948). By the time she got to film one of her most celebrated stage roles, that of Pegeen Mike in the 1962 version of *The Playboy of the Western World*, she was already too old for the part. Her film career is of much less significance than her theatrical legacy. KR

Other Films Include: *The Lost People* (1949); *King of Kings* (1961, US); *Of Human Bondage* (1964); *Doctor Zhivago* (1965, US).

McLAREN, Norman

Stirling, Scotland 1914 – Montreal, Canada 1987

British animator, whose best-known British work, *Hell Unltd.* (1936), was made with his colleague at Glasgow Art School, Helen Biggar. (Stewart McAllister, who went on to become Humphrey Jennings'* editor and collaborator, was a contemporary.) Biggar and McLaren were members of the left activist film group Glasgow Kino, and their film is an attack on the growing arms trade of the 1930s coupled with an appeal for working-class solidarity. It attracted the attention of John Grierson*, who invited McLaren to join the GPO Film Unit (Biggar remained in Glasgow). Before joining the unit, McLaren went to Spain with Ivor Montagu* and was cameraman on *In Defence of Madrid* (1936). Again at the invitation of Grierson, McLaren joined the National Film Board of Canada in 1941 and became director of its animation unit. He continued to develop the technique of drawing directly on to film, the method invented by Len Lye*, producing both abstract and representational art animation. He also worked in live-action animation, and his film *Neighbours* (1952) received an Academy Award as well as a screening in the Free Cinema* season. JC

Other Films Include: **In Britain** – *7 till 5* (1933); *Camera Makes Whoopee, Colour Cocktail* (1935). **In US** – *Stars and Stripes* (1939); *Dots, Loops, Boogie Doodle* (1940). **In Canada** – *V for Victory* (1941); *Begone Dull Care* (1949); *Rhythmetic* (1956); *Mosaic* (1965); *Pas de Deux* (1968); *Spheres* (1969); *Striations* (1970).

MALLESON, Miles

Croydon 1888 – London 1969

British actor, **scriptwriter and playwright**. Malleson is probably most familiar as the genteel hangman of *Kind Hearts and Coronets* (1949) or as Canon Chasuble in *The Importance of Being Earnest* (1952), or in a wide range of small but distinctive character parts in postwar films ranging from *Geordie* (1955) to *Peeping Tom* (1960). He was also, however, on the advisory council (along with George Lansbury, James Maxton and Sybil Thorndike) of the Masses Stage and Film Guild established by the Independent Labour Party (ILP) in 1929 to bring 'plays and films of an international character to working-class audiences'; he was the author of a play on the Tolpuddle Martyrs supported by the Trades Union Congress; and, simultaneously, he was one of Herbert Wilcox's* leading scriptwriters in the 1930s, with credits including such hits as *Nell Gwyn* (1934) and *Peg of Old Drury* (1935), the patriotic celebrations of monarchy, *Victoria the Great* (1937) and *Sixty Glorious Years* (1938), and, for Alexander Korda*, *The Thief of Bagdad* (1940), in which he also played the Sultan. JC

MASON, James

Huddersfield 1909 – Lausanne, Switzerland 1984

British actor, and major British and American star, the softness of whose voice often belied the steel in his character's soul. Though he became respectable in *Odd Man Out* (1947), it was in the Gainsborough melodramas* that Mason emerged as a star, ousting George Formby* from the top of the British popularity charts in 1943.

The Man in Grey (1943), *Fanny by Gaslight* (1944), *The Seventh Veil* (1945) and *The Wicked Lady* (1945) established him in the vein of erotic and aristocratic cruelty: most aristocratic in *The Man in Grey* and *Fanny by Gaslight*, most cruel in *The Seventh Veil* and most erotic in *The Wicked Lady*, where his taking of Margaret Lockwood* is conducted as a sexual transaction in which he is the loser. *Odd Man Out*, directed by Carol Reed*, offered him a more culturally prestigious role in a quality film. In 1949 he went to Hollywood, where he made two films with Max Ophuls*, *Caught* and *The Reckless Moment* (both 1949), played Rommel twice, in *The Desert Fox* (1951) and *The Desert Rats* (1953), played Brutus to Marlon Brando's Anthony in *Julius Caesar* (1953), and starred with Judy Garland in *A Star is Born* (1954). He returned to Britain in 1953 to make *The Man Between*, again with Carol Reed. He continued to play significant roles on both sides of the Atlantic until his death, winning a posthumous UK Film Critics award in 1985 for his part in *The Shooting Party*. JC

Bib: Sheridan Morley, *James Mason: Odd Man Out* (1989).

Other Films Include: *Blind Man's Bluff* (1936); *The Mill on the Floss, Fire Over England* (1937); *Hatter's Castle* (1941); *The Night Has Eyes, Thunder Rock* (1942); *The Bells Go Down* (1943); *They Were Sisters* (1945); *Madame Bovary* (1949); *Pandora and the Flying Dutchman* (1951); *Bigger Than Life* (1956, US); *North by Northwest* (1959, US); *The Trials of Oscar Wilde* (1960); *Lolita* (1962); *The Pumpkin Eater* (1964); *Lord Jim* (1965); *Georgy Girl* (1966); *Age of Consent* (1969, Australia); *Child's Play* (1972, US); *Autobiography of a Princess, Mandingo* [US] (1975); *Voyage of the Damned* (1976); *Cross of Iron* (1977); *Heaven Can Wait, The Boys from Brazil* (1978, both US); *Salem's Lot* (1979, US); *The Verdict* (1982, US).

MATHIESON, Muir

Stirling, Scotland 1911 – Oxford 1975

British music director. Though hardly a household name, Muir Mathieson's name must surely appear on the credit lists of more British films than that of any other individual. A Scot, trained at the Royal College of Music, he joined Alexander Korda* at Denham in 1934, worked for various government film units during the war, and was musical director at Rank from 1945 until 1970. His first credit as music director was for *The Private Life of Don Juan* (1934); he persuaded Arthur Bliss to compose music for *Things to Come* (1936) and William Walton to compose the famous score for *Henry V* (1945). He also commissioned first scores from Vaughan Williams, Arnold Bax and Malcolm Arnold*. In all, it is estimated he initiated and conducted over a thousand scores. JC

MATTHEWS, Jessie London 1907 – Pinner 1981

British actress, who made her film debut in 1923 at the age of sixteen, and became one of the top three British stars of the 1930s. Whereas Gracie Fields* and George Formby* had a predominantly working-class appeal derived from northern music hall, Matthews was the 'Dancing Divinity' of the sophisticated musical. She was the only one of the trio to achieve real success in America. While the ordinariness of the other two inspired affection in the domestic audience, Matthews offered fantasy and an extraordinary sexuality. In dance numbers, her pretty face and prim little mouth seemed unaware of what the rest of her body was doing in its slinky gowns and silky, liquid movements. She may not have had the choreography of Ginger Rogers, and she certainly lacked an adequate male partner, but she made up for it with the unselfconscious sensuality of her movement. In the three musicals she made with Victor Saville*, the fantasy was played out as masquerade flirting with the perverse: in *Evergreen* (1934) she poses as her own mother and falls in love with the young man who is posing as her son; in *First a Girl* (1935), based on the German film *Viktor und Viktoria* (1933), she double-cross-dresses and, of course, falls in love; and in *It's Love Again* (1936) she impersonates a celebrated adventuress. Matthews was at her best directed by Saville, her popularity declining towards the end of the decade when her direction was taken over by her husband, Sonny Hale. Her film career went into decline after the war, but she returned from relative obscurity in 1963 to play Mrs Dale in the BBC radio serial, *Mrs Dale's Diary*. JC

Bib: Jeffrey Richards, *The Age of the Dream Palace: Cinema and Society in Britain, 1930–1939* (1984).

Other Films Include: *Out of the Blue* (1931); *The Midshipmaid* (1932); *The Man from Toronto, The Good Companions* [Saville], *Friday the Thirteenth* [Saville] (1933); *Waltzes from Vienna* [Hitchcock] (1934); *Head over Heels* [Hale], *Gangway* [Hale] (1937); *Sailing Along* [Hale], *Climbing High* (1938); *Forever and a Day* (1943, US); *Victory Wedding* [short; dir. + role] (1944); *Tom Thumb* [cameo] (1958); *The Hound of the Baskervilles* [cameo] (1978).

MERCHANT–IVORY
IVORY, James Berkeley, California 1928;
MERCHANT, Ismail Bombay, India 1936;
JHABVALA, Ruth Prawer Cologne, Germany 1927

American/Indian director-producer-writer team. Formed by an American director (Ivory), an Indian producer (Merchant), and a German-born writer of Polish descent who became Indian by marriage

(Jhabvala), Merchant-Ivory during the 1980s has luxuriated in Englishness, becoming a brand-name for the 'heritage film'. The company was formed in the 1960s in India. Its first notable production was *Shakespeare Wallah* (1965, India), which dealt with the English in India through a travelling theatre company, and the partnership continued in the US in the 1970s, producing independent American films like *Roseland* (1977). In Britain, their series of adaptations began in 1979 with *The Europeans*, continued with *The Bostonians* (1984, US), turned to E. M. Forster with *A Room with a View* (1985), and followed its success with *Maurice* (1987) and *Howards End* (1991). The Forster cycle discovered a rich seam of English nostalgia which had already been mined on television with *Brideshead Revisited* (1981) and on film with *Chariots of Fire* (1981) and was revisited again by Charles Sturridge with adaptations of Forster's *Where Angels Fear to Tread* (1991) and Evelyn Waugh's *A Handful of Dust* (1987). The 'heritage film', which is now firmly identified with Merchant–Ivory, is characterised by a rich visual style and a loving recreation of the Edwardian period which replaces the irony of the original novels with a longing for England's past. [> HERITAGE CINEMA IN EUROPE] JC

Bib: Andrew Higson, 'Re-presenting the national past: nostalgia and pastiche in the heritage film', in Lester Friedman (ed.), *British Cinema and Thatcherism: Fires Were Started* (1983).

MILLS, (Sir) John — Felixstowe 1908

British actor, one of the more appealing representatives of British decency in wartime and postwar cinema. It is surely culturally significant that in 1947 the decent, unassuming and likeable John Mills displaced the wicked James Mason* from the top of the popularity charts.

Mills started in the chorus line of musical revue, and his screen debut was opposite Jessie Matthews* in *The Midshipmaid* (1932). In the 1930s, his association with the patriotic valour of the common man was established in the role of seaman Albert Brown in *Forever England* (1935). In *In Which We Serve* (1942), *This Happy Breed* (1944) and *Waterloo Road* (1945), Mills represented the 1940s version of the working-class hero: the little man caught up by war or the threat of war but with no aspiration to be other than he is, no imaginings other than to sort things out back home. Unlike Stanley Baker*, who also represents class difference in the war film, the Mills character seems to have no inner anger or spite. In civilian clothes, he is Mr Polly in *The History of Mr Polly* (1949) or Charles Laughton's* biddable son-in-law in *Hobson's Choice* (1954). As he grew older, Mills rose through the ranks and gained authority, a swagger stick and a moustache. He was, however, still able to return to his humble origins in *Ryan's Daughter* (1970), for which he received an Oscar as Best Supporting Actor. He was knighted in 1976. JC

Other Films Include: **As Actor** – *O.H.M.S.* (1937); *The Young Mr Pitt, The Big Blockade* (1942); *We Dive at Dawn* (1943); *Victory Wedding* [dir. Jessie Matthews, short] (1944); *The Way to the Stars* (1945); *Great Expectations* (1946); *Scott of the Antarctic* (1948); *Morning Departure* (1950); *The Colditz Story* (1954); *Above Us the Waves* (1955); *Ice Cold in Alex, I Was Monty's Double* (1958); *Tiger Bay* (1959); *Tunes of Glory* (1960); *King Rat* (1965, US); *The Wrong Box, The Family Way* (1966); *Oh! What a Lovely War* (1969); *Young Winston* (1972); *Lady Caroline Lamb, Oklahoma Crude* (1973, US); *The Human Factor* (1975); *Gandhi* (1982). **As Director**: *Sky West and Crooked* [+ prod.] (1965).

MIRREN, Helen London 1945

British actress, who has moved with equal success between theatre, film and television since the late 1960s. She was a member of the Royal Shakespeare Company, making her film debut in Peter Hall's *A Midsummer Night's Dream* (1968), and accompanying Peter Brook on his tour of Africa with *The Conference of the Birds* in 1972. Mirren brings to her performances on film, and more recently on television, a combination of strength, sexuality and sheer skill. A strongly sensual actress in, for example, Michael Powell's* *Age of Consent* (1969, Australia), she could also burlesque sensuality in *O Lucky Man!* (1973) or in a superb performance as Titania in a television version of *A Midsummer Night's Dream* (1981). She received a Cannes film festival award for her performance in *Cal* (1984), and appeared with Harrison Ford in Peter Weir's underrated *The Mosquito Coast* (1986, US). In the 1990s she won a well-deserved BAFTA award for her performance in the television police serial *Prime Suspect* (1991). She received an Oscar nomination as Best Supporting Actress for her role as Queen Charlotte in *The Madness of King George* (1994). JC

Other Films Include: *Savage Messiah* (1972); *The Long Good Friday, Excalibur* (1981); *White Nights* (1985, US); *Pascali's Island* (1988); *The Cook the Thief His Wife & Her Lover* (1989); *Cortesie per gli ospiti/ The Comfort of Strangers* (1990, It./UK); *Where Angels Fear to Tread* (1991); *The Hawk* (1992).

MONTAGU, Ivor London 1904 – Watford 1984

British producer, **writer and director**. Communist, aristocrat, son of the banker Lord Montagu, the Hon. Ivor Montagu was a leading figure in left-wing film activity in the 1930s. One of the founders of the London Film Society* in 1924, in 1934 he organised the Progressive Film Institute (PFI) as a producing and distributing body for the Communist Party. The PFI sent a crew (including Thorold Dickinson* and Norman McLaren*) to Spain during the Civil War, where Montagu produced and directed *In Defence of Madrid* (1936). *Peace and Plenty* (1939), directed by Montagu for the Communist Party, followed McLaren's *Hell Unltd.* (1936) in using graphics, puppets and animation to attack Chamberlain's appeasement policy. Montagu was editor and title writer for Alfred Hitchcock's* *The Lodger* (1926), associate producer of *The Man Who Knew Too Much* (1934) and *The 39 Steps* (1935), and first film critic of the *Observer* and the *New Statesman*. He was a friend and translator of Eisenstein*, and accompanied him on his visit to Hollywood and Mexico, recording the trip in his book *With Eisenstein in Hollywood* (1968). During World War II he worked for the Ministry of Information, and he was a scriptwriter at Ealing after the war. He was awarded the Lenin Peace Prize in 1959. JC

Bib: Ivor Montagu, *The Youngest Son: Autobiographical Sketches* (1970).

MORE, Kenneth   Gerrards Cross 1914 – London 1982

British actor, one of the league of likeable gentlemen of postwar British cinema. He began in stage revue and worked in the mid-1930s at the Windmill Theatre. He retained his comic ability in his film career, and two of his most popular films were *Genevieve* (1953) and *Doctor in the House* (1954). In his dramatic roles, he projected a matter-of-fact heroism or an ability to get the job done. Like many British actors, he commuted between film and theatre, playing the lead in both the stage and screen versions of Terence Rattigan's play *The Deep Blue Sea* (1955), his screen performance winning him a Best Actor award at Venice. Very much an icon of decency in the 1950s in cinema, he moved into television in the 1960s, renewing his popularity with his role in the BBC serialisation of *The Forsyte Saga* (1967). JC

Other Films Include: *Look Up and Laugh* (1935); *Scott of the Antarctic* (1948); *Morning Departure* (1950); *The Franchise Affair* (1951); *The Yellow Balloon* (1952); *Reach for the Sky* (1956); *The Admirable Crichton* (1957); *A Night to Remember, The Sheriff of Fractured Jaw* (1958); *North West Frontier, The 39 Steps* (1959); *Oh! What a Lovely War* (1969).

MORRISON, George   Tramore 1922

Irish director and archivist. Morrison's film-making career is indelibly linked to two major actuality films, *Mise Eire/I Am Ireland* (1959) and *Saoirse?/Freedom?* (1961), which not only traced the struggle for Irish independence up to the outbreak of Civil War in 1922, but helped save

The Garden (Derek Jarman, 1990).

Margaret Rutherford and Alastair Sim in *The Happiest Days of Your Life* (Frank Launder, 1950).

Malcolm McDowell and Christine Noonan in *If…* (Lindsay Anderson, 1968).

Edith Evans, Dorothy Tutin, Joan Greenwood, Michael Redgrave, Michael Denison, Margaret Rutherford, Miles Malleson in *The Importance of Being Earnest* (Anthony Asquith, 1952).

John Mills, Noel Coward, Bernard Miles in *In Which We Serve* (Noel Coward/David Lean, 1942).

Peter O'Toole in *Lawrence of Arabia* (David Lean, 1962).

Listen to Britain (Humphrey Jennings, 1942).

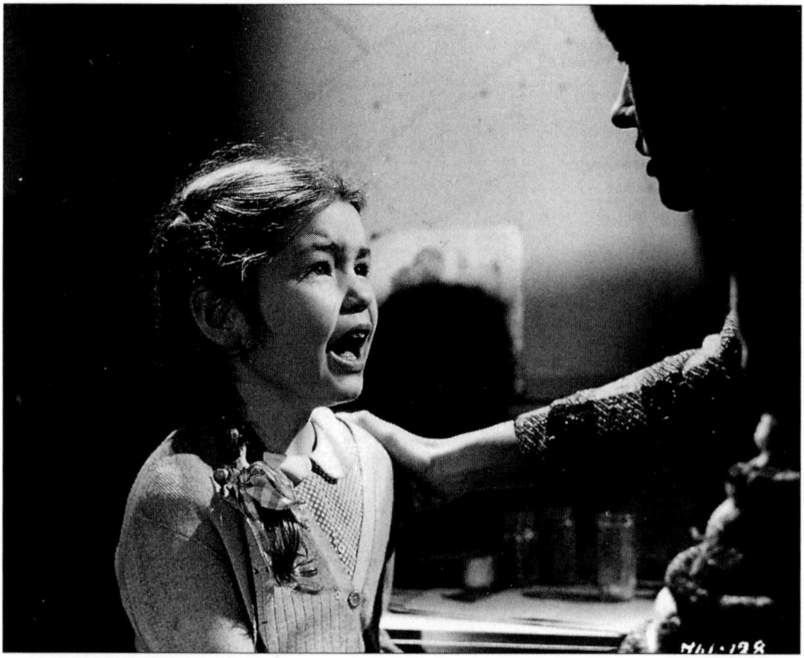

Mandy Miller and Phyllis Calvert in *Mandy* (Alexander Mackendrick, 1953).

Stephen Archibald in *My Childhood* (Bill Douglas, 1972).

Arthur Lucan (right) in *Old Mother Riley in Business* (John Baxter, 1940).

Alec Guinness in *Oliver Twist* (David Lean, 1948).

Tilda Swinton and Quentin Crisp in *Orlando* (Sally Potter, 1993).

Leslie Howard in *Pimpernel Smith* (Leslie Howard, 1941).

Charles Laughton in *The Private Life of Henry VIII* (Alexander Korda, 1933).

John Gielgud in *Prospero's Books* (Peter Greenaway, 1991).

Paul Robeson (right) in *The Proud Valley* (Pen Tennyson, 1940).

a large portion of contemporary Irish newsreel film from being lost or destroyed. In the process, national consciousness was raised about this period of Irish history and the valuable use which could be made of archival material. The films are now viewed in a more critical light, and their often simplistic nationalist views and use of images of nature to naturalise historical difference are seen as representative of an earlier official Irish nationalist historiography. Morrison went on to make other documentaries, but none of them matched the impact of his first two films. KR

MOVIE

British journal. Established in 1962, *Movie* was responsible for translating the *politique des auteurs** from *Cahiers du Cinéma** to a British context, marrying it to the close textual reading of British literary criticism, and arguing for serious critical attention to be extended beyond the permissible range of 'quality' criticism to include *auteurs* like Frank Tashlin and Jacques Tourneur. *Movie* was motivated by 'a desire to investigate the way [films] worked ... the best antidote to the prevalent woolliness about the cinema seemed to us to lie in detailed, descriptive criticism.' The cinema which they championed was Hollywood, particularly those directors who were associated with *mise-en-scène*: Alfred Hitchcock*, Vincente Minnelli, Otto Preminger, Nicholas Ray. The cinema which came off worst was British cinema. In 1962, in the context of the British New Wave*, an editorial article declared, 'All we can see is a change of attitude, which disguises the fact that the British cinema is as dead as before. Perhaps it was never alive. Our films have improved, if at all, only in their intentions. We are still unable to find evidence of artistic sensibilities in working order.' *Movie* was most influential in the 1960s and early 1970s, and continues to appear intermittently. JC

MULVEY, Laura
WOLLEN, Peter

Oxford 1941 and London 1938

British directors and theorists. As independent avant-garde filmmakers, Mulvey and Wollen are best known for two films which they co-directed in the 1970s: *Penthesilea: Queen of the Amazons* (1974) and *Riddles of the Sphinx* (1977). Both films use formal experiment to investigate theoretical and practical issues raised by the women's movement, addressing both the construction of sexuality through myth and history, and practical problems of child care. In *Amy!* (1980), a short film based on the life and legend of Amy Johnson, they address the myths of modernity, and in later work such as *Crystal Gazing* (1982) and *The Bad Sister* (1983) they use video to consider structures of fantasy. Their film-making is informed by their theoretical writing on semiotics, psychoanalysis, modernism and the avant-garde. Mulvey's 1975 *Screen** article, 'Visual Pleasure and Narrative Cinema' (probably the most cited article in feminist film theory), proved seminal for psychoanalytic debates about sexuality, subjectivity and cinema; Wollen's article 'The Two Avant Gardes' in *Studio International* (1975) was an important intervention in British avant-garde film theory and practice. Mulvey, with Claire Johnston and Linda Myles, organised the Women's Event at the Edinburgh Film Festival in 1972, and Wollen organised the Avant-Garde Event at the same festival in 1975. Laura Mulvey now teaches film studies in Britain. Her most recent film is *Fallen Idols* (1994). Peter Wollen teaches in California at UCLA, and continues to direct films and videos, including *Friendship's Death* (1987). JC

Bib: Laura Mulvey, *Visual and Other Pleasures* (1989); Peter Wollen, *Readings and Writings: Semiotic Counter-strategies* (1982).

MURPHY, Pat — Dublin 1951

Irish director and scriptwriter. Murphy has made only two feature films: *Maeve* (1981), with co-director John Davies, and *Anne Devlin* (1984), but they are among the most culturally critical films of the new Irish cinema. *Maeve* explores the relationship between republicanism and feminism in Northern Ireland and poses this usually disguised problematic: even if republicans 'win', what type of society will it be for women as long as this male-dominated movement remains largely unengaged with women's concerns? In *Anne Devlin*, Murphy sought to uncover the 'hidden history' of a woman who was associated with the 1803 rebellion against British rule in Ireland, but whose role has been submerged by the elevation to mythic status of the rebellion's leader, Robert Emmet. In common with most independent Irish film-makers in the late 1980s and early 1990s, she has faced extreme difficulty in continuing to make films. KR

Bib: Luke Gibbons, 'The Politics of Silence: *Anne Devlin*, Women and Irish Cinema', *Framework* 30–31 (1986).

N

NEAGLE, (Dame) Anna

Florence Marjorie Robertson; London 1904 – Surrey 1986

British actress, whose career was developed almost exclusively from 1932 until 1959 by the director and producer Herbert Wilcox*, who became her husband in 1940. Associated with historical roles in the 1930s, she graduated from an irrepressible *Nell Gwyn* (1934) to become a dignified Queen Victoria in the patriotically popular *Victoria the Great* (1937) and its sequel, *Sixty Glorious Years* (1938). A top box-office star of the 1940s, she played a wide range of strong independent women, from Edith Cavell in *Nurse Edith Cavell* (1939, US) to Amy Johnson in *They Flew Alone* (1942), or from a spy in *The Yellow Canary* (1943) to a hero of the Resistance in *Odette* (1950). She is, however, most associated with the dramas and musical romances of the upper classes known as the 'Mayfair' cycle: *I Live in Grosvenor Square* (1945), *Piccadilly Incident* (1946), *The Courtneys of Curzon Street* (1947), *Spring in Park Lane* (1948) and *Maytime in Mayfair* (1949). She was made a Dame of the British Empire in 1969. JC

NEESON, Liam

Ballymena, Northern Ireland 1953

Irish actor. Neeson's early career in Ireland included work at the Lyric Players Theatre, Belfast, and the Project and Abbey Theatres, Dublin. He made his feature film debut in John Boorman's* *Excalibur* (1981, US). Tall and ruggedly handsome, Neeson has mostly worked in the British and American film industries, where he has played a variety of roles, often as a lover: to Diane Keaton in *The Good Mother* (1988, US) and to Mia Farrow in *Husbands and Wives* (1992, US). His Irish roles have included *Lamb* (1985), in which he plays a Christian Brother who takes a boy away from a penal educational institution and goes on the run; an IRA hit man in *A Prayer for the Dying* (1987); and a ghost in Neil Jordan's* *High Spirits* (1988). Seeking to avoid being typecast as an 'Irish' actor, he has distanced himself from straight Irish roles. After a period in the doldrums, Neeson was rescued by the theatre through his performance in *Anna Christie* on Broadway, for which he won a Tony Award in 1993. This role also brought him to the attention of Steven Spielberg, who cast him in the title role in *Schindler's List* (1993, US), for which Neeson was nominated for an Oscar. He played the noble savage in *Rob Roy* (1995, US) as if he, at least, believed in it, but he was left high and dry in a film which as Kim Newman said, 'redeemed itself by the quality of its perfidy'. KR

Other Films Include: *The Bounty* (1984); *The Innocent* (1985); *Duet for One* (1986); *The Mission* (1986); *Suspect* (1987, US); *The Dead Pool, Satisfaction* (1988, both US); *Next of Kin* (1989, US); *The Big Man* (1990); *Darkman* (1990, US).

NEWTON, Robert

Shaftesbury 1905 – Beverly Hills, California 1956

British actor. Newton's career is dominated by two roles, Bill Sikes in David Lean's* *Oliver Twist* (1948) and Long John Silver in the Disney version of *Treasure Island* (1950). The wonderful hamming of the latter in particular became part of the cultural luggage of schoolboys in the 1950s, and was perpetuated in a sequel, *Long John Silver* (1955, Australia), and an Australian television series, *The Adventures of Long John Silver* (1955). The image of the shameless scene-stealer, however, belies the quiet control of his acting in other films. In *This Happy Breed* (1944), Newton's scrupulously economical performance is invisibly woven into the fabric of lower middle-class respectability between the wars. JC

Other Films Include: *Fire Over England* (1937); *Jamaica Inn* (1939); *Gaslight* (1940); *Major Barbara, Hatter's Castle* (1941); *Henry V* [as Pistol] (1945); *Odd Man Out* (1947); *Tom Brown's Schooldays* (1951); *Les Misérables, Blackbeard the Pirate* (1952, both US); *The Desert Rats, Androcles and the Lion* (1953, both US); *The Beachcomber* (1954); *Around the World in Eighty Days* (1956, US).

NIVEN, David

Kirriemuir, Scotland 1910 – Château-d'Œx, Switzerland 1983

British actor, who began his Hollywood career as an extra after resigning a commission with the Highland Light Infantry. His Sandhurst military school training and inherited membership of the officer class equipped him for many of the parts he was to play: charming, dapper and sophisticated with a dash of light-hearted sexual roguishness. He had parts in a number of notable Hollywood films of the 1930s: *The Charge of the Light Brigade* (1936), *Dodsworth* (1936), *The Prisoner of Zenda* (1937) and *The Dawn Patrol* (1938). Signed to Goldwyn, he followed a supporting role in *Wuthering Heights* (1939) with his first starring role as Raffles (*Raffles*, 1940) in a remake of the Ronald Colman* original. Returning to the British army during the war, he was given leave to appear in Leslie Howard's* *The First of the Few* (1942) and Carol Reed's* *The Way Ahead* (1944). On his discharge as a colonel he played the poet-airman caught between life and death in *A Matter of Life and Death* (1946), one of his most effective roles. He spent the rest of his career consistently in demand on both sides of the Atlantic, an international imaginary Englishman whose debonair dash occasionally slipped to reveal emotional vulnerabity. He won an Oscar and a New York Film Critics award for his performance in Delbert Mann's *Separate Tables* (1958). JC

Bib: David Niven, *The Moon's a Balloon* (1971) and *Bring on the Empty Horses* (1975) (both republished 1985).

Other Films Include (UK Unless Indicated): *Bonnie Prince Charlie* (1948); *The Elusive Pimpernel* (1950); *Happy Go Lovely* (1951); *The Moon is Blue* (1953, US); *Carrington V.C.* (1954); *The King's Thief* (1955, US); *Around the World in Eighty Days* (1956, US); *My Man Godfrey* (1957, US); *Bonjour Tristesse* (1958); *The Guns of Navarone* (1961); *55 Days at Peking* (1963, US); *The Pink Panther* (1964, US); *Casino Royale* [as James Bond] (1967); *Paper Tiger* (1975); *Death on the Nile* (1978); *Rough Cut* (1980, US); *Curse of the Pink Panther, Trail of the Pink Panther* (1982).

NORTHERN IRELAND AND FILM

Northern Ireland is familiar to most people through the regular diet (especially in Britain) of television footage of bombings, shootings and funerals, or of a narrow range of films dealing with political violence: *Odd Man Out* (1947), *The Gentle Gunman* (1952), *Hennessy* (1975), *Angel* (1982), *A Prayer for the Dying* (1987). An indigenous independent film-making practice has developed since the 1970s, though films had been made prior to that, the most prolific period being the 1930s when a number of 'quota quickies' were produced by Donovan Pedelty and Richard Hayward. These films include the horse-racing comedy *The Luck of the Irish* (1935), and *The Early Bird* (1936), in which villagers rebel against a puritanical woman.

During the 1970s and 1980s a number of independent production companies were formed, such as those of documentarists John T. Davis – *Shell Shock Rock* (1979), *Power in the Blood* (1989), *Dust on the Bible* (1990) – and David Hammond, a prolific independent television producer. Fiction film-makers have included the late Bill Miskelly, whose feature, *The End of the World Man* (1985), won first prize at the Children's Festival at Berlin in 1985.

Channel 4* has played an important role in supporting independent production through its workshop programme. Formed in 1984, Derry Film and Video Workshop produced tapes and films, and out of this context Margo Harkin was able to make the incisive *Hush-A-Bye-Baby* (1989), which set a story of teenage pregnancy against the background of the British occupation of Northern Ireland and of conservative institutional and moral attitudes. Though produced through John Davies' Frontroom Productions, a London company, *Acceptable*

Levels (1983) was also a Workshop project and remains one of the most interesting films to come out of the North. It follows the fortunes of a television documentary crew as they weave their way through political and institutional pressures and compromises to construct a version of the events in Northern Ireland which bears little relation to what they experience.

Financial support for film-making has been small-scale, with the Arts Council of Northern Ireland providing only limited support. With the extension of the British Film Institute's* charter to Northern Ireland, the North's marginal status in British and Irish film culture is changing. As significant has been the decision to establish the independent Northern Ireland Film Council, which is developing a broad range of film cultural activities. It was awarded production finance from the Arts Council in 1993, and is also being funded by the Northern Ireland Department of Education. KR

NOVELLO, Ivor

David Ivor Davies; Cardiff, Wales 1893 – London 1951

British actor, who, like Noël Coward*, with whom he is often compared, was also a director on stage and screen, a playwright, a scriptwriter and a songwriter whose most famous song is 'Keep the Home Fires Burning'. Elegantly and excessively beautiful, he was a matinee idol of the West End stage in the 1910s and 1920s, making his film debut in France under the direction of Louis Mercanton with *L'Appel du sang/The Call of the Blood* (1920). He played romantic leads throughout the 1920s, often adapting his films from his own plays. He created the character of Pierre Boucheron/The Rat in a series directed by Graham Cutts*: *The Rat* (1925), *The Triumph of the Rat* (1926) and *The Return of the Rat* (1929). *The Lodger* (1926), one of two Alfred Hitchcock* films in which he starred (the other being *Downhill*, 1927), is probably now his best-known film. Directed by D. W. Griffith in *The White Rose* in 1923, he failed to achieve Hollywood stardom. In 1934 he gave up cinema and returned to the theatre. JC

Other Films Include: *Miarka, la fille à l'ours/Miarka, Daughter of the Bear* (1920, Fr.); *Bonnie Prince Charlie, The Man Without Desire* (1923); *The Vortex* (1927); *The Constant Nymph* (1928); *Once a Lady* (1931, US); *The Lodger* [remake] (1932); *Sleeping Car, I Lived With You* [from his own play] (1933); *Autumn Crocus* (1934).

OBERON, Merle

Estelle Merle O'Brien Thompson; Bombay, India 1911 – Los Angeles, California 1979

British actress of great beauty, whose British career is associated with Alexander Korda*, her husband from 1939 to 1945. Most famously, she played Anne Boleyn opposite Charles Laughton* in *The Private Life of Henry VIII* (1933), and it was her near fatal car crash in 1937 which caused the abandonment of *I, Claudius*. After playing Cathy to Laurence Olivier's* Heathcliffe in the Goldwyn production of *Wuthering Heights* (1939, US) she moved to Hollywood, where she starred in a number of films, notably Ernst Lubitsch's *That Uncertain Feeling* (1941), *Forever and a Day* (1943) and Charles Vidor's *A Song to Remember* (1945). JC

O'CONNOR, Pat

Ardmore 1943

Irish director.O'Connor came to prominence as a television director, especially with *The Ballroom of Romance* (1982), for which he won a BAFTA award. The film recreated 1950s rural Ireland and explored the suppressed sexuality of the people attending the local dance-hall. His first feature film, *Cal* (1984), which was set in Northern Ireland, told of the relationship between the driver of an IRA unit and a widow whose policeman husband was killed by the unit. As John Hill observes, 'the film's inability to invest its view of the "troubles" with any degree of political complexity is confirmed by the retreat into metaphysics'. O'Connor's other Irish feature, *Fools of Fortune* (1990), is set among the Anglo-Irish in rural Ireland during the War of Independence. Their world is shattered as the events impinge on their lives, but as in *Cal*, O'Connor's concerns are less with the political and historical events than with an exploration of a love affair and the possibilities of redemption through retribution. O'Connor has worked most frequently in Britain and America, where he lives with his actress wife Mary Elizabeth Mastrantonio, who has also appeared in his films. KR

Bib: Kevin Rockett, Luke Gibbons, John Hill, *Cinema and Ireland* (1987).

Other Films Include: *A Month in the Country* (1987); *Stars and Bars* [UK], *The January Man* (1988, US); *Circle of Friends* (1995, Ireland/US).

O'LEARY, Liam

Youghal 1910 – Dublin 1992

Irish actor, director, archivist. Legendary film activist who began his career as a civil servant and worked in theatre and film from the early 1930s. One of the founders of the Irish Film Society in 1936, he worked as a director in both independent theatre and at the Abbey Theatre, often directing Irish-language plays. He began making documentaries in the 1940s, some of which were sponsored by government departments. He also made one of Ireland's most effective propaganda films, *Our Country* (1948), which was widely distributed and helped defeat the powerful Fianna Fail party in the 1948 general election. O'Leary acted in a number of films, including *Stranger at My Door/At a Dublin Inn* (1950), a thriller, and as a missionary priest in *Men Against the Sun* (1953). In 1953 he moved to London, where he worked as Acquisitions Officer at the National Film Archive until 1965. During this time his interest in the silent cinema was activated and his book *Silent Cinema* (1965) was influential in drawing attention to this neglected area. He had already written the first Irish book on the cinema, *Invitation to the Film* (1945), and later wrote the first biography (1980) of the Irish-born director of the 1920s and 1930s, Rex Ingram. On returning to Ireland in 1965 he worked as a Viewing Officer at Radio Telefis Eireann* (RTE). During this time he began collecting Irish film memorabilia and gathering data for a history of the cinema in Ireland which was never completed. Donald Taylor Black made a documentary on his life, *At the Cinema Palace: Liam O'Leary* (1983). KR

OLIVIER, (Sir) Laurence (Baron Olivier of Brighton)

Dorking 1907 – Steyning 1989

British actor and director. Already a star on Broadway and the West End in the 1930s (and for the next five decades), Olivier seemed destined for Hollywood stardom as well. Groomed by Hollywood in the early 1930s as a successor to Ronald Colman*, he was tested for *Queen Christina* (1933) but rejected by Garbo in favour of John Gilbert. In *Wuthering Heights* (1939), *Pride and Prejudice* (1940), *Rebecca* (1940) and *That Hamilton Woman/Lady Hamilton* (1941), however, he brought a troubled and austere romanticism to his roles which had all the marks of classic cinematic star quality. Returning to Britain during the war, Olivier put his romantic bravura at the service of patriotism in *Henry V* (1945), and continued after the war, sometimes to the dismay of purists, to bring his star quality to Shakespearean cinema. Like an old-fashioned actor-manager, he directed, produced and adapted *Henry V*, *Hamlet* (1948) and *Richard III* (1955) as star vehicles, creating popular cinema rather than simply filmed theatre.

Estimations of Olivier's acting vary, and critics are harsh on his playing to the gallery. Certainly, many of his appearances in the 1980s had the ring of the cash register about them. In his heyday, however, he brought a touch of glamour and slightly dangerous romance to a British cinema more used to geniality, restraint and responsibility.

Olivier was knighted in 1947, and received a life peerage in 1970. JC

Bib: Laurence Olivier, *Confessions of an Actor: An Autobiography* (1982).

Other Films (UK Unless Indicated): *Too Many Crooks* (1930); *Friends and Lovers* [US], *Potiphar's Wife* (1931); *Westward Passage* (1932, US); *Moscow Nights* (1935); *As You Like It, Conquest of the Air, Fire Over England* (1937); *The Divorce of Lady X* (1938); *Q Planes* (1939); *49th Parallel, Words for Battle* [commentary] (1941); *The Demi-Paradise* (1943); *The Magic Box* (1951); *Carrie* (1952, US); *The Beggar's Opera* [+ co-prod.] (1953); *The Prince and the Showgirl* [+ dir., prod.] (1957); *Spartacus* [US], *The Entertainer* (1960); *Term of Trial* (1962); *Bunny Lake is Missing, Othello* (1965); *Oh! What a Lovely War* (1969); *Three Sisters* [+ dir.] (1970); *Sleuth, Lady Caroline Lamb* (1973); *Love Among the Ruins (*1975, US); *Marathon Man* (1976, US); *A Bridge Too Far, A Long Day's Journey Into Night* [US] (1977); *The Boys from Brazil* (1978, US); *The Jazz Singer* (1980, US); *War Requiem* (1988).

O'SULLIVAN, Thaddeus — Dublin 1948

Irish director and cameraman. Since the 1960s O'Sullivan has lived in London, where he trained as a cameraman, working in particular with experimental film-maker Stephen Dwoskin in the 1970s. His debut film, *A Pint of Plain* (1975), and his feature *On a Paving Stone Mounted* (1978) used an experimental form as they sought to explore the Irish migrant's experience in London and the migrant's relationship to Ireland. As Marc Karlin noted of *A Pint of Plain*, 'all things denoting British Realism were being unusually mobile ... It was hallucinating to see the props of British Cinema drifting from their moorings as if a poltergeist had invaded the land' (*BFI Productions Catalogue 1977–78*). O'Sullivan's formal challenge to Irish film-makers has not in general been taken up and he himself has gradually shifted towards mainstream commercial cinema and television. His first 35mm short, *The Woman Who Married Clark Gable* (1985), was about a woman, played by Brenda Fricker*, who fantasises that her husband, Bob Hoskins*, is transforming into Clark Gable, until the reality of their childless lives impinges on the cinematic imagination. O'Sullivan's most accomplished, and commercially popular, film, *December Bride* (1990), was set in Northern Ireland and concerns the relationships in a largely Protestant community between a housekeeper and two brothers. Having children in turn with both men she, and they, remain uncompromising in the face of the social opprobrium of the local community. O'Sullivan has also worked in television, making *In the Border Country* (1991), about the border area between Northern Ireland and the Republic. He returns to the Northern Ireland setting in *Nothing Personal* (1995), an Anglo-Irish coproduction. KR

Bib: *British Film Institute Productions Catalogue 1977–78* (1978).

O'TOOLE, Peter
Connemara, Ireland 1932

British actor, born in Ireland, who made his film debut as Rob Roy in Disney's *Kidnapped* (1960). One of the new wave of actors to emerge in British theatre in the late 1950s, O'Toole came to critical attention in *The Long and the Short and the Tall* (1959), though the more bankable Laurence Harvey played the part in the film version. O'Toole leapt to fame in the title role of *Lawrence of Arabia* (1962), for which he won a British Academy award and an Oscar nomination, followed by starring roles in *Becket* (1964) and *Lord Jim* (1965). He has always been attracted to eccentric roles, and the eccentricity began to express itself in the 1970s in more mannered performances (unwisely in a musical version of *Goodbye, Mr. Chips*, 1959, with Petula Clark, and outrageously in *The Ruling Class*, 1972), and in a public persona which moved from star acting to scandalous celebrity. He received a US Film Critics award for *The Stunt Man* (1979, US), and gave a restrained performance as the tutor in Bertolucci's *The Last Emperor* (1987, It.). JC

Other Films Include: *What's New Pussycat*; *La Bibbia/The Bible In the Beginning* ... [as three angels; It./US], *The Night of the Generals* (1966); *Casino Royale* (1967); *The Lion in Winter* (1968); *Under Milk Wood* (1971); *Man of la Mancha* (1972, US); *Rosebud* (1975, US); *Man Friday* (1976); *Caligula* (1980, US/It.); *My Favorite Year* (1982, US); *The Rainbow Thief* (1990).

P

PARKER, Alan

London 1944

British director. Parker is one of a group of directors and producers, which includes Ridley Scott* and Tony Scott, Adrian Lyne, Hugh Hudson and David Puttnam*, who graduated from the British advertising industry in the late 1960s. His first feature, *Bugsy Malone* (1976), was a musical gangster spoof with an all-children cast, and with the sweet smell of success in his nostrils he turned to Hollywood. His next feature, *Midnight Express* (1978), scripted by Oliver Stone, won Academy Awards for Screenplay and Music Score, and a nomination for Best Director. Like a number of Parker's films, it is stronger on action and visual dynamism than on political sensitivity. Most of Parker's subsequent work has been in America, though he still plays the role of the Islington 'turnip-head' (his contribution to a 1986 television series on British cinema was called 'A Turnip-Head's Guide to British Cinema'), and enjoys an occasional round of anti-intellectualism with anyone who regards cinema as an intellectual activity. JC

Bib: Jonathan Hacker and David Price, *Take 10: Contemporary British Film Directors* (1991).

Other Films Include: *Fame* (1980, US); *Shoot the Moon* (1981, US); *Pink Floyd The Wall* (1982); *Birdy* (1984, US); *Angel Heart* (1987, US); *Mississippi Burning* (1988, US); *Come See the Paradise* (1990, US); *The Commitments* (1991, UK/Ir.); *The Road to Wellville* (1994, US).

PAUL, R. W.

London 1869–1943

British pioneer inventor and producer, who may be responsible for the first British 'made-up film', *The Soldier's Courtship*, a comic narrative scene made in March 1896, and for the first covered studio, which he built at Sydney Road, New Southgate, London in 1899. Paul was an instrument maker, whose camera design, according to Barry Salt, was the one used by Georges Méliès* for superimpositions and who invented the first panning head to allow him to film the processions at Queen Victoria's Diamond Jubilee in 1897. His interest in film was scientific rather than artistic, and he retired from film in 1910, returning to instrument making and other scientific interests. JC

Bib: Barry Salt, *Film Style and Technology: History and Analysis* (1983).

PEARSON, George London 1875 – Malvern 1973

British director, who entered the film industry from school-teaching in 1912. During the early years of World War I, he made 'topicals' such as *Incidents of the Great European War* (1914), and directed the six-reel *A Study in Scarlet* (1914). He created the 'Ultus' thriller series, encouraged by Léon Gaumont to duplicate the success of Louis Feuillade's *Fantômas* series in France. In 1918, Pearson formed the Welsh-Pearson Company with his partner, Thomas Welsh. His popularity was ensured when he discovered Betty Balfour*, the most successful female star of the 1920s, and launched her into the 'Squibs' series. Pearson, however, aspired to an artistic cinema in films like *Love, Life and Laughter* (1923) and, particularly, *Reveille* (1924), claimed by one critic as 'the greatest achievement of the British silent cinema'. *The Little People* (1926) was made in France with Thorold Dickinson* as assistant and Alberto Cavalcanti* as designer, and his adaptation of John Buchan's *Huntingtower* (1927) had Sir Harry Lauder as the retired Glasgow grocer, Dickson McCunn. Pearson was relegated to 'quota quickies' during the 1930s, but joined the Colonial Film Unit in 1940 and used his experience to train a new generation of film-makers. JC

Bib: George Pearson, *Flashback: An Autobiography of a British Film Maker* (1957).

PINTER, Harold London 1930

British playwright and scriptwriter (and originally actor) best known in the cinema for his collaboration with Joseph Losey* on *The Servant* (1963), *Accident* (1967) and *The Go-Between* (1970). His play *The Caretaker*, staged in 1960 and filmed in 1963, was inspired more by Samuel Beckett than by the social realism of the British (theatrical or cinematic) New Wave*. Pinter's plays, like his scripts for Losey, are allusive and elliptical, with an unstated menace hiding in the cracks. He adapted *The Birthday Party* (1968) and *The Homecoming* (1973, US/UK) for the screen. His interest in complex temporal structures is evident in his treatment of *The French Lieutenant's Woman* (1981), but most developed in *The Proust Screenplay* (1977), a project begun with Losey but which has not been produced. For Volker Schlöndorff he wrote the screenplay of *The Handmaid's Tale* (1990, US/Ger.), based on Margaret Atwood's novel, and for Paul Schrader he adapted Ian McEwan's *The Comfort of Strangers/Cortesie per gli ospiti,* 1990, It./UK). Pinter won a New York Film Critics award for *The Servant,* and British Academy awards for *The Pumpkin Eater* (1964) and *The Go-Between.* He directed *Butley* (1973, US/UK/Canada), adapted from Simon Gray's stage play, in 1976. JC

PLEASENCE, Donald

Worksop 1919 – St. Paul de Vence, France 1995

British actor, whose general appearance seems to fit him for bank manager roles, but whose lizard eyes, steely gaze and tightly constricted voice were increasingly exploited in horror movies. A station manager in Yorkshire in the mid-1930s, he began acting in theatre in 1939, but did not make his film debut until 1954. Mainly a character actor in supporting roles in the 1950s and 1960s, he was given a lead role in the screen adaptation of Harold Pinter's* *The Caretaker* (1963) and appeared in Roman Polanski's *Cul-de-Sac* (1966). During the 1970s and 1980s he was increasingly associated with the more eccentric and bizarre elements of crime and horror, culminating in an association with John Carpenter in *Halloween* (1978, US) and its sequels. JC

POTTER, Sally

London 1947

British director, whose background in avant-garde music, dance and performance art plays an important part in the construction of her films. Her short film *Thriller* (1979) became one of the classics of British feminist independent cinema. Replete with references to *film noir*, and using a music track which combines Bernard Herrmann's score from *Psycho* with Puccini's *La Bohème*, the film is an investigation into why Mimi had to die. Her first feature, *The Gold Diggers* (1983), again investigates the conventions of narrative cinema to expose their construction of women, and was made with an all-woman crew on which everyone – including Julie Christie* – received the same daily rate. With *Orlando* (1992, UK/USSR/Fr./It./Neth.), adapted from Virginia Woolf, starring Tilda Swinton*, co-produced between St Petersburg, Rome, Paris and Maarsen, gloriously shot on location in England and Russia, with a compelling score co-written by Potter and David Motion, she addresses a wider art cinema audience while retaining the integrity of her exploration of gender and identity. JC

POWELL, Dilys

Bournemouth 1902 – London 1995

British film critic, who, with C. A. Lejeune* at the *Observer*, dominated British film reviewing during and after World War II. She was film critic of the *Sunday Times* from 1939 until 1976, a regular broadcaster long after that, and her influential book, *Films Since 1939*, published in 1947, established many of the values of 'quality cinema'. These values were rooted in the documentary movement, and the cinema which she advocated was one which brought 'documentary truth' to the fiction film. Sharing many of Lejeune's tastes and prejudices, she was dismissive of triviality, and contemptuous of, for example, the excess of the Gainsborough* melodramas. At the same time, many of her critical judgments ran against the grain of contemporary opinion: she admired Michael Powell* and Emeric Pressburger before it was fashionable to do so; she supported Alfred Hitchcock* when *Sight and Sound** still wrote him off as a mere 'master of suspense'; and she wrote approvingly of Diana Dors* when she was treated as a joke by the rest of the press. Dilys Powell was awarded a BFI* Fellowship in 1986, and received the Critics' Circle Film Section award in 1988. JC

Bib: Christopher Cook (ed.), *The Dilys Powell Film Reader* (1991).

POWELL, Michael — Canterbury 1905 – Avening 1990
and
PRESSBURGER, Emeric — Miskolc, Hungary 1902 – Aspall 1988

British director, producer and writer team (Pressburger of Hungarian origin). Opinion has fluctuated on Powell and Pressburger. At the popular level, *A Matter of Life and Death* (1946) was chosen for the first Royal Command Performance, but Powell fell from grace after the 'scandal' of *Peeping Tom* (1960), whose disturbed, sadistic serial killer outraged critical and public opinion. Critically, the editors of *Movie**, in their 1962 chart of British *auteurs*, placed Powell in the 'Competent or ambitious' category along with Michael Anderson and Robert Day. More recently, however, as critical taste has moved away from realism, Powell and Pressburger have been reclaimed as the jewels in the crown of British cinema.

Powell began as an assistant in Rex Ingram's studio in Nice in 1925, and his own 'un-British' style carries traces of Ingram's stylish expressionism. He learned his craft in 'quota quickies', directing twenty-three films between 1931 and 1936. In 1937, he went to the remote island of Foula in the Shetland archipelago to direct *The Edge of the World*, and in 1940 he was one of the directors on Alexander Korda's* *The Thief of Bagdad*. Pressburger, born in Hungary, had been a scriptwriter in Germany, Austria and France before arriving in England as a contract writer for Korda in 1936. Korda put Powell and Pressburger together for *The Spy in Black* in 1939, and the two worked together for the next seventeen years, forming 'The Archers' company in 1942 and sharing writing, directing and producing credits on all their films between *The Life and Death of Colonel Blimp* (1943) and *Ill Met by Moonlight* (1957). After they split up, Powell continued to direct, including such distinctive films as *Peeping Tom* and *Age of Consent* (1969, Aust.), and Pressburger directed *Twice Upon a Time* (1953), but it is The Archers period which forms the core of their work, cutting a bright dash in the utility realism of postwar British cinema.

Together, Powell and Pressburger received a Special Award from the BFI* in 1978, and a Golden Lion award at Venice in 1982. In 1981, Powell became Senior Director in Residence at Coppola's Zoetrope Studios. In his autobiography, *A Life in the Movies* (1986), he wrote:

> 'I love England. I have mirrored England to the English in my films. They have not understood the image in the mirror. I am writing these lines in a foreign country [...] because for the last ten years I have been made to feel an outcast by my own people. I was "too big a risk". I was "too independent". I wanted my own way. I was all the things that have made my films different from my contemporaries' films. I have grown up. Audiences have grown up. Films have stayed in the nursery.' JC

Bib: Ian Christie, *Arrows of Desire: The Films of Michael Powell and Emeric Pressburger* (1985).

Other Films: **Powell As Director**, **Pressburger As Writer** – *Contraband* (1940); *49th Parallel* (1941); *...One of Our Aircraft is Missing* (1942). **As 'The Archers'** – *The Volunteer* [short] (1943); *A Canterbury Tale* (1944); *I Know Where I'm Going!* (1945); *Black Narcissus* (1947); *The Red Shoes* (1948); *The Small Back Room* (1949); *Gone to Earth*, *The Elusive Pimpernel* (1950); *The Tales of Hoffmann* (1951); *Oh ... Rosalinda!!* (1955); *The Battle of the River Plate* (1956); *They're a Weird Mob* (1966, Aust./UK); *The Boy Who Turned Yellow* (1972). **Films Directed By Michael Powell Include** – *Two Crowded Hours* [first feature] (1931); *The Fire Raisers* (1933); *Red Ensign* (1934); *Luna de Miel/Honeymoon* (1959, Sp./UK); *The Queen's Guards* (1961); *Herzog, Blaubarts Burg/Bluebeard's Castle* (1964, Ger.); *Return to the Edge of the World* [for BBC] (1978).

PUTTNAM, (Sir) David — London 1941

British producer, who was hailed as the saviour of the commercial British film industry in the early 1980s, when it seemed, for a brief moment, that it would be saved. Coming to film from advertising, he brought to the cinema a number of other first-time directors from the world of advertising: Alan Parker*, Ridley Scott*, Hugh Hudson. His first production, *S.W.A.L.K./Melody* (1971), was written by Parker, with whom he went on to produce *Bugsy Malone* (1976) and *Midnight Express* (1978). He engaged Scott to direct *The Duellists* (1977), the first production of Puttnam's own production company, Enigma; and hired Hudson to direct *Chariots of Fire* (1981). The Best Picture Oscar for *Chariots of Fire*, followed by the success and cultural prestige of *Local Hero* (1983) and *The Killing Fields* (1984), both of which he produced for Goldcrest*, seemed to herald a renaissance in the British commercial feature film, which in the event proved to be short-lived. They did, however, establish him as a major force in the British film industry. Puttnam has been compared to Michael Balcon*, with his productions in the 1980s reflecting his own liberal morality and mildly suburban sentimentality: an Ealing for the Thatcher years most apparent in the 'First Love' films which Enigma produced for Channel 4*. He is, however, unambiguously commercial, targeting and tailoring his films as entertainment for an international market. In the late 1980s he had a brief, and unhappy, flirtation with Hollywood as head of production for Columbia Pictures, before returning to Britain as a producer and campaigner (with Richard Attenborough*) for the revitalisation of Britain as a centre of European film production. He was knighted in 1995. JC

Q

QUINN, Bob

Dublin 1939

Irish director and writer. The most prolific Irish film-maker, who worked in Radio Telefis Eireann* (RTE) in the 1960s before establishing an independent production company, Cinegael, in an Irish-speaking area of the West of Ireland, because it is 'isolated by its language from the English-American world'. He made the first Irish-language fiction film, *Caoineadh Airt Ui Laoire/Lament for Art O'Leary* (1975), which explored the relationship between the eighteenth century and the present in a formally innovative manner, casting the English playwright John Arden and his wife Margaretta D'Arcy in the unfamiliar roles of colonialist oppressors. His *Poitin* (1978) inserted a realist aesthetic into a West of Ireland previously populated by '*Quiet Man*' quaintness and '*Man of Aran*' celebration of land and sea. Continuing to work in often quirky contrast to other Irish film-makers, Quinn made a three-part television series, *Atlantean* (1984), which sought to overturn the Celtic myth of Irish origins and argued that the Irish came via the Atlantic from North Africa. Quinn's largely silent feature, *Budawanny* (1987), unconventionally explored the publicly unacknowledged reality of a supposedly celibate priest having a relationship with a woman. In one of the film's wittiest sequences the priest announces from the pulpit to his bewildered parishioners that 'soon you'll have another reason to call me Father'. Continuing with this theme, *The Bishop's Story* (1994) is a version of the controversy surrounding the real-life Bishop Casey, forced to resign as Bishop of Galway in 1992 after it became known that he had had a child in the 1970s. The film confirms Quinn's continuing challenge to established views and institutions. KR

R

RADIO TELEFIS EIREANN (RTE)

Irish television service. The public broadcasting television service, originally founded as a radio station in 1926, began television transmission in 1961. Historically, it has been the most important employer in the Irish audio-visual sector, and, with the absence of formal film training until recent years, the training ground for many film-makers, including Bob Quinn* and Pat O'Connor*. Its support for independent film and television production has been sporadic, but following a ministerial directive its IR£3.5 million contribution to the sector in 1993 increased to £5 million in 1994 and it will invest IR£12.5 million by 1999, about 10 per cent of its current budget. Its own soaps, dramas, documentaries and other programmes are consistently more popular than imported programmes, indicating, as with Irish-theme theatrical films, that Irish audiences in general engage with Irish material when given the chance.

During the 1960s RTE provided an important forum for hitherto publicly unarticulated views and as a result aided the process of modernisation and internationalisation of Irish culture and society. Its strengths during the 1960s and 1970s lay in such areas as successfully combining light entertainment with controversial discussion, most especially in the long-running *The Late Late Show*; current affairs, where numerous challenges were made to governments and other interest groups through investigative reporting; and in both rural and urban soap operas such as *The Riordans, Glenroe* and *Fair City*. By the 1980s RTE seemed to have lost its programming direction, especially its commitment to drama, which was a result in part of an engineer-dominated management structure. Its weak challenges to increased demands for the privatisation of its service, and its unenthusiastic engagement with independent film-makers, also lost it residual public and critical support as an institution. KR

Bib: Martin McLoone and John MacMahon (eds.), *Television and Irish Society: 21 Years of Irish Television* (1984).

RANK, J. Arthur — Hull 1888–1972

British film financier, and founder of the Rank Organisation, which, from the beginning of World War II, became the dominant force in British cinema, exercising near monopolistic control over production, distribution and exhibition. His biographer, Alan Wood, says that Rank's 'greatest virtue of all was undoubtedly the fact that he knew nothing whatever about making films.' A millionaire flour miller from Yorkshire and a devout Methodist, Rank first became involved in film through a desire to promote Christian values. In 1934 he and his business partner Lady Yule formed British National and built Pinewood Studios. Infuriated by the lack of distribution for their critically acclaimed first feature, *Turn of the Tide* (1935), he acquired a controlling interest in General Film Distributors. When his partnership with Lady Yule dissolved, she retained her interest in British National and he kept Pinewood. In 1938, Rank relieved the financially embarrassed Alexander Korda* of Denham Studios, and acquired the new studios at Elstree. When the war started, the industry anticipated a downturn and Rank was able to gain control, at knockdown prices, of two of the three largest cinema circuits, Odeon and Gaumont-British (which also brought him control of Gainsborough Pictures). In fact, cinema attendance spiralled upwards, and Rank's profits soared, forcing him to expand his investments in production to avoid tax, and fuelling what now looks like a golden age. By the end of the war, through his subsidiary, Independent Producers Ltd., Rank was financing independent production companies such as The Archers (Michael Powell* and Emeric Pressburger), Cineguild, Two Cities, Individual and Ealing. At the same time, seeking outlets for the films in which he was investing, Rank had acquired holdings in cinema chains in Australia, New Zealand, Canada and South Africa, and had become the largest single shareholder in Universal, offering him a platform from which to challenge Hollywood itself. Unfortunately, Labour government policy intervened in 1947 with import taxes and other restrictions, causing an Atlantic war of attrition with boycotts on both sides. It was a war which Rank could not win, and though, when the dust settled, select films like *Hamlet* (1948) and *The Red Shoes* (1948) continued to do well in select cinemas, J. Arthur Rank posed no future threat to American market dominance. The Rank Organisation became a finance house, exerting its main influence through the duopoly in exhibition which it shared with ABC, and subseqently EMI, and making its real profits from its acquisition of Xerox. In 1980, eight years after the death of its founder, Rank announced it was pulling out of film production altogether. JC

Bib: Geoffrey Macnab, *J. Arthur Rank and the British Film Industry* (1993).

REA, Stephen

Belfast 1946

Irish actor. When Rea came to international prominence with his performance in Neil Jordan's* *The Crying Game* (1992), for which he was nominated for an Oscar, he was already an experienced stage, television and film actor. He played in Jordan's *Angel* (1982) in a role not dissimilar to that in *The Crying Game*, and, in a rather different vein, he played a supporting role in Jordan's *Interview with the Vampire: The Vampire Chronicles* (1994, US). As a director of the Field Day Theatre Company, based in Derry, he has helped to rejuvenate Irish theatre. His television work includes the role of a local council employee in *Bad Behaviour* (1993). KR

Other Films Include: *The House* (TV), *The Company of Wolves* (1984); *Life is Sweet* (1990); *Angie* (1994, US); *Princess Caraboo* (1994, US); *All Men are Mortal* (1995, UK/Neth./Fr.).

REDGRAVE, (Sir) Michael

Bristol 1908 – Denham 1985

British actor. Co-founder (with Rachel Kempson) of the Redgrave 'dynasty' (which includes daughters Vanessa* and Lynn and son Corin), educated at Cambridge where he wrote film reviews, and a member of John Gielgud's* famous Old Vic theatre company from 1937, Redgrave claimed an ambivalence about his success in the cinema, insisting that he only ever took his debut lead role in Alfred Hitchcock's* *The Lady Vanishes* (1938) because he had a family to support. Ambivalence may be the key to his persona. Never an aggressively romantic hero, nor quite one of the league of postwar chaps, the character which Redgrave projected simply seemed unsure of himself and looking for something else – either out of idealism or discomfort. This might express itself through a frustrated passion, as in the socially idealistic but domestically inept mine-worker's son of *The Stars Look Down* (1939), the excruciating distraction of Barnes Wallis in *The Dam Busters* (1955), or the eccentric dithering of his lighter roles, *The Lady Vanishes* for example. Though he may have been doubtful about cinema, apparently finding it suspiciously easy, Redgrave's later filmography does not reveal quite so many embarrassments as those of some of the other theatrical knights.

Redgrave was nominated for an Oscar for his performance as Orin in *Mourning Becomes Electra* (1947, US). He was knighted in 1959. JC

Bib: Michael Redgrave, *In My Mind's I: An Actor's Autobiography* (1983).

Other Films Include: *Climbing High* [with Jessie Matthews] (1938); *Kipps* (1941); *The Big Blockade, Thunder Rock* (1942); *Dead of Night, The Way to the Stars, A Diary for Timothy* [narrator] (1945); *The Captive Heart* (1946); *Fame is the Spur* (1947); *Secret Beyond the Door* (1947, US); *The Browning Version* (1951); *The Importance of Being Earnest* (1952); *Oh ... Rosalinda!!, The Dam Busters, Confidential Report/Mr Arkadin* [Sp./Switz.] (1955); *1984* (1956); *Time Without Pity* (1957); *The Quiet American* [US], *Law and Disorder, The Immortal*

Land [narrator] (1958); *The Wreck of the Mary Deare* [US], *Shake Hands with the Devil* (1959); *The Innocents* (1961); *The Loneliness of the Long Distance Runner* (1962); *Young Cassidy, The Hill* (1965); *Oh! What a Lovely War, Goodbye, Mr Chips* (1969); *The Go-Between* (1970).

REDGRAVE, Vanessa London 1937

British actress, who made her London stage debut in 1958 and had a distinguished career in London and Stratford (including a famous Rosalind in *Much Ado About Nothing*) before making an impact in cinema in 1966, first with Karel Reisz's* *Morgan a Suitable Case for Treatment* and then in Michelangelo Antonioni's *Blowup* (1967). As with Redgrave* *père*, there is a tentativeness in her acting, an edge of self-conscious awkwardness, which gives a fragile complexity to the independent and forthright women she plays. Andy Medhurst refers to 'a lingering sense of something great' which is never quite realised, and it is true that her screen performances give off a sense of energy with not enough to work on. Some of the energy is diverted into left-wing political activity, much of it funded from her earnings, and into her commitment to the Palestinian cause which has frequently lost her a sympathetic audience in the US. She won Best Actress awards at Cannes for *Morgan* and for *Isadora* (1969), an Oscar for Best Supporting Actress for *Julia* (1977, US), and a New York Film Critics' Best Supporting Actress award for her role as Peggy Ramsay in *Prick Up Your Ears* (1987). She was nominated for a Best Actress Oscar in the Merchant-Ivory* *The Bostonians* (1984), and for Best Supporting Actress in their *Howard's End* (1992). She was given a BFI* Fellowship in 1988. JC

Bib: *Vanessa Redgrave: An autobiography* (1991).

Other Films Include: *A Man for All Seasons* (1966); *Camelot* [US], *The Sailor from Gibraltar* (1967); *The Charge of the Light Brigade, Un Tranquillo posto di campagna/A Quiet Place in the Country* [It./Fr.] (1968); *The Sea Gull* (1969); *Oh! What a Lovely War* [as Sylvia Pankhurst] (1969); *La vacanza/Vacation* [It.], *The Devils* (1971); *The Trojan Women, Mary Queen of Scots* (1972); *Murder on the Orient Express* (1974); *The Palestinian* [prod.] (1977); *Agatha* [US], *Yanks* (1979); *Wetherby, Steaming* (1985); *Comrades* (1986); *The Ballad of the Sad Café* (1991, US/UK); *Mother's Boys* (1993, US).

REED, (Sir) Carol London 1906–76

British director. The son of the famous theatrical actor-manager Herbert Beerbohm Tree, Carol Reed was a stage actor and director before directing his first feature, *Midshipman Easy*, in 1935. During the 1930s he directed Jessie Matthews* and Michael Redgrave* in the musical comedy *Climbing High* (1938), but he was principally identified with the realism of ordinary lives and everyday settings: *Laburnum Grove* (1936), *Bank Holiday* (1938) and *Penny Paradise* (1938). *The Stars Look Down* (1939), a remarkably committed account of working-class life and trade union activity adapted from A. J. Cronin, won well-deserved critical praise, and *Night Train to Munich* (1940) and *The Young Mr Pitt* (1942) gave him an international audience. During the war, Reed worked on propaganda documentaries. In 1945, with Garson Kanin, he co-directed *The True Glory*, a feature-length compilation charting the progress of the war from D Day to VE Day. In the postwar cinema, Reed, like David Lean*, comes close to being a 'classic' British film-maker, his acknowledged classics being *The Way Ahead* (1944), *Odd Man Out* (1947), *The Fallen Idol* (1948) and his best-known film, *The Third Man* (1949), the last two scripted by Graham Greene*, with whom he also made *Our Man in Havana* (1960). These films confirmed his critical reputation as a leading director of British quality cinema, a reputation which was enhanced by *Outcast of the Islands* (1951) and *The Man Between* (1953). He received the Academy Award as Best Director for *Oliver!* in 1968. He was knighted in 1952. JC

Bib: Nicholas Wapshott, *The Man Between: A Biography of Carol Reed* (1990).

REED, Oliver — Wimbledon 1938

British actor, whose first starring role was as the werewolf in Terence Fisher's* *The Curse of the Werewolf* (1961). If there is a tradition of decency and restraint in British postwar cinema, Reed belongs to that of excess, which would also contain Hammer horror* and Ken Russell*, for whom Reed starred in *Women in Love* (1969), *The Devils* (1971) and *Tommy* (1975). Reed was one of Richard Lester's* musketeers in *The Three Musketeers* (1974, Panama) and *The Four Musketeers* (1975, Panama/Sp.). He is the nephew of Carol Reed*, for whom he played a notable Bill Sikes in *Oliver!* (1968). He appeared in *The Brood* (1978, Canada) for David Cronenberg and in *Castaway* (1986) for Nicolas Roeg*. Much loved by the popular press as a source of scandal, he is given to displays of boozy masculinity on television chat shows. JC

REISZ, Karel — Ostrava, Czechoslovakia 1926

British director of Czech origins who came to England as a refugee at the age of twelve. He worked with Lindsay Anderson* on the Oxford journal *Sequence**, and was involved in Free Cinema*. The short documentary which he co-directed with Tony Richardson*, *Momma Don't Allow* (1956) and *We are the Lambeth Boys* (1959), were shown in the Free Cinema season at the National Film Theatre, London. Reisz published the influential *The Technique of Film Editing* in 1953. His first feature, *Saturday Night and Sunday Morning* (1960), was both a critical and a commercial success, and a landmark in the British New Wave*. Reisz was to have directed *This Sporting Life* (1963), but elected to produce, with Anderson directing. *Morgan a Suitable Case for Treatment* (1966) has a certain cult status for those who still believe in the mythology of the 1960s. Outside the context of British social realism, Reisz's work has been consistently interesting – *The Dog Soldiers/Who'll Stop the Rain* (1978, US), *The French Lieutenant's Woman* (1981) – but never overwhelming. Like many other British directors, he was forced to turn to Hollywood in the 1970s and 1980s. JC

Bib: Karel Reisz, *The Technique of Film Editing* (1953).

Other Films: *Night Must Fall* (1964); *Isadora* (1968); *The Gambler* (1974, US); *Sweet Dreams* (1985, US); *Everybody Wins* (1990, US).

RELPH, Michael – see DEARDEN, Basil

RICHARD, (Sir) Cliff Harry Webb; Lucknow, India 1940

British singer and actor, and idol of the pre-Beatles pop scene in the early 1960s. He made four successful films between 1959 and 1962, *Expresso Bongo* (1959), *The Young Ones* (1961), *Wonderful Life* (1964) and *Summer Holiday* (1963). Modelled on Elvis Presley's movies in the US, Cliff's films were a wonderfully British variant: like a pop version of Ealing*, they placed civic-spirited youth against weary bureaucrats and businessmen of The Older Generation. The music was good, the direction was lively, and there was just enough teenage rebellion to make parents anxious and thus ensure Cliff the enthusiastic approval of their kids. He went on to make two further films, *Finders Keepers* (1966) and *Take Me High* (1973), but the times they had a-changed and the youth audience had moved on, leaving Cliff stranded at home with the grown-ups. JC

RICHARDSON, (Sir) Ralph Cheltenham 1902 – London 1983

British actor, who made his stage debut in *Les Misérables* in 1921, and with John Gielgud* and Laurence Olivier* formed the leading triumvirate of theatrical knights for five decades. Despite turning up to rehearsals on his motorbike in his seventies, Richardson seems never to have been completely young, and his 1930s persona already contains the seeds of his dotage. In his second film, Victor Saville's* *Friday the Thirteenth* (1933), Richardson partnered Jessie Matthews* as the proper schoolmaster to her exuberant showgirl, and in *The Divorce of Lady X* (1938) he was already the dotty aristocrat who reappears forty-six years later in *Greystoke, The Legend of Tarzan Lord of the Apes* (1984). Karol Kulik, in her biography of Alexander Korda*, compares Richardson's swaggering Chief in *Things to Come* (1936) to a mixture of Charles Laughton* and W. C. Fields, a mixture which reputedly did not please Mussolini on whom the characterisation was based. But the eccentric dottiness and apparent befuddledness did not undermine the strength of his characters. His performance as the Tory squire in Saville's *South Riding* (1938), caught between conscience and straitened circumstances, is richly drawn. However recognisable and consistent Richardson's characterisations were, they were never dull or predictable, and each performance was precisely measured. In 1952 he directed himself in *Home at Seven* (1952), an unpretentious murder mystery, and in 1962 he played James Tyrone in the screen adaptation of *A Long Day's Journey into Night* [US]; but for the most part his postwar film career was in distinctive supporting roles and character parts. JC

Bib: Garry O'Connor, *Ralph Richardson: An Actor's Life* (1982).

Other Films Include: *The Man Who Could Work Miracles* (1936); *The Citadel* (1938); *The Four Feathers, The Lion Has Wings* (1939); *The Silver Fleet* (1943); *School for Secrets* (1946); *Anna Karenina, The Fallen Idol* (1948); *The Heiress* (1949, US); *Outcast of the Islands* (1951); *The Sound Barrier* (1952); *Richard III* (1955); *Our Man in Havana, Exodus* [US] (1960); *Doctor Zhivago* (1965); *Campanadas a medianoche/Chimes at Midnight* [narrator] (1966, Sp./Switz.); *Oh! What a Lovely War* (1969); *Tales from the Crypt* (1972); *O Lucky Man!, A Doll's House* (1973); *Time Bandits* (1981).

RICHARDSON, Tony

Cecil Antonio Richardson; Shipley 1928 – Los Angeles, California 1991

British director, who was a leading figure in the British New Wave* in both cinema and theatre. After Oxford, Richardson worked in BBC television drama, and in 1955 formed the English Stage Company with George Devine at the Royal Court Theatre. It was his production of John Osborne's *Look Back in Anger* (1956) – or at least Kenneth Tynan's review of it – which set the theatre 'new wave' in motion and gave birth to the 'angry young men'. Simultaneously, the documentary which he co-directed with Karel Reisz*, *Momma Don't Allow* (1955), was appearing in the Free Cinema* season. In 1958, Richardson formed Woodfall Productions with Osborne, to translate the new wave to cinema, and in 1959 his film directing debut, *Look Back in Anger,* began a series of adaptations: *The Entertainer* (1960) from Osborne's play, *A Taste of Honey* (1961) from Shelagh Delaney's play, and *The Loneliness of the Long Distance Runner* (1962) from a short story by Alan Sillitoe. Richardson's career with Woodfall ended exuberantly with *Tom Jones* (1963), which won the Oscar for Best Director. Much of the rest of Richardson's career was in Hollywood, but it failed to build on the verve of *Tom Jones*. In *The Charge of the Light Brigade* (1968), however, he almost produced a national epic of triumphant defeat. His last film, *Blue Sky* (1991) was released posthumously. JC

Other Films Include: *The Loved One* (1965, US); *The Sailor from Gibraltar* (1967); *Hamlet* (1969); *Ned Kelly* (1970); *A Delicate Balance* (1974, US); *Joseph Andrews* (1977); *The Border* (1982, US); *Hotel New Hampshire* (1984, US).

ROBERTS, Rachel

Llanelli, Wales 1927 – California 1980

British actress. Though primarily a stage actress, Rachel Roberts gave two of the most memorable female performances in the British New Wave* cinema. In *Saturday Night and Sunday Morning* (1960) she played a mature, defeated woman trapped in an empty marriage and an affectionless and humiliating relationship with a younger lover (Albert Finney*). In *This Sporting Life* (1963), her Mrs Hammond is unremitting in her refusal of life, affection or sexual pleasure, or of Frank Machin (Richard Harris*), whose response is rape. The Roberts character is, in fact, the most painful of the sacrificial victims of the misogynist current in the British New Wave. Her performances in *Saturday Night and Sunday Morning* and *This Sporting Life* received Best Actress awards from the British Academy, from whom she also won a Best Supporting Actress award for *Yanks* (1979).

She had a troubled relationship with Rex Harrison*, moved to California, suffered from alcoholism, and died of an overdose in 1980. JC

Bib: Alexander Walker (ed.), *The Rachel Roberts Journals* (1984).

Other Films Include: *The Good Companions* (1957); *The Reckoning* (1970); *O Lucky Man!, The Belstone Fox* (1973); *Murder on the Orient Express* (1974); *Picnic at Hanging Rock* (1975, Australia); *Charlie Chan and the Curse of the Dragon Queen* (1980, US).

ROBESON, PAUL

Princeton, NJ, USA 1898 – Philadelphia 1976

American singer/actor. Robeson was based in Britain during much of the 1930s while he developed his European singing and acting career (appearing with Peggy Ashcroft* in a 1930 production of *Othello*), and he appeared in a number of films which exploited his colour and his singing voice to mixed effects. He had already appeared in Oscar Micheaux's *Body and Soul* (1925, US). His appearance, with his wife Eslanda, in Kenneth Macpherson's *Borderline* (1930, Switz.) placed him in contact with the British avant-garde group around the magazine *Close Up**. He was tempted into Zoltan Korda's *Sanders of the River* (1935) by the promise of authentic African music and tribal life, but the result was a vindication of paternalistic colonialism, and Robeson attempted to prevent the film's release. Stevenson's *King Solomon's Mines* (1937) had more adventure but little more enlightenment. *Song of Freedom* (1936) and *The Big Fella* (1937), both directed by J. Edgar Wills and featuring Elizabeth Welch, were low-budget features, but *Song of Freedom*, at least, was welcomed by the Harlem press (and Langston Hughes) for its representation of the black man. Most successful, but no less compromised in its representation of race, was *The Proud Valley* (1940), directed by Pen Tennyson, which integrates Robeson effortlessly into a Welsh mining community through his singing voice, but still leaves him in the anteroom when the miners negotiate with the bosses. JC

Bib: Martin Bauml Doberman, *Paul Robeson* (1989).

ROBSON, (Dame) Flora

South Shields 1902 – Sussex 1984

British actress, renowned as one of the great character players of the British theatre and cinema. At the age of 32, Robson played the old Empress Elizabeth in Alexander Korda's* *Catherine the Great* (1934); she played Queen Elizabeth I in *The Sea Hawk* (1940, US); but most famously she played the same role in *Fire Over England* (1937), uttering the lines which have become part of Elizabethan mythology: 'I know I have the body of a weak and feeble woman, but I have the heart and valour of a King. Aye, and of a King of England too.' After the war, demonstrating her range, she appeared in *Holiday Camp* (1947), the first of a series of films which featured the very ordinary Huggett family; as the Mother Superior in Michael Powell* and Emeric Pressburger's *Black Narcissus* (1947); as a magistrate in *Good-time Girl* (1948); as a prospective Labour MP in Basil Dearden's* excellent *Frieda* (1947); and in Dearden's costume melodrama, *Saraband for Dead Lovers* (1948). For the rest of her career she remained in the theatre, though she gave a memorable performance in John Ford's *7 Women* (1966, US). She was made a Dame in 1960. JC

ROEG, Nicolas

London 1928

British director. Roeg seems like a product of the 1960s art schools, but is in fact a product of the Marylebone dubbing studios from 1947, camera operator from 1958 on, for example, Roger Corman's *The Masque of the Red Death* (1964), second unit camera on *Lawrence of Arabia* (1962), and cinematographer on such films as the screen adaptation of Harold Pinter's* *The Caretaker* (1963), François Truffaut's *Fahrenheit 451* (1966) and John Schlesinger's* *Far from the Madding Crowd* (1967). His directing debut, *Performance* (1970), co-directed with Donald Cammell and starring Mick Jagger and James Fox, became a cult movie of the 1970s. Roeg's films are characterised by intricately edited time warps in which opposing worlds clash. With *Walkabout* (1971), set in the Australian outback, the cultural clash and the temporal ellipses were still connected, in *Don't Look Now* (1973) the gap between this world and the other was chilling, and in *The Man Who Fell to Earth* (1976) there was a sense of ideas just beyond the edge of the screen. But the later films often seem, in Chuck Kleinhans' phrase, 'permutations without profundity'. Roeg seems to inhabit a peculiarly British territory, an art cinema (like Peter Greenaway's*) whose cleverness leaves it stranded between pretentiousness and seriousness. JC

Bib: Jonathan Hacker and David Price, *Take 10: Contemporary British Film Directors* (1991).

Other Films Include: *Bad Timing* (1980); *Eureka* (1983); *Insignificance* (1985); *Castaway* (1986); *Track 29* (1987).

ROTHA, Paul

Paul Thompson; London 1907 – Wallingford 1984

British director, **critic and author**, who had already written the first edition of his influential *The Film Till Now: A Survey of World Cinema* (1930) when he joined John Grierson* at the Empire Marketing Board (EMB) in 1932. The book, which was updated in 1948 and 1958, was the first of several, including *Documentary Film* (1935), an influential expression of what Michael Balcon* later characterised as 'the documentary attitude' in British cinema, the ethos of a cinema of moral and social responsibility. Rotha sought to maintain independence from government and the 'official' British Documentary Movement*, and only remained at the EMB for a few months. He established Strand

Films in 1935, producing sponsored documentaries such as *Today We Live* (1937) on unemployment in the mining industry; and founded the *Documentary News Letter* in 1939. During the war he made documentaries for the Ministry of Information. After the war, as well as documentaries, he made three feature films. From 1953 until 1955 he was Head of the Documentary Film Department at the BBC, and oversaw the production of a number of early dramatised documentaries. He received British Film Academy awards for *The World is Rich* (1947) and *World Without End* (1953), the latter co-directed with Basil Wright*. JC

Bib: Paul Morris (ed.), *Paul Rotha* (1982).

Other Films Include: **Documentaries** – *Contact* (1932); *Shipyard* (1933); *The Future's in the Air* (1936); *New Worlds for Old* (1939); *World of Plenty* (1943). **Features** – *No Resting Place* (1951); *Cat and Mouse* (1958); *De Overval/The Silent Raid* (1962, Neth.).

RTE – see RADIO TELEFIS EIREANN

RUSSELL, Ken

Southampton 1927

British director. The excess and 'bad taste' of Russell's later work is in sharp contrast to the 'good taste' of his work in the early 1960s for the television arts series *Monitor*, where he directed lyrical documentaries on romantic composers. His critical reputation in cinema was established by *Women in Love* (1969). He hit problems with the censors on *The Devils* (1971), and outraged music lovers everywhere with the Tchaikovsky biopic, *The Music Lovers* (1970), and with subsequent 'outrageous' film biographies of the sexual and political deviances of romantic composers: *Mahler* (1974) and *Lisztomania* (1975). His obsession with the romantics turned to gothic horror in the 1980s with *Gothic* (1986) and *The Lair of the White Worm* (1988). Russell is a self-confessed cultural conservative. While there may be subtleties and contradictions in his attitude to sexuality, his very unsubtle presentation of it looks like misogyny. Though his visual imagination is often striking, it leaves little room for the imagination of the spectator, and his erotic imagery ends up being curiously and unsensuously intellectual. His bad taste ought to be a relief from the proprieties of a cinema of restraint, but ends up being rather wearying. JC

Bib: Barry Keith Grant, 'The Body Politic', in Lester Friedman (ed.), *British Cinema and Thatcherism* (1993).

Other Films Include: *Amelia and the Angel* [short] (1957); *French Dressing* (1964); *Billion Dollar Brain* (1967); *The Boy Friend* (1971);

Savage Messiah (1972); *Tommy* (1975); *Valentino* (1977); *Altered States* (1980, US); *Crimes of Passion* (1984, US); *Salome's Last Dance* (1987); *The Rainbow* (1988); *Whore* (1991, US).

RUTHERFORD, (Dame) Margaret

London 1892 – Chalfont St Peter 1972

British actress, who became one of the best-loved eccentric character actresses in the postwar cinema. As Sylvia Paskin has suggested, 'character actress' is 'a term applied to women not considered attractive enough to be the love interest in films', but Rutherford seemed to accept the role with particular gusto and considerable craft, sporting her tweediness with pride. While her ample frame lacked the conventional appearance of the female star, her performances never lacked sparkle, though her gung-ho ebullience was often laced with something quite touching. Some of her finest parts came from theatre – she had already played Madame Arcati and Miss Prism on the stage before she repeated the roles in the screen adaptations of *Blithe Spirit* (1945) and *The Importance of Being Earnest* (1952). She was mystically dotty in *Blithe Spirit*, academically dotty in *Passport to Pimlico* (1949), domestically dotty in *I'm All Right Jack* (1959), classically dotty as Mistress Quickly in Welles' *Campanadas a medianoche/Chimes at Midnight* (1966, Sp./Switz.), and inquisitively dotty as Agatha Christie's Miss Marple in the series of films she made for MGM in the early 1960s – *Murder She Said* (1961), *Murder at the Gallop* (1963), *Murder Most Foul* (1964), *Murder Ahoy* (1964) and *The Alphabet Murders* (1965). She received an Oscar as Best Supporting Actress for *The V.I.P.s* (1963). JC

Bib: Dawn Langley Simmons, *Margaret Rutherford: A Blithe Spirit* (1983).

S

SABU

Sabu Dastagin; Karapur, Mysore, India 1924 – Hollywood 1963

Indian/British actor, who was 'discovered' by Robert Flaherty* for the title role of *Elephant Boy* (1937), and brought to Britain to play Prince Azim in Zoltan Korda's *The Drum* (1938) and Abu in *The Thief of Bagdad* (1940). He went to Hollywood to play similar exotic roles, and was brought back to Britain to play the young Indian prince in Michael Powell* and Emeric Pressburger's *Black Narcissus* (1947). By the time he was 25, however, there was no longer a call for young Indian princes. He tried unsuccessfully to establish himself in Italian exotica in *Buongiorno, Elefante!* (1953, It.), returned to Hollywood for *Jungle Rampage* (1962) and *A Tiger Walks* (1963), but died of a heart attack at the age of 39. JC

SAVILLE, Victor

Victor Salberg; Birmingham 1897 – London 1979

British director, who was prominent as both director and producer in the 1930s. Saville entered the film industry in 1917 as the manager of a cinema in Coventry, and in 1920 he formed a small renting firm in Birmingham in partnership with Michael Balcon*. In the late 1920s he was a producer and writer, directing his first feature, *The Arcadians*, an adaptation of the stage success, in 1927. His major successes came in the 1930s, beginning with *The Good Companions* (1933), the first of five highly popular films he directed with Jessie Matthews*: the others were *Friday the Thirteenth* (1933), *Evergreen* (1934), *First a Girl* (1935) and *It's Love Again* (1936). Saville was at home with the Hollywood-style sophisticated musical, but his range extended to the thriller with *I Was a Spy* (1933), which made Madeleine Carroll* an international star; to political comedy with the fascinating *Storm in a Teacup* (1937), addressing fascism in the guise of Scottish nationalism; and to social drama with the excellent *South Riding* (1938), described by Jeffrey Richards as the supreme example of the 1930s 'consensus film'. Saville moved to Hollywood as a producer and director for MGM in 1939. JC

Bib: Jeffrey Richards, *The Age of the Dream Palace: Cinema and Society in Britain, 1930–1939* (1984).

SCHLESINGER, John

London 1926

British director. Schlesinger graduated to film after acting (his credits include *The Battle of the River Plate* [1956] and *Brothers in Law* [1957]), and directing television documentaries in the late 1950s for *Tonight* and *Monitor*. In 1961 his documentary on the daily life of Waterloo Station, *Terminus*, made for Edgar Anstey* at British Transport Films, won an award at Venice. His first features, *A Kind of Loving* (1962) and *Billy Liar* (1963), inhabit the territory of the British New Wave*, but Schlesinger seemed less committed to it than the other 'angry young men'. In *Darling* (1965), he turns to the new, consumerist middle class, with Julie Christie* representing both the destructiveness of 'Swinging Sixties' values and the desire for something else, and in *Sunday Bloody Sunday* (1971) he returns to the same concerns at a more intimate and enclosed level. Since the 1960s, and following the success of *Midnight Cowboy* (1969), which won Oscars for Best Director, Best Screenplay and Best Film, Schlesinger has found it easier to make films in the US than in Britain, and even *Yanks* (1979), though set in the North of England, had to raise its finance in America and Germany. He has directed a number of films for television, including the award-winning *An Englishman Abroad* (1983). JC

Other Films Include: *Far from the Madding Crowd* (1967); *The Day of the Locust* (1975, US); *Marathon Man* (1976, US); *Honky Tonk Freeway* (1981, US); *The Falcon and the Snowman* (1985, US); *The Believers* (1987, US); *Madame Sousatzka* (1988); *Pacific Heights* (1990, US); *The Innocent* (1993, UK/Ger.).

SCOTLAND AND FILM

If, as Benedict Anderson suggests, a nation is an 'imagined community', the question for Scottish cinema might be, 'Who imagined Scotland?'. In the standard version, Sir Walter Scott established the main outlines of the mythology: Scotland as the frontier territory of Europe, playing out the epic struggles of nature and culture; the Highlands as the sublime wild place of Romanticism faced with the encroachments of administrative rationality and industrial revolution. J. M. Barrie (*The Little Minister*), at the end of the nineteenth century, added the self-deprecating whimsy of small-town sensibility, and Hollywood, Ealing* and Dr Finlay did the rest : *Rob Roy* (1954, US; 1995, US/Scotland); *Kidnapped* (1938, US; 1948, US; 1960, US; 1971, US); *Master of Ballantrae* (1953, US; 1984, TS); *The Little Minister* (1934, US); *Whisky Galore* (1949, Ealing); *The Maggie* (1954, Ealing); *Dr Finlay's Casebook* (1959–66, BBC; 1994–5, STV). The infamous *Brigadoon* (1954, US) set the whole thing to music, earning it the undying affection of lovers of Hollywood musicals, the enduring hatred of lovers of Scotland, and intellectual contortions from anyone who has the misfortune to love both.

The problem is, of course, that like most other small countries – or, more accurately, 'stateless nations' – Scotland has had a limited capacity to represent itself in feature films. The appetite for film was prodigious from the start, and in the 1930s Glasgow had the largest cinema in Europe – Green's Playhouse – and more cinema seats per capita than any other city in Europe. Production, however, was restricted almost exclusively to documentaries and educational films – and to politically motivated activists and inspired amateurs: there was an active Left film movement represented by Glasgow Kino; Norman McLaren* and Helen Biggar made the innovative animation *Hell Unltd* (1936) as a campaigning film against the arms trade; and Jenny Gilbertson made striking anthropological documentaries in Shetland

and Greenland. For a while Scotland shared in John Grierson's* success in securing state sponsorship for documentary production, and after the war his biographer, Forsyth Hardy, established Films of Scotland as an agency for commercial and industrial sponsorship. It was not till the 1970s that Bill Douglas* became the first Scottish film-maker to make a major contribution to European narrative cinema with his autobiographical trilogy, *My Childhood* (1972), *My Ain Folk* (1978) and *My Way Home* (1978). Bill Forsyth* (who served his apprenticeship in sponsored documentaries) claims *That Sinking Feeling* (1979) as the first Scottish feature film to be funded wholly from within Scotland (a claim which has to be qualified by the fact that it used non-professional actors, begged or borrowed almost everything, and cost almost nothing).

Forsyth's success, confirmed by *Gregory's Girl* (1980), coincided with the opening of Channel 4* in 1982, and laid the foundations of an aspiring Scottish film industry. The Scottish Film Production Fund was established in 1982 through the cooperation of the Scottish Arts Council and the Scottish Film Council to provide development funding, and Scottish feature films, commissioned by Channel 4, began to appear in the commercial cinema. The Workshop Movement* had a less tenuous hold in Scotland than in many of the English regions, though the Edinburgh Film Workshop Trust provided an important entry point for community video, animation and documentary. Throughout the 1980s, a close-knit community of independent film-makers became increasingly articulate in their demands, and began to breathe a sense of urgency into the cultural and commercial bureaucracies, who, by the 1990s, were in any case beginning to recognise the potential of the media industries for inward investment, employment, economic regeneration, and (dread word) tourism. The Glasgow Development Agency established a Glasgow Film Fund, administered through the Scottish Film Production Fund, one of whose early investments was in *Shallow Grave* (1994). The international success of that film led to the same team (Boyle, Macdonald, Hodge) making *Trainspotting* (1996). Ken Loach was attracted to Scotland to make *Carla's Song* (to be released, 1996), a film set in both Glasgow and Nicaragua. The Lottery Fund administered by the Scottish Arts Council and the Scottish Film Council made awards to film production, its first major awards including £1 million for an adaptation of Alasdair Gray's *Poor Things*. Scottish Screen Locations marketed Scottish locations, bringing Franco Zeffirelli and Mel Gibson to Aberdeenshire to make *Hamlet* (1990) and Peugeot to the West Highlands to shoot commercials. Scottish Broadcast and Film Training provided in-service training and re-training. Both BBC Scotland and Scottish Television established series allowing first time directors to make short narrative films, and the Gaelic Film Fund extended film production to the Gaelic-speaking areas.

There are reasons to be cheerful. Hollywood's rediscovery of Scotland has more to do with the incentives of inward investment than with cultural commitment, and it will move on (as it did with *Braveheart*) when it finds a more favourable tax environment. Its images may bring more benefits to tourism than to national self-awareness, *but they are no longer the only images*, and can consequently be enjoyed (or not) for what they are. New people are finding entry points, new voices are heard, and not every film has to redress the grievances of the past or recast its myths. While it is still too early to talk of a Scottish film industry, the peculiar conditions of a post-industrial economy seem to be producing the conditions in which feature films, short films and documentaries can be produced in Scotland which begin to proliferate and complicate the ways in which Scotland can be imagined.

Bib: Colin McArthur (ed.), *Scotch Reels: Scotland in cinema and television* (London: BFI Publishing, 1982); Eddie Dick (ed.), *From Limelight to Satellite: A Scottish film book* (Glasgow/London: Scottish Film Council and BFI Publishing, 1990). JC

SCOTT, Ridley

South Shields 1939

British director. Scott is representative of a group of British directors who emerged from advertising in the 1970s and gravitated towards Hollywood in the 1980s. A graduate of the Royal College of Art (and described by David Puttnam* as 'a painter who happens to use film'), Scott made his first short film, *Boy and Bicycle*, funded by the BFI* Experimental Film Fund, in 1966: 'An ambitious first film that combines adventurous camerawork with a voice-over monologue by Tony Scott [his brother], exploring the sensibility of a schoolboy.' He started in television as a set designer turned director. He left television in 1967 to direct commercials, winning awards for, among others, the Hovis Bread series, and, incidentally, employing Hugh Hudson, later director of *Chariots of Fire* (1981). In 1977, he was engaged by Puttnam, also a former advertising man, to direct *The Duellists*, to which he brought the period style of the Hovis ads, toughened up by strong performances from Harvey Keitel and Keith Carradine into an intriguing male melodrama. In Hollywood, he has managed to make at least one very good film per decade: *Alien* (1979), *Blade Runner* (1982), and *Thelma & Louise* (1991), each marked by the visual style and narrative shocks of the art school and the television commercial. There is always the danger, however, that his pictures will swamp his stories, as in the Christopher Columbus extravaganza, *1492 Conquest of Paradise* (1992, UK/Fr./Sp.). JC

SCREEN

British journal. Started in 1960 by the Society for Education in Film and Television (SEFT), *Screen* in the early 1970s became the leading international journal of film theory in the English language. '*Screen* theory' combined the semiotics of Metz, Kristeva and Barthes, the psychoanalysis of Freud and Lacan, and the marxism of Althusser, to which were added, sometimes uneasily, the advances of feminist theory and of independent and avant-garde film practice. The journal imported the excitement of post-'68 French theory not only to film studies, to which it gave the academic respectability necessary to establish it in higher education, but to a wider sphere of critical studies, and it exported theory to North America and Australia. SEFT, a grant-in-aid body of the British Film Institute*, also published *Screen Education*, which extended debates to education and cultural studies. *Screen* was frequently accused of jargon, intellectual terrorism and political naivety, but its success in the 1970s was in creating a constituency, through weekend schools as well as through the journals, and in defining debates. The constituency and the debates became more multiple in the 1980s, and the agenda more inclusive. In 1989 the BFI withdrew funding from SEFT, and *Screen* moved to an academic base in the John Logie Baird Centre in Glasgow. JC

SELLERS, Peter

Richard Henry Sellers; Southsea 1925 – London 1980

British actor, who first rose to fame on radio as the source of several idiotic voices in *The Goon Show*, a national cult in the mid-1950s. It was as an impersonator that he was most skilled, and it was sometimes difficult to dissociate his skills as a mimic from his dramatic performance. Even in *I'm All Right Jack* (1959), where his satiric role as the Stalinist Fred Kite brought him a British Academy Best Actor award, there is the sense of Peter Sellers, the Goon, putting on a funny voice to 'do' a trade unionist, just as he 'did' Asians in *The Millionairess* (1960) and *The Party* (1968, US). In the context of Stanley Kubrick's* *Dr Strangelove* (1963), Sellers' mimicry in multiple roles works brilliantly, but in the same director's *Lolita* (1962) it simply pulls the film out of focus. His performance in the dramatic role of Chance in *Being There* (1979) was well received critically, but his lasting achievement may be the creation of Inspector Clouseau in Blake Edwards' *Pink Panther* series, a legendary comic creation whose disastrously misplaced aplomb (pronounced 'aplöm') has entered popular memory and whose misplaced 'French' vowels have entered the vocabulary. JC

Bib: Alexander Walker, *Peter Sellers: The Authorised Biography* (1981).

Other Films Include: *The Ladykillers, The Case of the Mukkinese Battle-horn* [short] (1955); *The Naked Truth* (1957); *Carlton-Browne of the F.O., The Mouse That Roared* (1959); *The Battle of the Sexes* (1960); *Mr Topaze* [+ dir.] (1961); *The Wrong Arm of the Law* (1962); *The Pink Panther* (1963, US); *A Shot in the Dark* (1964, US); *What's New Pussycat* (1965, US/UK/Fr.); *The Wrong Box* (1966); *Casino Royale* (1967); *I Love You, Alice B. Toklas* (1968, US); *There's a Girl in My Soup* (1970); *The Optimists of Nine Elms* (1973); *The Return of the Pink Panther* (1975); *The Pink Panther Strikes Again* (1976); *Revenge of the Pink Panther* (1978); *Trail of the Pink Panther* (1982).

SEQUENCE

British journal (1947–52), published initially at Oxford University, and subsequently in London. Edited by Gavin Lambert, Lindsay Anderson* and Penelope Houston, with contributions from Karel Reisz*, *Sequence* formed the breeding ground of Free Cinema* and the British New Wave*. It was also, like *Close Up** before it and *Movie** after, a reaction against the dominant traditions of British film criticism and the postwar quality cinema which it supported. The journal set itself against the 'sociology' of the British Documentary Movement* and British realist cinema, seeking out the 'living poetry' which came from 'creative direction', a poetry which it was as likely to find in John Ford's Westerns as in the cinema of important themes favoured by *Sight and Sound**. It anticipated *Movie* in its careful analyses, though not in the breadth of its tastes. Gavin Lambert became editor of *Sight and Sound* in 1950, and the poachers became the gamekeepers for the next generation. JC

SHERIDAN, Jim — Dublin 1949

Irish director and writer. Sheridan's career began in the 1970s as a theatre director and playwright. Eight of his own plays have been produced, especially when he was a director at the Project Arts Centre, the main alternative venue for theatre, visual arts and film at the time. He moved to New York where he was Artistic Director of the Irish Arts Centre and studied film at New York University. He spent many years attempting with producer Noel Pearson to gain backing for his adaptation of the autobiography of writer Christy Brown, which became eventually *My Left Foot* (1989). It was the first Irish-produced film to be nominated for five Oscars (only to be exceeded by Neil Jordan's* *The Crying Game*, 1992) and it won two: for actors Daniel Day-Lewis* and Brenda Fricker*.

The Browns are depicted in *My Left Foot* as a Dublin working-class family struggling to overcome adversity, with the mother binding the family together despite hints of violence from the father. The film avoids the more uncomfortable realities of a large family in a society where contraception was illegal. Sheridan's second film, *The Field* (1990), was also nominated for an Oscar: for Richard Harris'* performance as Bull McCabe, a farmer who is seeking to purchase a field he has long tilled. The film radically altered the play by John B. Keane from which it was derived, by shifting the story from the late 1950s/early 1960s to the 1930s, and changing the Bull's rival from English to Irish-American (Tom Berenger) – changes dictated by the foreign funding of the film. The need to retain audience recognition for a character and the reinforcement of a pre-modern, pastoral view of Ireland, as historically constructed in the international cinema, requires a film-maker such as Sheridan, despite his earlier success, to compromise in a manner that largely neutralises its cultural impact in Ireland. Sheridan's third feature, *In the Name of the Father* (1993), explores the Guildford Four miscarriage of justice case when Irish people were wrongly convicted of terrorist offences and as a result spent fifteen years in jail. KR

SIGHT AND SOUND

British journal, established in 1932, and taken under the wing of the British Film Institute* in 1933. Both came out of an Institute of Adult Education commission set up in 1929 to 'consider suggestions for improving and extending the use of films for educational and cultural purposes and to consider methods for raising the standard of public appreciation of films'. In the 1930s and 1940s, *Sight and Sound*'s main constituencies were education and the film societies, and its influence on the national cinema was limited. Since the late 1940s, however, *Sight and Sound*, has been the rock of official film culture against which succeeding waves and new waves have crashed. Under the editorship of Gavin Lambert (1949–56) and Penelope Houston (1956–90), it spoke with some authority in the debates of the 1950s and early 1960s, but it seemed out of touch with the radical, oppositional and multicultural currents which emerged in the 1970s and 1980s. In 1991, a new series was launched which has sought an eclectic mix of international popularity, domestic influence, critical diversity, and financial viability. The jury is still out. JC

SIM, Alastair — Edinburgh 1900 – London 1976

British actor, who spiced British comedy with a gallery of Dickensian eccentrics. In the late 1930s, he was inclined towards the sinister with films like *The Terror* (1938), but he also appeared with George Formby* in *Keep Your Seats Please* (1936), with the Crazy Gang in *Alf's Button Afloat* (1938), and with Jessie Matthews* in *Climbing High* (1938). During the war, he gained recognition as Sergeant

Bingham in the Inspector Hornleigh films, but it was after the war that he developed his true eccentric genius. Though he could be the benign doctor of *Waterloo Road* (1945), and is probably best remembered for his doubling and cross-dressing in *The Belles of St. Trinian's* (1954), a sinister element remained in many of his best parts. His charm could be of the leering sort, and his eyes could flicker in a moment from sunny geniality to languid malignity. His Henry Squales in *London Belongs to Me* (1948) is one of the classic creations of dark comedy. Only one of his Frank Launder and Sidney Gilliat* films, *Geordie* (1955), is actually set in Scotland, but he seldom disguises his Scottish accent: it is simply another feature which he draws on to colour, and perhaps explain, his eccentricity. JC

Other Films Include: *Green for Danger* (1946); *Captain Boycott, Hue and Cry* (1947); *The Happiest Days of Your Life, Stage Fright* (1950); *Laughter in Paradise, Scrooge, Lady Godiva Rides Again* (1951); *Folly to be Wise* (1952); *Innocents in Paris* (1953); *An Inspector Calls* (1954); *Blue Murder at St Trinian's* (1957); *The Doctor's Dilemma, Left, Right and Centre* (1959); *School for Scoundrels, The Millionairess* (1960); *The Ruling Class* (1972); *Royal Flash* (1975).

SIMMONS, Jean — London 1929

British actress, who became a major star in Hollywood after moving there in the early 1950s. In Britain, she made her debut at the age of 14 as Margaret Lockwood's* sister in *Give Us the Moon* (1944). Following a brief but effective appearance as a singer in *The Way to the Stars* (1945), she made a considerable impact as the young Estella in David Lean's* *Great Expectations* (1946) before Estella grew up and became Valerie Hobson. Michael Powell* put her into slightly embarrassing make-up to play an Indian seductress in *Black Narcissus* (1947), but at least he recognised the power of her sexuality, just as Laurence Olivier* recognised the power of her vulnerability when he cast her as Ophelia in his *Hamlet* (1948), a role for which she won an Oscar nomination and a Best Actress award at Venice. She starred in *The Blue Lagoon* (1949), one of J. Arthur Rank's* many attempts to break into the American market, and appeared with Dirk Bogarde* in *So Long at the Fair* (1950), but Hollywood beckoned – and with seriously starring roles in big pictures: *Angel Face* (1953), *The Robe* (1953), *Guys and Dolls* (1955), *The Big Country* (1958), *Spartacus* (1960) and *Elmer Gantry* (1960). She returned to Britain to play Susan Lampton in the not very distinguished *Life at the Top* (1965). JC

SLOCOMBE, Douglas London 1913

British cinematographer, who began his career as a photo-journalist for *Life* and *Paris-Match*, becoming a newsreel camera operator during World War II before making his debut as a lighting cameraman at Ealing on *Dead of Night* (1945). Slocombe deserves much of the credit for the distinctive, unpretentious look of Ealing, his work being seen at its best perhaps in *It Always Rains on Sunday* (1947) and, in particular, in the luminous Romney Marsh locations of *The Loves of Joanna Godden* (1947). After Ealing, his career developed as a freelance cinematographer on both sides of the Atlantic, with British Academy awards for *The Servant* (1963), *The Great Gatsby* (1974, US) and *Julia* (1977, US). Since the late 1970s he has shot a number of films for Spielberg, most notably *Close Encounters of the Third Kind* (1977, US), *Raiders of the Lost Ark* (1981, US) and *Indiana Jones and the Temple of Doom* (1984, US). JC

Other Films Include: *The Captive Heart* (1946); *Hue and Cry* (1947); *Saraband for Dead Lovers* (1948); *Kind Hearts and Coronets* (1949); *The Lavender Hill Mob, The Man in the White Suit* (1951); *Mandy* (1952); *The Titfield Thunderbolt* (1953); *The Young Ones* (1961); *Freud* [US], *The L-Shaped Room* (1962); *Guns at Batasi, A High Wind in Jamaica* (1965); *Dance of the Vampires* (1967); *The Music Lovers* (1970); *Travels with My Aunt* (1972, US); *Jesus Christ Superstar* (1973, US); *Rollerball* (1975, US); *Never Say Never Again* (1983).

SMITH, (Dame) Maggie Ilford 1934

British actress. To anyone who recalls Maggie Smith's highly charged Shakespearean roles in the theatre of the 1960s, her tragic Desdemona repeated on film (*Othello*, 1965), or even the vivacity of her cameo trouper in *Oh! What a Lovely War* (1969), her mutation into the perpetual 'neurotic spinster' may be a disappointment. The success of her best known screen role in *The Prime of Miss Jean Brodie* (1969) locked her into the stereotype, demonstrating her ability to draw a triumphant pathos out of comic mannerisms and a slightly ludicrous sensitivity. The role has been repeated with varying blends of triumph, pathos and comedy, and always with consummate skill. In Jack Clayton's low-key *The Lonely Passion of Judith Hearne* (1987) she animates the type with real feeling, but rather too often, as in her playing of the lonely Charlotte Bartlett in *A Room with a View* (1985), there is a sense of watching Maggie Smith doing her thing, and her later career in the cinema seems to strain a little less than it might against the leash. *Hook* (1992, US), *Sister Act* (1991, US) and *Sister Act 2* (1993, US) do little to extend her. She is, however, a highly respected actress, winning Oscars as Best Actress for her Miss Jean

Brodie, and as Best Supporting Actress for *California Suite* (1978), and receiving a BAFTA Lifetime Achievement award in 1993. JC

Other Films Include: *Go to Blazes* (1962); *The V.I.P.s* (1963); *The Pumpkin Eater* (1964); *Travels with My Aunt* (1973, US); *Death on the Nile* (1978); *Clash of the Titans, Quartet* (1981, UK/Fr.); *Evil Under the Sun, The Missionary* (1982); *A Private Function* (1984).

SMITH, G. A.

George Albert Smith; Brighton 1864 – Hove 1959

British pioneer inventor and producer, who was one of the leading figures, with James Williamson* and Esme Collings, of the 'Brighton School'. A portrait photographer, he developed his own camera in 1896, and went on to anticipate Georges Méliès in many of the advances in trick photography. The catalogue description of Smith's *The Corsican Brothers* (July 1898) leads Barry Salt to credit him with using superimposition, or 'spirit photography', before Méliès and Smith are believed to have corresponded with each other. Salt also credits Smith with the first 'true temporal and action continuity' in *The Kiss in the Tunnel* (1899) and the first scene dissection in *Grandma's Reading Glass* (1900), in which a boy looks at various objects through a magnifying glass. In association with Charles Urban, Smith patented Kinemacolor, the only commercially viable two-colour process before Technicolor, and he spent much of the rest of his career developing it, with Urban, in the Natural Colour Kinematograph Company, using colour most effectively in the feature-length *The Durbar at Delhi* (1911). JC

Bib: Barry Salt, *Film Style and Technology: History and Analysis (*1983)

STAMP, Terence

London 1938

British actor, who became one of the icons of 'swinging London' in the 1960s in both his screen appearances and his public life. Stamp won an Oscar nomination for Best Supporting Actor for his first film, *Billy Budd* (1962), and a Best Actor award from Cannes for *The Collector* (1965). He chose his films and his directors carefully, working with William Wyler, Joseph Losey*, Ken Loach*, John Schlesinger*, Pier Paolo Pasolini and Federico Fellini in the space of three years. For Pasolini, he was particularly striking in *Teorema/Theorem* (1968, It.), and much of his best work in the early 1970s was done in France or Italy. In his 1960s roles, Stamp's ethereal beauty and striking blue eyes were used to create a dangerous innocence, an almost sinister naivety. In his more commercial roles in Hollywood since General Zod in *Superman* (1978), the eyes have become harder but no less striking. His performance as Sir Larry Wildman in Oliver Stone's *Wall Street* (1987, US) threatened to steal the movie, but he has had a shortage of movies worth stealing. He gives, however, an excellent performance as a transsexual in the Australian cross-dressing comedy *The Adventures of Priscilla, Queen of the Desert* (1994). JC

Bib: Terence Stamp, *Stamp Album* (1987); *Coming Attractions* (1988); *Double Feature* (1989).

Other Films Include: *Modesty Blaise* (1966); *Far from the Madding Crowd, Poor Cow* (1967); *Blue* [US], *Histoires extraordinaires/Spirits of the Dead* ['Toby Dammit' episode; dir. Fellini] (1968, Fr./It.); *The Mind of Mr Soames* (1969); *Hu-nan* (1975, Fr.); *Divina Creatura* (1976, It.); *Meetings with Remarkable Men* (1979, US); *Superman II* (1981, US); *The Hit* (1984); *Legal Eagles* (1986, US); *The Sicilian* (1987, US); *Alien Nation, Young Guns* (1988, both US).

SWINTON, Tilda — Scotland 1961

British actress. Swinton, who appeared in a number of Derek Jarman* films in the 1980s, established herself as one of the most interesting actresses in current British cinema as Queen Isabella in his *Edward II* (1991), and confirmed her strength in the title role of Sally Potter's* *Orlando* (1992). An actress of great economy and concentration, in *Edward II* she suffers the indignities of Galveston and the rejection of Edward with moving dignity, then transforms herself into a chilling parody of Margaret Thatcher with no apparent change of gear. In *Orlando*, as Virginia Woolf's androgynous hero/heroine, she gives a lighter performance with knowing winks to the audience, but maintains a strong screen presence. The blankness of her expression and stillness of her concentration give her a fluidity perfectly suited to a cinema which is exploring sexual difference and identity. JC

T

TERRY-THOMAS Thomas Terry Hoar-Stevens; London 1911 – Godalming 1990

British actor, of the comic rotter school, particularly associated with the Boulting Brothers* comedies in the 1950s. Postwar British film comedy, with its links back to radio and music hall, produced a stable of actors who became comic types (Wilfrid Hyde-White, Arthur Mullard, Irene Handl). Terry-Thomas' type was a combination of the raffish World War II pilot and the upper-class cad who spent too much time at the racecourse, a type which exported well when he played the RAF pilot, alongside Bourvil and Louis de Funès, in *La Grande vadrouille/Don't Look Now ... We're Being Shot At* (1963, Fr./UK), one of the most popular French films ever. His flamboyant moustache, his gap-tooth, his cigarette holder, his sports cars and his tendency to dress on the loud side were the familiar emblems of 'class' trying too hard to be 'classy'. His popularity as a comic cad was ensured by his ultimate ineptitude and underlying innocence. JC

Other Films Include: *Private's Progress, The Green Man* (1956); *Brothers in Law, Lucky Jim, Blue Murder at St Trinian's, The Naked Truth* (1957); *Too Many Crooks, Carlton-Browne of the F.O., I'm All Right Jack* (1959); *School for Scoundrels* (1960); *How to Murder Your Wife, Strange Bedfellows* [US], *Those Magnificent Men in their Flying Machines* (1965); *Diabolik* (1967, It.); *Monte Carlo or Bust!* (1969); *The Abominable Dr Phibes* (1971); *Le braghe del padrone/The Master's Pants* (1978, It.); *The Hound of the Baskervilles* (1978).

THOMPSON, Emma 1959

British actress. A graduate of Cambridge University Footlights and the University's first all-female troupe, Woman's Hour, Thompson worked in theatre in the early 1980s with Kenneth Branagh's Renaissance Theatre Company. She appeared first on television in 1987, playing a spiky Glasgow waitress in John Byrne's six-part drama, *Tutti Frutti,* a wonderfully surreal and tragic musical comedy of Scottish rock'n roll and masculinity. Thompson's performance was arresting: a star quality touched with a dangerous eccentricity, a characteristic that has been masked by the rather more predictable good taste with which she has come to be associated. In the same year, she played opposite Kenneth Branagh* in the television adaptation of Olivia Manning's *The Fortunes of War,* a casting which began a screen association both with Branagh and with classic adaptation. Moving into cinema, she played Katherine to Branagh's Henry in his *Henry V* (1989) and Beatrice to Branagh's Benedick in his *Much Ado About Nothing* (1993). It is not clear whether they were haunted by shades of Laurence Olivier* and Vivien Leigh* or were courting them, but the connection was inescapable and they became (for their relatively brief allotted span) a golden couple for the upwardly mobile. Independently of Branagh, Thompson's association with quality adaptation led to an Oscar for Best Actress in the Merchant-Ivory *Howard's End* (1992), an Oscar nomination for Best Actress in the Merchant-Ivory *The Remains of the Day* (1993), a Golden Globe award for Best Screenplay, an Oscar nomination for Best Actress and an Oscar for Best Screenplay for her own adaptation of *Sense and Sensibility* (Ang Lee, 1996). Her attempts at versatility have met with less critical or popular approval: given her own television show at an early stage in her career, *Thompson* (BBC, 1988), she paid the price of hubris and over-exposure; Branagh's *Dead Again* (1991) and *Peter's Friends* (1992) won her few fans; and her appearance in *In the Name of the Father* (1993) seemed worthy but miscast. The intelligence of her acting is beyond doubt. Her problem will be to resist the narrowing of her range to the English virtues of quality and good taste that Hollywood rewards, going beyond mere versatility to rediscover some of the earlier danger. JC

Other Films Include: *The Tall Guys* (1989); *Junior* (1994); *My Father, My Hero* (1994, US); *Carrington* (1995).

TODD, Ann

Hartford 1909 – London 1993

British actress, probably best known for her role in two Sydney and Muriel Box* productions, both directed by Compton Bennett: *The Seventh Veil* (1945) and *Daybreak* (1946). If Margaret Lockwood* claimed the high ground of wicked lady in the women's films of the 1940s, Todd inhabited the realms of neurosis, sensitivity and instability familiar from American *film noir*. She had already played Ralph Richardson's* 'mad wife in the attic' in *South Riding* (1938), and in *The Seventh Veil* she plays the tyrannical James Mason's* victim/protégée: a pianist pursued by young men, dominated by the Mason father figure, and finally restored to health and romantic love by the intervention of psychoanalysis. *Daybreak* also has *film noir's* predilection for figures caught in the past, with Todd escaping through suicide. Todd married David Lean* in 1949, and made three films with him: *The Passionate Friends* (1949), *Madeleine* (1950) and *The Sound Barrier* (1952). In the 1960s and 1970s she wrote, produced and directed a number of travel documentaries. JC

Other Films Include: *The Ghost Train* (1931); *The Return of Bulldog Drummond* (1934); *Things to Come* (1936); *Perfect Strangers* (1945);

Gaiety George (1946); *The Paradine Case* (US, 1947); *Time Without Pity* (1957); *Il figlio del Capitano Blood/The Son of Captain Blood* (1962, It./Sp.).

TOYE, Wendy London 1917

British director. One of very few women directors in British cinema, Toye began as a dancer at the age of seven, staging a performance at the London Palladium when she was ten. She appeared as a dancer in *Invitation to the Waltz* (1935), and toured Europe with her own ballet company, Ballet-Hoo, in the late 1940s. She directed a widely acclaimed short fantasy, *The Stranger Left No Card* (1953), and on the strength of its success was given a contract by Alexander Korda* at London Films, where she made *The Teckman Mystery* (1954). Her films include such comedies as *Raising a Riot* (1955) and *All for Mary* (1955), but she mostly worked in theatre and opera. She has directed occasionally for television since 1955, including a remake of *The Stranger Left No Card* (called *Stranger in Town*, 1982) for the Anglia television series 'Tales of the Unexpected'. JC

Other Films Include: *Three Cases of Murder* [ep.] (1955); *True as a Turtle* (1957); *We Joined the Navy* (1962); *The King's Breakfast* (1963).

U

UNSWORTH, Geoffrey London 1914 – France 1978

British cinematographer, who began as camera operator on *The Drum* (1938) and continued with such films as *The Thief of Bagdad* (1940), *The Life and Death of Colonel Blimp* (1943) and *A Matter of Life and Death* (1946). He became a cinematographer for Gainsborough in the mid-1940s, with *Jassy* (1947) as one of his early credits. He is possibly best known as a technical innovator for his collaboration with Douglas Trumbull on *2001: A Space Odyssey* (1968), for which he invented a special front-projection system. His craftsmanship as a colour cinematographer was widely respected, winning him Academy Awards for his work on *Cabaret* (1972, US) and *Tess* (1981). JC

Other Films Include: *The Blue Lagoon, Scott of the Antarctic* (1948); *The Spider and the Fly* (1949); *Simba* (1955); *A Town Like Alice* (1956); *A Night to Remember* (1958); *Becket* (1964); *Half a Sixpence*

(1967); *Cromwell* (1970); *Love and Pain and the Whole Damn Thing* (1973, US); *Zardoz, Murder on the Orient Express* (1974); *The Return of the Pink Panther, Royal Flash* (1975); *A Bridge Too Far* (1977); *Superman* (1978).

USTINOV, (Sir) Peter London 1921

British actor, director and scriptwriter – and broadcaster, raconteur, playwright, theatre director, opera director and novelist. Ustinov seems to be the inspired amateur of British cinema, hard to categorise under the usual professional labels. Of Russian and French parentage, he is one of the more European figures of British cinema, appearing in a number of French, Italian and Spanish films, including two with Max Ophuls* in France: as the narrator in *Le Plaisir/House of Pleasure* (1952), and as the ringmaster in *Lola Montès* (1955). As he never seems to take himself too seriously, the seriousness of his career is always surprising. He co-scripted *The Way Ahead* (1944), won Best Supporting Actor Academy Awards for *Topkapi* (1964, US) and for *Spartacus* (1960, US), scripted, directed and starred in *Romanoff and Juliet* (1961), adapted from his own stage play, and co-scripted *Billy Budd* (1962), adapted from Herman Melville. JC

Bib: Peter Ustinov, *Dear Me: An Autobiography* (1977).

Other Films Include (As Actor Unless Indicated): *Let My People Sing, The Goose Steps Out, ... One of Our Aircraft is Missing* (1942); *The True Glory* (1945); *School for Secrets* [+ dir., sc., prod.] (1946); *Private Angelo* [+ co-dir.] (1949); *Odette* (1950); *Quo Vadis* [US], *The Magic Box* (1951); *I Girovaghi/The Wanderers* (1956, It.); *Un angel paso sobre Brooklyn/An Angel over Brooklyn* [Sp./It.], *Les Espions/The Spies* [Fr.] (1957); *The Sundowners* (1961, UK/Aust.); *Lady L* [+ dir., sc.] (1965); *Hammersmith is Out* [+ dir.] (1972); *Death on the Nile, Doppio delitto* [It.] (1978); *Charlie Chan and the Curse of the Dragon Queen* [US], *Evil Under the Sun* (1982); *Memed My Hawk* [+ dir., sc.] (1984); *Appointment with Death* (1988).

WALES AND FILM

If Scotland's founding moment in the international imagination lies in the Celtic twilight and the lost romance of the Highlands, the mythology of Wales in cinema had to wait till the twilight of the industrial revolution. Classically, Wales is figured in the small, stalwart mining communities of the Valleys, the pit-head towers silhouetted against the sky, the blackened miners emerging from the cages, the wives waiting, the potential for disaster always in the air, and, always, the community unifying itself in song. John Ford brought to the mining community of *How Green Was My Valley* (1941) the same sensibility which he later brought to the Irish rural community of *The Quiet Man* (1952), drawing on Welsh stereotypes which were already in circulation in English films like *The Citadel* (1938) and *The Proud Valley* (1940), and fixing them in the popular imagination. However impressive the work within the Fordian canon, it did for Wales what *Brigadoon* did for Scotland. A more complicated and less epic view of the community and the industry undergoing change is found in the neglected *Blue Scar,* directed by Jill Craigie in 1949.

Until the 1980s the image of Wales in the feature film was constructed mainly from the outside. There were a few exceptions – Karl Francis's *Above Us the Earth* (1977), for example, a drama-documentary funded by the BFI Production Board – but, in general, Welsh cultural agencies showed little enthusiasm for film. The introduction of Channel 4* in 1982, however, as well as diversifying the funding for British film in general, brought to Wales Sianel Pedwar Cymru (S4C), a separate fourth channel devoted to Welsh-language production, the result of a hard-fought battle by the Welsh language lobby and threats of a hunger strike by the leader of Plaid Cymru. After a somewhat shaky start, and a predilection for the very distant past, S4C began to set up the conditions in which feature films could be made in Wales, and the Wales Film Council was established in 1993 through a collaboration between S4C, the Welsh Arts Council and BBC Wales. Production was, predictably, limited by budget, never quite achieving the sense of a dynamic which appeared in Irish cinema in the early 1980s. Stephen Bayly's *Rhosyn a Rhith/Coming Up Rose* (1987), a comedy made for under £400,000, and Karl Francis's *Milwr Bychan/ Boy Soldier* (1987), the drama of a Welsh soldier in Northern Ireland, became the first Welsh–English bilingual films to play outside Wales. Steve Gough's *Elenya* (1992) was supported by the British Film Institute*, S4C and the German ZDF, and Paul Turner's *Hedd Wyn* (1993), in Welsh with English subtitles, was nominated for an Oscar as Best Foreign Language Film. Chapter Arts Workshop and Red

Flannel, both established with the support of Channel 4 in 1982 as part of the Workshop Movement* (and the latter operating as a franchised all-women film and video collective), further extended the diversity of entry points into film production. Chris Monger, one of Chapter's early directors who now divides his work between Wales and Hollywood, made *The Englishman Who Went Up a Hill, But Came Down a Mountain* (1995), set in a Welsh community, whose international release may have owed something to the temporary notoriety of its star, Hugh Grant. One of the surprise achievements of recent Welsh filmmaking has been animation, stimulated perhaps by the popularity and inventiveness of S4C's *SuperTed*, but supported by the development of Chapter Animation Workshop in the late 1980s.

In the 1990s, Wales, alone among the Celtic countries, has not attracted the attention of Hollywood that has been the good or bad fortune of Scotland; nor has it produced directors with the international profile of Bill Forsyth or Neil Jordan, or films which have received the hype of *Shallow Grave* (1995) or *Trainspotting* (1996). The infrastructure is still precarious, but Wales shares with the rest of the UK the fragile benefits of small-scale, dispersed independent production, no longer wholly dependent on the outside for its images.

Bib: David Berry, *Wales and Cinema: The First Hundred Years* (Cardiff: University of Wales Press, in cooperation with the Wales Film Council and the BFI, 1994). JC

WARNER, Jack London 1896–1981

British actor, whose career on both film and television made him an icon of responsible postwar ordinariness. His role as the paterfamilias of the Huggetts in the series of Gainsborough films which grew out of *Holiday Camp* (1947) represented the values of working-class decency and community inspired by the Attlee Labour government. As Robert Murphy suggests, the Huggetts anticipated such television families as the Appleyards and the Groves of the 1950s, and the community values of the early *Coronation Street*. Despite his role as an embittered and heartless killer in *My Brother's Keeper* (1948), Warner's role as PC George Dixon in *The Blue Lamp* (1950) established him as the image of benevolent community policing. Translated to television in 1955 as *Dixon of Dock Green*, his Saturday night homilies on order, justice and the British way of life ran until 1976, by which time both Jack Warner (who played the part until he was 80) and the image of the police which he represented were ready for retirement. JC

Bib: Jack Warner, *Jack of All Trades: The Autobiography of Jack Warner* (1975).

Other Films Include: *The Captive Heart, Dear Murderer, Hue and Cry* (1947); *Here Come the Huggetts* (1948); *Vote for Huggett* (1949); *The Huggetts Abroad* (1949); *The Square Ring, Albert RN, The Final Test* (1953); *The Quatermass Experiment, The Ladykillers* (1955); *Carve Her Name with Pride* (1958).

WATT, Harry Edinburgh 1906 – Amersham 1987

British director, who was a prominent member of the British Documentary Movement* throughout the 1930s. He assisted Robert Flaherty* on *Man of Aran* (1934), directed *North Sea* (1938), and co-directed *Night Mail* (1936) with Basil Wright*, and *London Can Take It!* (1940) with Humphrey Jennings*. During the early years of the war he was associate producer of the Crown Film Unit, scripting and directing the hugely successful *Target for To-night* (1941), described by Watt as 'an understated and unemotional account of an average air raid'. He joined Ealing Studios in 1942, directing all his feature films in either Australia or Africa, including *The Overlanders* (1946), which he wrote and directed in Australia. He joined Granada Television as a producer in 1955. JC

Bib: Harry Watt, *Don't Look at the Camera* (1974).

Other Films Include: *BBC: Droitwich* [co-d.] (1934); *The Saving of Bill Blewitt* (1936); *The First Days* [co-d.] (1939); *Squadron 992* (1940); *Christmas Under Fire* (1941); *Nine Men* (1943); *Fiddlers Three* (1944); *Eureka Stockade* (1949); *Where No Vultures Fly* (1951); *West of Zanzibar* (1954); *The Siege of Pinchgut* (1959).

WHITELAW, Billy Coventry 1932

British actress. Whitelaw is well respected for her work on television and theatre, where she is renowned both in working-class realism and as the leading female interpreter of Samuel Beckett, with whom she collaborated. She has made surprisingly few films, often in supporting character roles. She received a British Film Academy award for her part in Albert Finney's* *Charlie Bubbles* (1967), played opposite Finney in Stephen Frears'* *Gumshoe* (1971), and, more recently, gave an utterly convincing performance as the matriarch in Peter Medak's *The Krays* (1990). JC

Other Films Include: *Miracle in Soho* (1957); *Make Mine Mink* (1960); *Twisted Nerve* (1968); *Leo the Last* (1970); *Frenzy* (1972); *The Omen* (1976, US); *An Unsuitable Job for a Woman* (1982).

WILCOX, Herbert

Cork, Ireland 1891 – London 1977

British producer/director. 'The guiding principle of my company,' Wilcox said in 1935, 'will be productions based on outstanding star personalities with music, romance and comedy as the basic ingredients.' In the 1920s he had already tested the formula, adapting proven stage successes such as *Chu Chin Chow* (1923) and engaging Dorothy Gish to star in four films, including the highly successful *Nell Gwyn* (1926). *Dawn* (1928), with Sybil Thorndike as Nurse Edith Cavell, was the subject of a censorship case initiated by the German embassy, but was highly praised in *Close Up**. In the 1930s Wilcox discovered his star and future wife in Anna Neagle*, casting her first in *Goodnight Vienna* (1932) and remaking *Nell Gwyn* with her in 1934. He unashamedly cashed in on public patriotism with *Victoria the Great* (1937) and *Sixty Glorious Years* (1938). Wilcox and Neagle spent the early years of the war in Hollywood, returning to Britain in 1942 and marrying in 1943. Wilcox maintained his success after the war with the 'Mayfair' cycle – *I Live in Grosvenor Square* (1945), *Piccadilly Incident* (1946), *The Courtneys of Curzon Street* (1947) and *Maytime in Mayfair* (1949) – but in the 1950s he began to lose his feel for what the audience wanted. He co-produced Peter Brook's *The Beggar's Opera* (1953) with Laurence Olivier*, but his long and successful career ended in bankruptcy in 1964. JC

Bib: Herbert Wilcox, *Twenty-Five Thousand Sunsets: The Autobiography of Herbert Wilcox* (1967).

Other Films Include: *Madame Pompadour* (1927); *The Triumph of the Scarlet Pimpernel* (1928); *The Woman in White* (1929); *The King's Cup, Bitter Sweet, The Little Damozel* (1933); *The Queen's Affair* (1934); *Peg of Old Drury* (1935); *London Melody* (1937); *No, No, Nanette, Irene* (1940, both US); *They Flew Alone* (1942); *Odette* (1950); *The Lady with a Lamp* (1951); *Trouble in the Glen* (1954); *King's Rhapsody* (1955); *These Dangerous Years* (1957); *The Lady is a Square* (1958).

WILLIAMSON, James

Scotland 1855 – 1933

British pioneer inventor and producer. A chemist with an interest in photography, Williamson became one of the members of the 'Brighton School' along with G. A. Smith* and others. He is credited by Barry Salt with the first action continuity sequence in *Stop Thief!* (1901), in which a thief is chased out of one frame and into the next in a different location, and is finally caught in the third frame. This became the basic grammar of the chase sequence. After 1904, Williamson concentrated on the manufacturing of equipment. JC

Bib: Barry Salt, *Film Style and Technology: History and Analysis* (1983).

WISDOM, Norman

London 1920

British actor. A late, postwar addition to the music-hall tradition, Wisdom did not make his music-hall debut until 1946, and it was through success on television from 1948 that he entered films. Like that of George Formby* or Will Hay*, his comedy is based on a stable character – 'the Gump' – subjected to disaster-laden situations which get in the way of his romantic intentions. His performance, however, is much more physical and slapstick (to the point of masochism), and Wisdom may have more in common with the Hollywood tradition of Chaplin, particularly as reworked by Jerry Lewis. Associated with two directors, John Paddy Carstairs and Robert Asher, he was at his best when Carstairs set tight limits to the sentimentality inherent in the character. JC

Films Include: *Trouble in Store* (1953); *One Good Turn* (1954); *Man of the Moment* (1955); *Up in the World* (1956); *Just My Luck* (1957); *The Square Peg* (1958); *Follow a Star* (1959); *There Was a Crooked Man, The Bulldog Breed* (1960); *On the Beat* (1962); *The Early Bird* (1965); *Press for Time* (1966); *The Night They Raided Minsky's* (1968, US); *Going Gently* [TV] (1981).

WITHERS, Googie

Georgette Withers; Karachi, India 1917

British actress, who learned her craft in 'quota quickies' during the 1930s and found her strongest roles with Ealing, and in particular with Robert Hamer*, in the 1940s. She made over thirty films between 1934 and 1941, including *Trouble Brewing* (1939) with George Formby*, a brief, giggly appearance for Alfred Hitchcock* in *The Lady Vanishes* (1938), and three 'quota quickies' directed by Michael Powell*: *The Girl in the Crowd* (1934), *The Love Test* (1935) and *Her Last Affaire* (1935). Powell rewarded her by giving her her first leading dramatic part in *One of Our Aircraft is Missing* (1942). At Ealing, she played a series of determined women struggling against the constraints of a conservative, respectable male society, her boldly drawn, assertive sexuality sitting uneasily with the image of Ealing's gentle revolution. For Hamer, she appeared in the 'Haunted Mirror' episode of *Dead of Night* (1945), *Pink String and Sealing Wax* (1945), and, probably her best film, *It Always Rains on Sunday* (1947). Hamer was also closely involved in Charles Frend's *The Loves of Joanna Godden* (1947) – her other best role as a Mildred Pierce of the Romney Marshes. Married to John McCallum, her leading man in her two best films, Googie Withers moved to Australia in the 1950s, where she continues to work – *Country Life* (1994). She returned to Britain in the 1980s and gave two fine television performances in *Hotel du Lac* (1986) and *Northanger Abbey* (1987). JC

Other Films Include: *The Silver Fleet* (1943); *On Approval, They Came to a City* (1944); *Miranda, Once Upon a Dream, Traveller's Joy* (1949); *Night and the City* (1950); *White Corridors, The Magic Box* (1951); *Derby Day* (1952); *The Nickel Queen* (1970, Australia).

WOLLEN, Peter – see MULVEY, Laura

WORKSHOP MOVEMENT

British movement, which became institutionalised with the arrival of Channel 4*, but had its roots in the politics of collective practice associated with 1968 and feminism. Early collectives, which included Cinema Action, Amber Films, the Berwick Street Collective, the London Women's Film Group and Four Corners, saw their work as politically oppositional rather than alternative. Film was conceived as a social practice, with Cinema Action using *Song of the Clyde* (1971) in support of the Upper Clyde Shipyards occupation, the Berwick Street Collective making *Nightcleaners* (1975) in support of a cleaners' strike, and the London Women's Film Group campaigning for equal pay with *The Amazing Equal Pay Show* (1974). Though distinct from the formal preoccupations of the London Film-makers Co-op, many of the groups became increasingly concerned with the politics of form, engaging particularly with the debates about Brecht and cinema which *Screen** was promoting. The films were distributed by The Other Cinema, formed in 1970 and opening its own cinema in 1976, and in 1974 the Independent Film-makers Association was formed to coordinate and promote the interests of the grant-aided sector.

The arrival of Channel 4 gave an institutional form to the Movement. An agreement between the ACTT (Association of Cinematograph, Television and Allied Technicians – the main trade union), the British Film Institute*, and Channel 4 known as the 'Workshop Declaration' accredited a number of 'franchised workshops', recognising them for the production of commissioned work for Channel 4 at lower than normal rates and crewing levels. The Declaration encouraged the formation of workshops within communities of region, race and gender. Some existing collectives were franchised, and new regional workshops were established in, for example, Cardiff, Birmingham and the East Midlands. Women's workshops were franchised in Leeds (the Leeds Animation Workshop) and Sheffield, and black workshops such as Sankofa, Ceddo and Black

Audio Film Collective were formed in the mid-1980s. Material was shown on the Channel 4 series, 'The Eleventh Hour', but the revenue funding was also intended to support educational and cultural work within the workshops' own communities. The system gave financial security to the participants, and brought new forms of film-making to a wider audience than could be reached through commercial cinema distribution.

There were, however, contradictions. A concern with the politics of form was a difficult training ground for television, and many programmes were criticised for being more concerned with form than with audiences. More insidiously, the institutionalisation of workshops had the effect of localising them within their communities, coherent as a unit but not as a movement. Nevertheless, at the local level the workshop system represented an astonishing form of social and cultural patronage from a commercial television channel.

By 1990 the climate and the economy had changed, and both the BFI and Channel 4 withdrew their guarantees of revenue funding, leaving the workshops to operate like any other small business seeking clients where it could find them. While many groups continue to produce interesting and even oppositional work, and while there is a sense of a greater access to production than at any time since the 1930s, the history of the Workshop Movement charts quite sharply a particular trajectory of British political culture and cultural politics since 1968. JC

Bib: Alan Lovell, 'That was the Workshops that was', *Screen* 31/1 (Spring 1990), and Rod Stoneman, 'Sins of Commission', *Screen*, 33/2 (Summer 1992).

WRIGHT, Basil — London 1907–87

British director and producer, and the first of John Grierson's* recruits to the Documentary Movement, joining him at the Empire Marketing Board in 1931. In 1934, with *Song of Ceylon,* Wright established the distinctive poetic quality which he brought to the British Documentary Movement*, and in 1936 he co-directed *Night Mail* with Harry Watt*. 'It is conceivable,' suggests Elizabeth Sussex, 'that [Wright] brought the one distinctive quality that actually put British documentary on the map.' He formed the Realist Film Unit with John Taylor and Alberto Cavalcanti* in 1937, and during the war worked at the Crown Film Unit, producing, for example, Humphrey Jennings'* *A Diary for Timothy* (1945). In 1953 he co-directed *World Without End* with Paul Rotha*. He taught at the University of California from 1960, and wrote *The Use of Film* (1948) and *The Long View* (1974). JC

Other Films Include: *O'er Hill and Dale* (1932); *Windmill in Barbados, Cargo from Jamaica, Liner Cruising South* (1933); *Children at School*

(1937); *The Face of Scotland* (1938); *This Was Japan* (1945); *Waters of Time* (1950); *Stained Glass at Fairford* (1955); *The Immortal Land* (1958).

YOUNG, Freddie   London 1902

British cinematographer, with a long and distinguished career stretching over half a century in British and Anglo-American films. His first film as co-cinematographer was *The Flag Lieutenant* (1926), and through the 1930s he was Herbert Wilcox's* principal lighting cameraman, shooting such films as *Goodnight Vienna* (1932), *Bitter Sweet* (1933), *Nell Gwyn* (1934), *Victoria the Great* (1937) and *Sixty Glorious Years* (1938). He continued to be associated with distinguished films during and after the war, working with such British directors as Michael Powell*, Carol Reed* and Anthony Asquith*, and Hollywood directors such as George Cukor, John Ford and Vincente Minnelli. In 1962, at the age of 60, he began an association with David Lean* which brought him Academy Awards for *Lawrence of Arabia* (1962), *Doctor Zhivago* (1965) and *Ryan's Daughter* (1970). He was the first recipient of the American Society of Cinematographers' International Achievement Award. JC

Other Films Include: *Goodbye, Mr Chips* (1939); *Contraband* (1940); *49th Parallel* (1941); *The Young Mr Pitt* (1942); *Caesar and Cleopatra* (1946); *The Winslow Boy* (1948); *Edward, My Son* (1949); *Treasure Island* (1950); *Lust for Life, Bhowani Junction* (1956, both US); *The Barretts of Wimpole Street, Gideon's Day, The Inn of the Sixth Happiness, Indiscreet* (1958); *Lord Jim* (1965); *You Only Live Twice* (1967); *Battle of Britain* (1969); *Nicholas and Alexandra* (1971, US); *Luther* (1973, US/UK/Can.); *The Tamarind Seed* (1974); *The Blue Bird* (1976, US/USSR). JC

BRITISH AND IRISH CINEMA IN EUROPE

Key European cinema concepts, genres and institutions

Avant-garde cinema in Europe
Emigration and European cinema
European art cinema
European cinema and Hollywood
European Community [now European Union] and the cinema
European film awards [FELIX]
Festivals
Heritage cinema in Europe
Lesbian and gay cinema in Europe
Sexuality, eroticism and pornography in European cinema

Key European cinema concepts, genres and institutions

This section gathers entries commissioned for the *Encyclopedia of European Cinema* on pan-European concepts, genres and institutions. They are included here as a useful and relevant background to the information contained in the preceding sections. The authors of these entries are named at the end of each one of them.

AVANT-GARDE CINEMA IN EUROPE

From our present postmodern vantage point, the concept of the avant-garde might appear as simultaneously archaic and elitist, now that it is behind us historically and seemingly beyond us politically. Two factors recur: the relationship of film to the other arts, and of aesthetics to politics, with the term 'avant-garde' breaking into the following registers of aspiration – experimentation and abstraction, independence and opposition.

Soviet montage, German expressionism, French impressionism and surrealism are traditionally considered the 'historical avant-gardes' of European cinema and the overlap of film with fine arts is characteristic of each of these founding moments. At its most militantly innovative and highly theorised in the work of Sergei Eisenstein and Dziga Vertov, Soviet montage was wrought from the combination of a modernist consciousness of the revolutionary moment – 1917, Bolshevism – and a fertile cross-pollination of film with Constructivist design, Futurist sound poetry and Suprematist experimentation with form. In France, impressionism and surrealism lacked the political impetus of the Soviets, but endorsed cinema as the manifestation of the Wagnerian idea of the *Gesamtkunstwerk*, the means of synthesising all the arts in the new, unique art of film, termed by Ricciotto Canudo 'the seventh art'.

The encounter between film and the fine arts has persistently characterised the abstract tendency of the European avant-garde. And while recent work in video-art can be seen as maintaining this tradition, it might equally be seen in the Structuralist/Materialist films of the 1970s. Malcolm Le Grice, one of the leading British exponents of such work, has identified abstract work as taking place as early as 1910–12 in the experiments of Bruno Corra and Arnaldo Ginna. Corra's theoretical text, *Abstract Cinema – Chromatic Music*, serves as an early indication of the enduring tendency in abstract film to seek aesthetic alliances with painting and music. This example predates the work of abstract animators Walther Ruttmann, Viking Eggeling, Hans Richter and Oskar Fischinger, often seen as inaugurating this aesthetic tendency. Richter gave perhaps the best summary of the abstract film position when he wrote: 'Problems in modern art lead directly into the film. The connection to theatre and literature was completely severed. Cubism, Expressionism, Dadaism, Abstract Art, Surrealism found not only their expression in film, but a new fulfilment on a new level.'

Two words serve to encapsulate the motivation of this first, historical phase of the European avant-garde: silence and 'specificity'. It is noticeable that this experimental phase ended with the coming of sound. While for the Soviet directors this can in part be attributed to Stalin's cultural policies of the late 1920s and early 1930s, the termination was also informed by the anti-realist agendas common to all the avant-gardes, with sound representing a decisively realist 'supplement' to the image. The change in the mode of production from the artisanal/patronage-based one enjoyed by the avant-garde to the labour and capital intensive base demanded by the new sound cinema also had a part to play in the end of the silent avant-gardes. The search for cinematic 'specificity' was polemical and separatist on the one hand – against theatrical and narrative models – synthesising and hybridising on the other, with models from painting and music.

The notion of the avant-garde in film was constructed around the idea of its oppositional status vis-à-vis the established cinematic order both generally and specifically in European cinema. This tendency can be defined in terms either of opposition or of independence, the former being predicated along militant political lines, the latter a means of constructing an alternative space for independent production, distribution and exhibition. This taxonomy works usefully in respect of the works of the 1960s and 1970s that best illustrate the bifurcation of European avant-garde practice into what Peter Wollen* christened in 1975 'the Two Avant-Gardes', one concerned with a politically oriented 'politics of form', the other with a formalist 'politics of perception'. The strand of European practice that came to be known as Counter-Cinema, while having its immediate origins in the political revolt of May 1968 in France, nevertheless took its conceptual and asthetic leads from a longer European tradition of radical, oppositional aesthetic practices, drawing on ideas from Brechtian dramaturgy – distanciation, the *Verfremdungseffekt* – and lauding Vertov over Eisenstein in the 'second discovery' of Soviet cinema of the mid- to late 1960s. While Jean-Luc Godard is most commonly associated with the counter-cinematic turning away from what he dubbed 'the Hollywood-Mosfilm' and towards a didactic cinema of '*films tableaux noirs*' (blackboard films), he was by no means alone in opting for this radical strategy. Chris Marker in France, Rainer Werner Fassbinder and Werner Schroeter in Germany, Věra Chytilová in Czechoslovakia and Dušan Makavejev in Yugoslavia experimented with a Brechtian challenge to narrative transparency against the perceived stylistic – hence ideological – hegemony of Hollywood cinema.

The other more Formalist/Structuralist-Materialist strand of avant-garde film-making rooted itself in an opposition to conventional narrative that owed much to the abstract cinema of the 1920s, although it might be said that the master-text of both the Structuralist-Materialist and counter-cinematic movements of the 1960s and 1970s remains Vertov's remarkable *Chelovek s kinoapparatom/The Man with the Movie Camera* (1929). The Co-op movements of the 1970s, particularly the London Film-makers Co-op*, represented the pursuit of a radical, independent practice both aesthetically and institutionally. Film-makers such as Malcolm Le Grice and Peter Gidal participated in a cinema of minimal effects concerned with the material properties of film – grain, emulsion, flicker, qualities of light – and in the spectatorial experience, experimenting with duration and performance-art styled interventions during projection. This strand arguably had more in common with the North American and Canadian avant-garde of Brakhage, Sharits and Snow than with the militancy of European counter-cinema. Godard himself attempted, in *Tout va bien* (1972), a Brechtian cinema-with-stars (Jane Fonda and Yves Montand), while other art cinema directors such as Yvonne Rainer and Chantal Akerman employed avant-garde strategies to question the sexual politics of cinematic representation, notably in Akerman's *Jeanne Dielman 23 Quai du Commerce 1080 Bruxelles* (1975), with its experimentation with duration.

With the advent of video technologies in the mid-1960s one would have imagined a revival of the European avant-gardes. However, in the hands of Godard and Marker, video has been used as a means of thinking cinema and of expressing an analytic relationship with the image. Marker's *Sans soleil/Sunless* (1983) and Godard's *Scénario du film Passion* (1982) are most representative of this application of video, the Marker film also being an eloquent piece of mourning-work for the lost illusions of 1960s political radicalism and so-called 'guerrilla film-making', while fully and euphorically exploiting the possibilities of video. European video-art *per se* has yet to achieve the international visibility of North American and Canadian video-artists such as Bill Viola, Gary Hill and Nam June Paik. However, the avant-garde has been – and, in the example of video-art, remains – an international, exportable phenomenon that cuts across both national, cultural and artistic boundaries, addressing a wide set of disparate art/film constituencies, in contrast to European popular cinemas that remain more firmly embedded in specific national traditions and hence export less effectively. (Chris Darke)

Bib: Peter Wollen, 'The Two Avant-Gardes', in *Readings and Writings: Semiotic Counter-Strategies* (1982).

EMIGRATION AND EUROPEAN CINEMA

The phenomenon of emigration both within Europe and from Europe greatly affected the cinema throughout its first century. Social factors (poverty and racism, especially anti-semitism) and historical events such as wars, revolutions and totalitarian regimes drove people from their home countries, usually west, towards Germany and the Netherlands, then France and the UK, and massively to the US. Economic and cultural factors specific to the film industry have also repeatedly drawn European film personnel to North America. There has been a small movement in the opposite direction, with American directors such as Joseph Losey* and Jules Dassin, and stars like Eddie Constantine and Paul Robeson* making a career in Europe.

Many Hollywood pioneers and movie moguls came from central Europe. Subsequently, Hollywood attracted film people who went either of their own volition or as a result of the studios' systematic policies of talent-scouting. Some made a first or second career there (Charlie Chaplin, Mihály Kertész [Michael Curtiz], Jean Negulescu [Negulesco], Ernst Lubitsch, Greta Garbo, Ingrid Bergman, Douglas Sirk [Detlef Sierck]) while for others Hollywood was a – more or less extended and more or less successful – episode: Victor Sjöström, Mauritz Stiller, Max Ophuls, Fritz Lang, René Clair, Julien Duvivier, Jean Renoir, S. M. Eisenstein, Louis Malle, Nestor Almendros and many others. The country most affected has been Germany. While directors, actors, scriptwriters, art directors and cameramen were forced to leave Germany when the Nazis came to power in 1933, others had already left. Those tempted, apart from Lubitsch, Sirk and Lang, included F. W. Murnau, William Dieterle, E. A. Dupont, Paul Leni, Ludwig Berger, Emil Jannings, Marlene Dietrich, Robert Siodmak, Pola Negri, Lya de Putti, Erich Pommer, Carl Mayer, Karl Freund, Joe May, Richard Oswald, Otto Preminger, Billy Wilder and Reinhold Schünzel. From 1 April 1933, Jews were systematically excluded from public life in Germany and consequently almost a third of Germany's film industry personnel fled to neighbouring countries and the US. France and Britain were especially important for émigré film-makers, since their film industries were then experiencing a period of dramatic growth. Consequently, producers like Pommer, Seymour Nebenzal and Alexander Korda* set up new production companies which provided work for fellow émigrés. Between 1933 and 1940, Lang, Siodmak, Ophuls, Kurt Bernhardt, G. W. Pabst, Anatole Litvak and others made nearly fifty films in France, including box-office hits such as *Mayerling* (1936), *Carrefour* (1938) and *Pièges* (1939), while in Britain Korda and Max Schach produced highly successful costume films for the international market.

Most émigrés resettled in the US, though few of those who arrived in Hollywood between 1933 and 1938 had a studio contract. After 1938–39, the number of refugees to the US increased dramatically. Altogether, about 500 German film-makers lived in Hollywood. In the 1920s–30s the German émigrés in Hollywood worked on films with a 'European flavour' and from the early 1940s film-makers such as Wilder, Siodmak and Lang contributed greatly to the development of *film noir* with such films as *Double Indemnity* (1944), *Phantom Lady* (1944), *Scarlet Street* (1945) and many others. German émigrés are also known for the sub-genre of the anti-Nazi film, of which about 180 were produced between 1939 and 1945 in the US, transmitting an anti-fascist message in traditional genre films such as spy thrillers (*Confessions of a Nazi Spy*, 1939), melodramas (*The Mortal Storm*, 1940) and comedies (*To Be or Not to Be*, 1942). In addition, German actors and their accents were much sought-after, ironically often to play Nazis (or their victims) in anti-Nazi films; Schünzel, Peter Lorre and Conrad Veidt were particularly successful in this respect. Only a handful of film-makers returned to Germany after World War II; most had settled permanently in the US and, furthermore, the German film industry was still run by those who had been successful in the Third Reich. Though it is impossible to speculate on what might have happened otherwise, there is no doubt that German film production suffered incalculably from this drain of talented film personnel.

Less visible because of the shared language has been the drain from the British film industry. Among the most famous British émigrés (or British personnel who worked substantially in Hollywood), apart from Chaplin, are: Julie Andrews, Cecil Beaton, Ronald Colman*, Alfred Hitchcock*, James Mason* and David Niven*. The important migrations mentioned above slowed down somewhat in the postwar period, as Hollywood itself went through a crisis and started investing in European productions [> EUROPEAN CINEMA AND HOLLYWOOD]. Since the 1980s, however, a renewed migration has taken place, with European film-makers seeking work abroad as their own national cinemas weaken; examples include Andrei Mikhalkov-Konchalovsky, Miloš Forman, George Sluizer, Wolfgang Petersen, Paul Verhoeven, Roman Polanski and Bernardo Bertolucci, as well as actors such as Rutger Hauer.

During the same period many other film-makers have turned to France, following another long tradition. In the 1920s, the French cinematic avant-garde was international, with film-makers such as Alberto Cavalcanti*, Carl Theodor Dreyer and Luis Buñuel among others [> AVANT-GARDE CINEMA IN EUROPE]. A significant group of émigrés had already arrived from Russia in the wake of the October revolution. The old Pathé studios in Montreuil became the centre of an active community. Iosif Yermolev [Joseph Ermolieff in France], an ex-Pathé employee, founded Ermolieff-film in 1920, with a team of prestigious directors including Yakov Protazanov [Jacob Protazanoff], Alexandre Volkov [Volkoff], Vjačelav Turžanskij [Victor Tourjansky], actor Ivan Mozzhukhin [Mosjoukine], set designers and cinematographers. Yermolev produced a dozen films before leaving for Berlin in 1922, and Ermolieff-film became Les Films Albatros, specialising in literary adaptations of French and Russian classics, with emphasis on nostalgia and exoticism, and producing prestigious films by Marcel L'Herbier, Jacques Feyder, René Clair, and others. Other firms, such as Ciné-France-Film, had a strong Russian contingent and produced French films, including Abel Gance's *Napoléon* (1926) and Volkov's *Casanova* (1927, starring Mosjoukine). The Russian influence continued in the 1930s when personnel included directors Fyodor Otsep [Fédor Ozep], Nicolas Farkas and Tourjansky and many others, as well as gifted cinematographers and set designers, generating the popular French genre of the 'Slav melodrama'. Lazare Meerson revolutionised set design and taught other designers such as Alexander Trauner and Georges Wakhevitch. New directors from Russia emerged, such as Litvak, and Władysław Starewicz [Ladislav Starevitch]. There were, during the same period, significant exchanges between France and Italy. Franco-Italian bilingual films were made, and several Italian directors worked in France: Mario Bonnard, Carmine Gallone and Augusto Genina.

Meanwhile, despite the threatening political climate, the attraction of better conditions in German studios remained strong, and French stars and directors became frequent travellers between Paris, Berlin and Munich. The coming of sound also contributed to the acceleration of cross-European journeys, with the making of multi-language versions by Ufa in Germany, Paramount in Paris and British International in London, between 1929 and 1932. Films were made in sometimes as many as a dozen versions (especially at Paramount) but more often in two or three, with German, French and English the most common languages, usually using the same decor but native stars (it was also at that time that Hollywood initiated the practice of remaking European films, especially French films, a phenomenon renewed with particular vigour in the 1980s and 1990s). As mentioned above, Paris in the 1930s also saw a major influx of German and central European personnel, the result of both economic and political emigration. During World War II, while some French film personnel left for Hollywood (Renoir, Duvivier, Jean Gabin, Michèle Morgan and others), French cinema lived in virtual autarchy.

In the postwar period, emigration to France took an individual character, with a wide range of personnel (Buñuel, Luis Mariano, Roman Polanski, Walerian Borowczyck, Eddie Constantine) working in Paris, though two strands can be detected. First, the intense programme of co-productions (especially with Italy) in the 1940s and 1950s brought many actors to France: Antonella Lualdi, Lea Massari, Gina Lollobrigida, Raf Vallone, Romy Schneider and Maria Schell among others. Secondly, the combination of generous French aid and of the break-up of the Eastern block, has produced another wave of eastern Europeans in France, among them Andrzej Wajda, Krzysztof Kieślowski and Otar Iosseliani, and, from other countries, directors such as Pedro Almodóvar and Manoel de Oliveira. No doubt the increasing 'Europeanisation' of European cinema, through co-productions and EU-backed projects, will further increase this transnational movement of personnel [> EUROPEAN COMMUNITY AND THE CINEMA]. (Ginette Vincendeau and Joseph Garncarz)

EUROPEAN ART CINEMA

We think we know what we mean by 'art cinema'. Yet in the European cinema of the 1990s, when directors as diverse in their preoccupations and styles as Krzysztof Kieślowski, Leos Carax and Pedro Almodóvar can be united by the same term, it would be more accurate to talk of 'art cinemas' to indicate the national and historical plurality concealed by the term. While being a means of defining and marketing a certain kind of European film, art cinema is also the institutional and aesthetic space into which the work of directors from beyond Europe has been integrated: for example, Kenji Mizoguchi from Japan, Satyajit Ray from India and, more recently, Zhang Yimou from China. Art cinema operates as a means of merging aesthetic and national 'difference', and of encouraging both.

Two moments can be loosely identified as having contributed to the formation of what Peter Lev calls 'a continuing impulse in film history', and to its association with Europe: the European avant-gardes of the 1920s and the New Waves that flourished from the late 1950s to the early 1970s [> BRITISH NEW WAVE, AVANT-GARDE CINEMA IN EUROPE]. The first of these moments includes the schools of Soviet montage, surrealism, French impressionism and German expressionism, all sharing a common search for creative and conceptual liaisons between the then silent medium and painting, music and poetry. In its earliest incarnation, then, art cinema implied an aesthetic project based in formal experimentation and innovation. Equally, as Steve Neale has observed, the concept of art cinema as an institutional space was developed by the national cinemas of Europe from the 1920s as 'attempts to counter both American domination of their indigenous markets in film and to foster a film industry and a film culture of their own'. The second, postwar, flourishing of art cinema can thus be seen as a consolidation of characteristics established in the 1920s.

The crucial role of Italian neo-realism in the development of postwar European art cinema is, as David Bordwell notes, in its being 'a transitional phenomenon' between the prewar and wartime national cinemas and those that were to develop after the war. The demise of the American studio system and the Paramount anti-trust decrees of 1948 created a shortage of films for international distribution. Equally, television was emerging both as a competitor for audiences and as a new market for films. This combination of factors meant that, from the mid-1950s onwards, films were increasingly made for international distribution. Italian neo-realism, then, can be seen as the forerunner of the art cinemas of the 1950s and 1960s, wherein the themes, styles and authorial address specific to a national cinema would find international audiences. 'The fullest flower of the art cinema paradigm', as Bordwell has called the postwar New Waves, 'occurred at the moment that the combination of novelty and nationalism became the marketing device it has been ever since'. The late 1950s/early 1960s thus brought the cinematic 'shocks' of the French New Wave, of Michelangelo

Antonioni's *L'avventura* (1960), Federico Fellini's *La dolce vita* (1960) and the international discovery of Ingmar Bergman, for many the archetypal European art cinema director.

The stylistic modes of art cinema – as opposed to Hollywood popular genres – traditionally privilege realism and ambiguity, two registers generally unified through the appeal to authorial expressivity. The notion of the *auteur* director as developed in *Cahiers du cinéma* in the 1950s, and then modified by Andrew Sarris in the US during the 1960s, speaks both of the critical support system that comes into being around art cinema and of the complexity of art cinema's internationalism. After all, the French New Wave defined itself positively in relation to American cinema and negatively in relation to the French cinema of the 1950s. Similarly, the New German Cinema of the late 1960s and 1970s established the *auteur* as 'public institution' in order to mark out a space for a national cinema founded on a combination of art cinema precepts: an aesthetics of personal expressivity supported by state funding. This tendency to 'institutionalise' the idea of the *auteur*, and with it an idea of a national art cinema, reached its apogee in the cultural policies of the French Minister for Culture, Jack Lang, in the 1980s when French *auteur* cinema was regarded as a significant part of the national cinematic patrimony. Perhaps the most high-profile example of this particular strategy is the French co-production of the French/Swiss/Polish *Trois couleurs/Three Colours* trilogy: *Bleu/Blue*, *Blanc/White* (both 1993) and *Rouge/Red* (1994) directed by Kieślowski, who represents the paradigm of the European *auteur*.

While Kieślowski, Carax and Almodóvar serve as significantly different versions of contemporary European art cinema directors, the specificity of European art cinema is increasingly unclear. Since the 'New American Cinema' of De Palma, Scorsese and Cimino took part of its inspiration from the European cinema of the 1960s, the idea of the *auteur* has become a critical/industrial commonplace. Yet since its heyday in the 1960s, art cinema has been understood, in some European film industries at least, as both a generic and an institutional option that, if no longer guaranteeing international visibility, at least preserves some of the cultural cachet associated with its past. (Chris Darke)

Bib: David Bordwell, *Narration in the Fiction Film* (1985).

EUROPEAN CINEMA AND HOLLYWOOD

Before 1914, France and Italy were the two main exporters of film. Between 1913 and 1925, however, American exports of film to Europe increased fivefold. If Hollywood secured its position as the world leader in film exports at the expense of a war-ravaged Europe, there was little American production involvement in Europe until 1945. European concern over the extent of the influx of American films began to take shape in the 1920s, with Germany the first major industry to take action against American films in the form of the Film Europe initiative spearheaded by Erich Pommer. Following the German example – whereby distributors were issued a permit to release a foreign film each time they financed and distributed a German one – France and Italy began to impose import restrictions, quotas, tariffs and quid pro quo conditions that sought to secure screen time for domestic production. In the UK, the 1927 Cinematograph Films Act instituted a quota on foreign film imports, which resulted in a flurry of British 'quota quickies' to satisfy quota demands. The Motion Picture Producers and Distributors of America (MPPDA; renamed the Motion Picture Association of America, MPAA, in 1945) gave what was to become the conventional American response to attempts by European countries to protect their industries, claiming that 'This government had adopted no restrictive regulations similar in any way to those enforced in certain foreign countries.' Nearly seventy years later, the same disingenuous free-trade rhetoric would be repeated in the 1993 Uruguay Round of the General Agreement on Tariffs and Trade (GATT).

American production involvement in Europe increased dramatically after World War II, the devistated continent now reliant on American aid and having little capacity or will to dictate strict import quotas. Equally, there were hundreds of American films, unreleased in Europe during the war, with which Hollywood could saturate European markets. At the same time, as Peter Lev has pointed out, 'European markets became a necessity, not a luxury, to American film companies in the 1950s, because the American audience for motion pictures was rapidly shrinking.' The Paramount decrees of 1948 which signalled the end of the vertical integration of Hollywood led to a drop in the number of films produced, and thus the increasing importance of the export market. In the face of the American strategy of market saturation, European countries returned either to quota systems or to a system of 'blocked funds' to try to counter American domination of domestic markets. The 1948 Anglo-American Film Agreement allowed US companies to withdraw only $17 million of their earnings, leaving over $40 million each year to accumulate in blocked accounts, the proviso being unlimited American access to the British market. The 1948 Franco-American Film Agreement allowed US firms to withdraw up to $3.6 million of their funds annually, leaving around $10 million blocked to be used for joint production with French companies and the construction of new studios, among other things. This latter agreement replaced the 1946 Blum-Byrnes trade agreement that had given America generous terms to export their films to France. Both 1948 agreements laid the ground for what became known as 'runaway productions', one of the three sorts of production that came to characterise the postwar relationship between Hollywood and Europe, the others being co-productions and what Peter Lev calls 'the Euro-American art film'.

With high unemployment in Hollywood in the 1950s and 1960s, and with lower production costs and more flexible labour regulations in Europe – especially Italy and Spain – the two immediate postwar decades saw a spate of European-American film production. 'Runaway productions' relied on a combination of European and American personnel and stars, were financed through blocked funds and tended towards the spectacular epic, films like *Alexander the Great* (1955), *Ben-Hur* (1959), *Lawrence of Arabia* (1962) or *55 Days at Peking* (1964); the ground-breaking Italian (so-called) 'Spaghetti' Westerns of the mid-1960s should also be included here. Co-production agreements were increasingly part of the production structure of such films; although they had been tried in the 1920s, they became common practice only after World War II. Jean-Luc Godard's *Le Mépris/Contempt* (1963) is both a satire on the exigencies of co-production – Georgia Moll as the harassed interpreter caught between Jack Palance's overbearing American producer, Fritz Lang's urbane European director, Michel Piccoli's French screenwriter and Brigitte Bardot's alienated sex goddess – and the very incarnation of the Euro-American art film. Such a film, according to Lev, 'attempts a synthesis of the American entertainment film (large budget, good production values, internationally known stars) and the European art film (auteur director, artistic subject and/or style) with the aim of reaching a much larger audience than the art film normally commands'. While the 1960s can be seen as the high point of such ventures, a nominal list of some of the more celebrated examples of the Euro-American art film indicates the longevity of this production style: *Blowup* (1967), *Ultimo tango a Parigi/Last Tango in Paris* (1972), *Paris, Texas* (1984), *The Last Emperor* (1987).

The 1993 GATT talks illustrated the extent to which the relationship between Europe and Hollywood remains 'a two-way fascination and a one-way exploitation', to use Godard's phrase. American objections to European film subsidies and 'protectionist' measures resulted in a piece of concerted brinkmanship by the French government – supported by a prestigious group of film-makers and stars – over the issue of 'cultural exception', which threatened to scupper the entire GATT agreement, of which film and audiovisual issues constituted only a small part. 'Cultural exception' was the idea that films and audiovisual material – because of their 'cultural specificity' to a particular nation – should not be governed by the same terms applied to foodstuffs, minerals, cars, etc. At the eleventh hour this principle was effectively acknowledged in a piece of EU/US political legerdemain: in order to save the GATT treaty, it was agreed simply to exclude film and audiovisual material from its terms. That the French government was so active in facing down American *laissez-faire* petitioning was accounted for by the French film critic Michel Ciment in December 1993 as follows: 'If French cinema has survived it is because of two measures that an American interpretation of GATT could decide were illegal. The first is the quota imposed on films shown on televison (60 per cent of them must be European). The second is a 13 per cent tax on all tickets sold at the box-office, which is used to subsidise innovative films, art-house cinemas, independent distributors, film festivals, film schools and East European and African production.' In retrospect, this aspect of GATT looks less resolved than simply put on hold, and the proliferation of cable and satellite channels promises to pose questions of broadcasting territory and intellectual property rights as well as to challenge definitions of the 'national' that underwrite positions such as those adopted by the French over their film industry.

Aesthetically speaking, the relay between Europe and Hollywood has had complex and diverse consequences, from the fascination and support evinced in the 1920s by American studios for German directors such as F. W. Murnau, Ernst Lubitsch and Paul Leni, to the sometimes uncomfortable exile that Hollywood offered to émigré European directors such as Lang, Jean Renoir, Douglas Sirk (Sierck) and Robert Siodmak in the 1930s and 1940s. A prime example of this international cross-pollination of film style can be seen in critical approaches to *film noir* as a hybridisation of American generic structures, German Expressionism and French Poetic Realism. The European New Waves and art cinemas of the 1950s and 1960s were often fascinated by Hollywood, a fascination epitomised by Godard's films, and in turn can be seen to have fed into the stylistics of American directors such as Martin Scorsese, Francis Ford Coppola and Brian De Palma of the 'New American Cinema' of the 1970s. This traffic of influence and mutual acknowledgment has been evident more recently in the American vogue for remaking successful European, and particularly French, films, for example Coline Serreau's *Trois hommes et un couffin/Three Men and a Cradle.* (1985) as *Three Men and a Baby* (1988), Luc Besson's *Nikita* (1990) as *The Assassin* (1993) and Daniel Vigne's *Le Retour de Martin Guerre* (1981) as *Sommersby* (1993). (Chris Darke)

Bib: Peter Lev, *The Euro-American Cinema* (1993).

EUROPEAN COMMUNITY [NOW EUROPEAN UNION] AND THE CINEMA

While European cinema production had previously fallen under general EC legislation and directives on trade and industry, it was not until the 1980s that the Brussels authorities developed a coherent policy specifically concerning film and other European media. The issue had been brought to a head by a 1984 proposal from French president François Mitterand to establish a pan-European co-production fund for work in cinema and television. Mitterand's plan was rejected but it had started the ball rolling.

In 1986 the Commission's Directorate for Information, Communication and Culture put forward its *Mesures pour Encourager le Développement de l'Industrie de Production Audio-Visuelle* (or MEDIA for short). Once accepted by the Council, MEDIA began a pilot phase in 1987, to last until 1990, under the control of the EC Ministers for Cultural Affairs. As a symbol of the EC's commitment to its MEDIA programme, 1988 was designated European Cinema and Television Year. Events included the first ever European Film Awards*, although somewhat ironically the Berlin ceremony garnered very little media attention. During the same year, in an attempt to emphasise the economic implications of MEDIA, the suffix '92' was added to the programme's acronym. MEDIA 92 was to be a high-profile test case for the new EC internal market, encouraging collaboration between the twelve member states.

The full MEDIA programme was adopted by the Council of Ministers of the EC in December 1990 and was retitled MEDIA 95. From 1991 to 1995, MEDIA was awarded a budget of 200 million ECU (roughly £340 million). Most of this money was designated as 'seed' funding, a system of repayable advances with the programme's initiatives sharing in any profit they had helped to create. Thus it was hoped that the MEDIA budget would largely become self-perpetuating in years to come. In an attempt to broaden the scope of MEDIA (and its funding), European states from outside the EC have been encouraged to join the programme's activities. In 1992 MEDIA initiatives were opened to five members of the European Free Trade Association (EFTA) – Austria, Finland, Iceland, Norway and Sweden – as well as to Poland, Hungary and Czechoslovakia.

MEDIA is made up of an ever-increasing programme of initiatives which support the development, production and distribution of European audiovisual culture. Of these, nineteen are partly or wholly concerned with film. The remit of the respective initiatives can usually be gleaned from their catchword titles. CARTOON, for example, comprises a package of measures to support European animation production, including a database of contacts and incentives to encourage cooperation between studios. The most important MEDIA initiative with regard to development is the European Script Fund (SCRIPT). Recognising that securing finance for the development of projects is often the biggest hurdle faced by European film-makers, SCRIPT provides loans and advice to help get proposals up and running. The loans, averaging 50 per cent of a project's pre-production budget, become reimbursable if the project goes into production. Completed films which have benefited from assistance by SCRIPT include *Acción Mutante* (1992, Spain), *Daens* (1992, Belgium/France/Netherlands) and *Naked* (1993, UK). For projects that have made it to the production stage, Euro Media Garanties (EMG) provides film-makers with a measure of financial security. Supporting ventures that involve producers from at least three Council of Europe members, EMG will guarantee up to 70 per cent of the loan finance taken out on the project.

Bruce Jones and Ricky Tomlinson in *Raining Stones* (Ken Loach, 1993).

Leonide Massine and Moira Shearer in *The Red Shoes* (Michael Powell/Emeric Pressburger, 1948).

Riddles of the Sphinx (Laura Mulvey/ Peter Wollen, 1977).

Ian McElhinney and Carol Scanlan in *Reefer and the Model* (Joe Comerford, 1988).

Julian Sands and Helena Bonham Carter in *A Room with a View* (Ismail Merchant/James Ivory, 1985).

Albert Finney in *Saturday Night and Sunday Morning* (Karel Reisz, 1960).

Wendy Craig, Dirk Bogarde, James Fox in *The Servant* (Joseph Losey, 1963).

Gracie Fields (front row) in *Sing as We Go* (Basil Dean, 1934).

Edward Rigby and Michael Redgrave in *The Stars Look Down* (Carol Reed, 1939).

Betty Balfour in *Squibs* (George Pearson, 1921).

Cliff Richard in *Summer Holiday* (Peter Yates, 1963).

Vivien Leigh and Laurence Olivier in *That Hamilton Woman* (Alexander Korda, 1941).

Joseph Cotten in *The Third Man* (Carol Reed, 1943).

George Formby and Peggy Bryan in *Turned Out Nice Again* (Marcel Varnel, 1941).

Sylvia Sims and Dirk Bogarde in *Victim* (Basil Dearden/Michael Relph, 1961).

We are the Lambeth Boys (Karel Reisz, 1959).

James Mason and Margaret Lockwood in *The Wicked Lady* (Leslie Arliss, 1945).

Valentine Nonyela and Mo Sesay in *Young Soul Rebels* (Isaac Julien, 1991).

Perhaps the biggest success story of the MEDIA programme, the European Film Distribution Office (EFDO) has helped many films reach wider markets, both within the continent and around the world. EFDO's main remit is to support distribution between EU member states, but through 'EFDO Abroad', which presents films at festivals outside Europe, it now also promotes European cinema to countries worldwide. With the vast majority of European cinema consisting of low-budget projects which are only ever distributed in their country of origin, EFDO has been particularly beneficial to smaller productions. In fact 80 per cent of EFDO's available funds are set aside for films costing no more than 2.25 million ECU (£3.825 million). Covering up to 50 per cent of distributors' pre-costs, EFDO offers interest-free loans to films which have secured a distribution deal for no less than three EU countries. Moreover, the loan is only repayable if the release is successful. Conversely, if a supported film does especially well at the box-office, EFDO becomes entitled to a small share of the profits, or 'success dividend', which can then be reinvested. Among the well-known films to have received support from EFDO are *Babettes gaestebud/Babette's Feast* (1987, Denmark), *Spoorloos/The Vanishing* (1987, Netherlands/France) and *Volere volare* (1991, Italy).

Another film to have benefited from EFDO money, *Toto le héros/Toto the Hero* (1991, Belgium/France/Germany), serves as a testament to the package of MEDIA initiatives and the spirit of cooperation they have fostered within European cinema. A co-production of three member states, *Toto* was aided at every stage by European funding, beginning with support from SCRIPT and ending with the promotion of the video release by Espace Vidéo Européen (EVE). Yet one of the film's major sources of funding came from outside the MEDIA programme, via an initiative of the Council of Europe, EURIMAGES.

Set up in 1988, EURIMAGES is a co-production fund in the mould of that proposed by François Mitterand four years earlier. Providing financial support for films made by production partners from at least three member countries, the fund initially comprised twelve Council countries. A notable absentee from the final agreement, though, was the UK. Displaying the all too prevalent combination of ignorance about what is happening in Europe and a belief that the British still lead the way, the UK government soon established its own European Co-Production Fund (ECF). In the meantime EURIMAGES has gone from strength to strength and the UK finally joined in 1993.

European government initiatives aimed at the media industries are completed by the Audiovisual EUREKA programme (AVE). Again proposed by Europe's prime mover in this field, François Mitterand, AVE's remit is somewhat less specific than those of MEDIA or EURIMAGES. AVE exists primarily to encourage the development and application of advanced audiovisual technology. It also differs from the other major programmes in that it has a wider membership base of nearly thirty countries and responds to specific proposals from the industry rather than attempting to initiate projects itself.

At the time of writing (early 1995), the MEDIA programme is preparing to enter a new phase, MEDIA 2. Although details are still to be confirmed, MEDIA 2 looks quite different from its predecessor, reducing the nineteen initiatives to three strands: training, development and distribution. MEDIA 2 should also have a considerably larger budget for its next five-year programme, but the decision not to provide any specific measure in favour of exhibition has already proved controversial.

Each EU country now has a Mediadesk to provide information and answer queries about the MEDIA programme. (Simon Horrocks)

EUROPEAN FILM AWARDS (FELIX)

Established in 1988 as part of the European Community's Cinema and Television Year, the FELIX awards were intended as a European rival to the Oscars. Yet their initial impact can be measured from the challenge made by Sean Day-Lewis after the first ceremony in Berlin went almost unnoticed: 'Hands up anybody who can name one of the winners or, come to that, anybody who knows whether the epoch-making occasion happened at all.'

FELIX largely follows the format of its Hollywood counterpart, awarding its major prizes in the categories of Best Film, Best Actor/Actress and so on. One innovation is the prise for Best Young Film, recognising the achievements of up-and-coming talents in European cinema. Suitably, the first recipient of this award was the *enfant terrible* of Spanish film, Pedro Almodóvar, for his *Mujeres al borde de un ataque de nervios/Women on the Verge of a Nervous Breakdown* (1988). As if to emphasise the 'European-ness' of the awards, the annual FELIX ceremony does not have a permanent home, visiting Berlin, Paris and Glasgow in its first three years. Reinforcing FELIX's identity, the prefix 'European' was added to the award categories from 1990, Best Film becoming European Film of the Year, etc. In 1991 responsibility for FELIX was assumed by the newly founded European Film Academy (EFA), bringing with it the respected name of the Academy's president, Ingmar Bergman*. But perhaps the most significant change was made to the awards in 1993. While the European Film of the Year continues to be judged on artistic merit, potential winners now have to achieve a designated amount of box-office revenue before qualifying for nomination. FELIX thus recognises that commercial viability is as important as critical acclaim if European cinema is to resist Hollywood's continued domination of the market. Although the European Film Awards have undoubtedly made significant progress since their inception, FELIX has a long way to go before it can hope to compete with the Oscars in the popular imagination. In the words of EFA chairman Wim Wenders*, 'our handicap is that the awards should have started at least twenty years ago'. (Simon Horrocks)

The winners in the major FELIX categories so far are as follows:

Best Film (European Film of the Year from 1990)

1988 *Krótki Film o Zabijaniu/A Short Film About Killing* (Krzysztof Kieślowski; Poland)
1989 *Topio stin Omichli/Landscape in the Mist* (Thodoros Angelopoulos; Greece/France/Italy)
1990 *Porte aperte/Open Doors* (Gianni Amelio; Italy)
1991 *Riff-Raff* (Ken Loach; UK)
1992 *Il ladro di bambini/Stolen Children* (Gianni Amelio; Italy/France)
1993 *Urga. Territoriya lyubvi/Urga. Territory of Love* (Nikita Mikhalkov; Russia/France)
1994 *Lamerica* (Gianni Amelio; Italy)
1995 *Land and Freedom* (Ken Loach; UK/Spain/Germany)

Best Young Film (Young European Film of the Year from 1990)

1988 *Mujeres al borde de un ataque de nervios/Women on the Verge of a Nervous Breakdown* (Pedro Almodóvar; Spain)
1989 *300 Mil do Nieba/300 Miles to Heaven* (Maciej Dejczer; Poland/Denmark)
1990 *Henry V* (Kenneth Branagh; UK)
1991 *Toto le héros/Toto the Hero* (Jaco van Dormael; Belgium/France/Germany)
1992 *De Noorderlingen/The Northerners* (Alan van Warmerdam; Netherlands)
1993 *Orlando* (Sally Potter; UK/Russia/France/Italy/Netherlands)
1994 *Le Fils du requin* (Agnès Merlet; France) and *Woyzeck* (Janos Szasz; Hungary)
1995 *La Haine/Hate* (Mathieu Kassovitz; France)

Best Actor (European Actor of the Year from 1990)

1988 Max von Sydow for *Pelle Erobreren/Pelle the Conquerer* (Denmark)
1989 Philippe Noiret for *La Vie et rien d'autre/Life and Nothing But* (France) and *Nuovo Cinema Paradiso/Cinema Paradiso* (Italy)
1990 Kenneth Branagh for *Henry V* (UK)
1991 Michel Bouquet for *Toto le héros/Toto the Hero* (Belgium/France/Germany)
1992 Matti Pellonpää for *La Vie de bohème/Bohemian Life* (Finland/France/Sweden)
1993 Daniel Auteuil for *Un Cœur en hiver/A Heart in Winter* (France)
[From 1994: no award]

Best Actress (European Actress of the Year from 1990)

1988 Carmen Maura for *Mujeres al borde de un ataque de nervios/Women on the Verge of a Nervous Breakdown* (Spain)
1989 Ruth Sheen for *High Hopes* (UK)

1990 Carmen Maura for *¡Ay, Carmela!* (Spain)
1991 Clothilde Coreau for *Le Petit Criminel* (France)
1992 Juliette Binoche for *Les Amants du Pont-Neuf* (France)
1993 Maia Morgenstern for *Balanta/Le Chêne/The Oak* (Romania/France)
[From 1994: no award]

FESTIVALS

Film festivals gather films (as well as film-makers and stars) in one venue for the purpose of promotion and information. Although such events have taken place since the 1910s, the first festival in the modern sense of the term was Venice, opened in 1932, followed by Cannes in 1946 and Berlin in 1951. These three constitute the major league of European film festivals, joined by Karlovy Vary and Locarno in 1946, Edinburgh* in 1947, London in 1957, and a host of others. Festivals' *raison d'être*, apart from media and tourist appeal, is to be a market place for new product and, incidentally (and often controversially), a forum for critical evaluation. Many award prizes and a Cannes, Venice or Berlin prize carries promotional value. Since the early 1980s, as the theatrical market for film has shrunk, festivals in Europe have taken on a vital role, as the *only* place of exhibition for an increasing number of films, at worst creating the ghetto of the 'festival circuit', but at best a springboard for media exposure and occasional release: the films of Emir Kusturica and Kira Muratova are two examples of the latter. Concurrently a veritable explosion of smaller festivals has taken place, especially in western Europe, where they are substantially supported by central and local state funds, catering for a wide variety of specialisms (animation, horror, shorts, thrillers, women's films, gay and lesbian films, children's films, silent cinema, realist cinema, national cinemas, etc.). While the market value of the smaller events is negligible, they perform a crucial cultural function, continuing and to some extent replacing the work of film clubs as a forum for discovery and debate, and providing an opportunity to circulate other European and non-American films. (Ginette Vincendeau)

Below is a *selective* list of film festivals. When not attributed to a writer, information is from British Council and British Film Institute documentation. For further details, see: *Directory of International Film Festivals*, published by the British Council, and the *BFI Handbook* (both yearly).

Albania hosts a biennial national film festival in Tirana. **Austria** has three main annual film festivals. The Viennale – Internationale Filmfestwochen Wien (Vienna international film festival, every autumn) is subsidised by the Vienna City Council and a private sponsor, and includes symposia and publications. The other two festivals are dedicated to Austrian cinema: the Österreichische Film Tage Wels

(Austrian Film Days, in Wels) since 1984, and the Diagonale – Festival des Österreichischen Films (festival of Austrian cinema) held in Salzburg since 1993 and organised by the Austrian Film Commission. **Belgium**'s most famous, though short-lived, festival was Exprmntl (experimental films) at Knokke-le-Zoute which ran in 1949, 1958, 1963, 1967, 1971 and 1974, and remains legendary for both its films and its passionate climate of debates and 'happenings'. Out of the country's large number of festivals should be mentioned the Brussels international film festival (January), the Brussels international festival of fantasy and science-fiction film and thrillers (March), and, also in Brussels, Cinédécouvertes (cine-discoveries) in July and Filmer à tout prix ('To film no matter what') in October. In November, a festival of European film is held in Virton. Ghent holds the Internationaal Filmgebeuren (international film festival) in October and an art film festival in February. **Bulgaria**'s main festival is the international festival of comedy films in Gabrovo in May (odd years). There is also an animation festival in Varna in October (odd years). **Czechoslovakia**. First held in 1946 and established permanently in 1950, Karlovy Vary (now in the Czech Republic) has been the main festival. Until 1992 it alternated biennially with Moscow and functioned as the Communist block alternative to Cannes and Venice, showcasing Eastern European cinema, but also 'Third World' cinema. Bratislava (now Slovakia) holds several festivals, including the Forum (festival of first feature films, November–December). **Denmark**. The main festival is the Odense international film festival (August, odd years). There are also a film and video festival in Copenhagen (June, even years) and the Copenhagen gay and lesbian film festival (September, annually).

Finland. The Midnight Sun festival takes place every June (since 1986) in Sodankylä, a small Lapland community, focusing on new Finnish cinema and silent films. Espoo ciné, in southern Finland, started in 1990. Kettupäivät ('The Fox-days') in Helsinki in early November is a forum for new Finnish shorts, documentaries and videos. The international children's film festival (launched in 1982) takes place in Oulu in late November. The Tampere short film festival in early March (since 1970) is an important forum for new Finnish film-makers. MuuMedia in early March in Helsinki (since 1991) concentrates on video and the new media. **France**. Founded in 1938 to counter the fascist influences thought to contaminate Venice, Cannes' opening was delayed by World War II. Since 1946, it has been the international film industry's most prominent meeting place. The festival takes place in May. The most important specialist events are: the Annecy festival (January), the Clermont-Ferrand short film festival, the Cognac festival of thrillers, the Créteil international women's film festival (March–April), the Cinéma du réel (documentary) festival in Paris (March) and the Deauville festival of American cinema in September (notoriously boycotted in the early 1980s by French Minister of Culture Jack Lang). The Institut Lumière in Lyons and the Cinémathèque Française organise regular retrospective festivals, the latter in particular with Cinémémoire (Paris, November), which shows newly restored prints. **Germany**. The most important German Festival is in Berlin, founded in 1951. The Internationale Kurzfilmtage Oberhausen (Oberhausen international short film festival), held annually since 1955 (in April), exhibits a wide variety of short films. The Internationales Film-Festival Mannheim (November), established in 1952, emphasises debut features and documentaries. The Internationale Hofer Filmtage (Hof International Film Days) has since 1967 been a meeting place for younger German film-makers, especially film school graduates. The Leipzig festival (November–December), launched in 1957, is a forum for politically committed documentary film-making. Although its political focus has shifted since the end of the GDR to Third World film, it still functions as a window for central and eastern Europe. Germany has two major women's film festivals, Feminale (Cologne, May, since 1984) and Femme totale (Dortmund, since 1987). The Stuttgart animation festival has been running since 1982. **Greece**. The major cinematic event in Greece is the Thessaloniki festival, founded in September 1960. **Hungary**. The main festival is the Hungarian Film Week, which provides a survey of Hungarian cinema, including documentary, experimental and student films. It is usually held in February, a week before Berlin. **Ireland**: see Cork*.

Italy. For many years Venice was Italy's sole major film festival. Since the early 1960s many smaller festivals have emerged. A pioneering role was played, from 1960, by the Festival del Cinema Libero at the Apennine resort of Porretta Terme, for films made outside or on the fringes of the system. This was followed in 1965 by the Mostra del Nuovo Cinema at Pesaro (June). Founded by critic Lino Micciché, Pesaro has devoted itself to the discovery or rediscovery of *auteurs*, movements and national cinemas, promoted conferences, and produced a steady stream of important publications. Throughout the 1970s and early 1980s numerous local initiatives followed. Among the most important were the Salso Film and TV Festival at Salsomaggiore, devoted (until its demise in the 1990s) to research and experiment; Filmmaker in Milan, dedicated to independent production; the Festival Cinema Giovani in Turin, with retrospectives of the 'New Waves' of the 1960s; and the Bergamo Film Meeting, a festival-market for quality films awaiting distribution. Among specialist festivals the most noteworthy are Mystfest at Cattolica, near Rimini, for thrillers, and the Pordenone festival of early cinema (October). **Netherlands**. The three main festivals are the Netherlands Film Festival (formerly Dutch Film Days), in Utrecht (September), where an independent film festival (Cinemanifestatie) ran 1966–71; the documentary festival in Amsterdam (December); and the Rotterdam festival (January–February). **Norway**. The main Norwegian film festival is held in Haugesund annually (August–September). In addition, a festival takes place in Oslo in November, and a short films festival in Trondheim in June. **Poland** has four annual festivals. The festival of Polish feature films in Gdansk/Gdynia (September) presents Poland's latest productions, and holds the annual meeting of the Association of Polish Filmmakers. The Cracow festival of short films (late May) celebrated its thirty years as the major Polish short film festival in 1993. The Warsaw International Film Festival has grown in recent years from a student film club event to a well organised festival of recent international releases (modelled on London). The Lubuskie Lato Filmowe, run by the Association of Film Societies (Dyskysyjne Kluby Filmowe) at Lagow in western Poland, presents the latest films produced in Poland and eastern and central Europe.

Portugal. Among Portugal's numerous festivals are the Espinho festival (November) for animation, the Encontros Internacionais de Cinema Documental (documentaries) in Odivelas, the Fantasporto (fantasy films) in Oporto in February, the Figueira da Foz festival (September) and the Troia festival (June–July). **Romania**. There is a biennial animation festival in Mamaia; the national film festival has taken place at Costinesti since 1976, but its future is in doubt. **(Former) Soviet Union**. The major film festival of the Soviet Union has been Moscow, in July (odd years, alternating with Karlovy Vary), traditionally the showcase for Soviet and eastern European socialist cinema; other festivals are held in St Petersburg (June), Sochi (May–June) and Tashkent (May–June). Among other festivals in the ex-Soviet states are the International Film Forum 'Arsenal' in Riga (Latvia) in September, for experimental film, the 'Golden Taurus' festival in Kaunas (Lithuania) in June and the 'Molodost' international film festival in Kiev (Ukraine) in October. **Spain**. The San Sebastián Film Festival (annually in September, since 1953) initially contributed glamour and an indirect legitimacy to Franco's regime, showcasing films which were then further cut or prohibited in Spain. After the transition to democracy, it is still Spain's premier film event; under Pérez Estremera, San Sebastián presents a competitive section built around the pick of Spanish autumn releases and the best new Latin American films, plus major international titles. Under Fernando Lara, festival director since 1983, the Valladolid International Film Festival (October) premieres major art films, complemented by tributes and retrospectives. Spain's other large festivals are Sitges (October) for fantasy and horror, and Valencia for Mediterranean cinema.

Sweden's main festivals are in Stockholm (November) and Uppsala (October, specialising in short films); there is also a festival in Gothenburg (February). **Switzerland**. Apart from Locarno, founded in 1946 as a showcase for the international film market, the main festivals in Switzerland are Nyon and Solothurn. Emerging from the 'Festival du film amateur' (Rolle 1963–64, Nyon 1965–68), Nyon is concerned with documentary. Its director was Moritz de Hadeln (also Locarno's director 1972–77) until 1980, when Erika de Hadeln took over, pursuing the festival's remit of showing politically and socially committed films. Solothurn, or the Solothurner Filmtage (Solothurn Film Days), held annually in the last week of January since 1966, is the most important venue for domestic productions, together with theme-specific films by foreign directors, exhibitions and round-tables on issues of national film policy. Solothurn has since the early 1990s opened up towards video, television and co-productions. Video art finds a place at the Internationale Film- und Videotage in Lucerne, the International Video Week in Geneva and the Video Festival at Locarno. **UK**. Apart from Edinburgh* the major event is the London Film Festival (November), held at the National Film Theatre and other London cinemas, created as a non-competitive 'festival of festivals' to present material shown at other festivals earlier in the year, as well as films released in their own country but not in Britain. The National Film Theatre also hosts the London lesbian and gay film festival (March) and the Jewish film festival (October). Smaller film festivals in the UK include Aberystwyth (November), Birmingham (October), Brighton (May), Cambridge (July), Leeds (October), the Norwich Women's Film Weekend (May), Nottingham ('Shots in the Dark', a thriller film festival, May–June) and Southampton (September). (GV) **(Former) Yugoslavia**. There is an international festival of animated films in Zagreb (Croatia) in June (even years). The Pula (Croatia) festival was first held in 1954, as the national film festival of Yugoslavia. In 1993 it was remodelled the national Croatian film festival. Fest was established in Belgrade in 1970 as a 'festival of festivals' and it became a major gathering point for international filmmakers. It collapsed under the economic and cultural embargo of Serbia in 1993.

GAY CINEMA IN EUROPE – see LESBIAN AND GAY CINEMA IN EUROPE

HERITAGE CINEMA IN EUROPE

The term describes period films made since the mid-1970s. Characteristic, successful examples include *Jean de Florette* (1986, France), *A Room with a View* (1985, UK), *Babettes gæstebud/Babette's Feast* (1987, Denmark) and *Belle Epoque* (1992, Spain). The term suggests an affinity with what has been called the heritage industry, notably retro fashion and the popularisation of museums and historical sites through the use of simulacra, lighting and sound effects and actors in period costume. Films may be characterised by use of a canonical source from the national literature, generally set within the past 150 years; conventional filmic narrative style, with the pace and tone of '(European) art cinema'* but without its symbolisms and personal directorial voices; a museum aesthetic, period costumes, decor and locations carefully recreated, presented in pristine condition, brightly or artfully lit; a performance style based on nuance and social observation.

It is arguable whether this is a distinct phenomenon. There are precedents (for example, the French costume dramas of the 1950s such as *Les Misérables*, 1958), but heritage films may be distinguished from many period films in a number of ways. While displaying high production values, they are generally small-scale and intimate, not spectacular; they do not (on the whole) deal with the great events of history, as conventionally understood, or even, like *Senso* (1954, Italy) or *Angi Vera* (1978, Hungary), treat such events through their impact on personal lives; much less do they address the construction of historical representation, like *Ludwig – Requiem für einen jungfräulichen König/ Ludwig – Requiem for a Virgin King* (1972, Germany) or *Amarcord* (1974, Italy). However, it is not a uniquely European genre, except perhaps in the sense of Eurocentric, since it has been important to the cinema of most white settler nations, notably Australia, Argentina and Canada.

The focus of the films is, typically, on attractively presented everyday bourgeois life. Critically they are an interesting case study. Often hugely popular in their country of origin, they tend to be sold as art cinema outside it. Though the market research is not available, it seems likely that they are especially popular with middle-class audiences, in a period when this class has become the majority or at least a significant minority in many European countries. They are thus embraced by the same class from which the critical establishment is drawn, yet the latter has generally viewed them negatively. Often characteristics such as nostalgia or attention to fixtures and fittings are criticised without considering the potential of the former to be a critique of the present or the sensuousness of the latter and its iconographic expressivity (typically requiring the skilled reading of a female spectator). Equally, the genre has provided a space for marginalised social groups, a sense of putting such people back into history, for instance women: *Rouge Baiser* (1985, France), *Rosa Luxemburg* (1986, Germany), *Howards End* (1991, UK); lesbians and gay men: *El diputado/Congressman* (1978, Spain), *Ernesto* (1979, Italy), *Avskedet/The Farewell* (1980, Finland); even ethnic minorities (*Cheb*, 1990, France) and the disabled (*My Left Foot,* 1989, Ireland). None of this argues for the merit of the genre, but suggests a critical issue of some complexity that warrants exploration. (Richard Dyer)

Bib: Andrew Higson, 'Re-presenting the National Past: Nostalgia and Pastiche in the Heritage Film', in Lester Friedman (ed.), *British Cinema and Thatcherism* (1993).

LESBIAN AND GAY CINEMA IN EUROPE

It is generally assumed that European cinemas have a good track record on homosexuality: more images, sooner, less prejudiced, more often produced by openly lesbian/gay people. This account needs qualification and explanation, and more research.

Lesbian/gay representation has been all but entirely absent from East European cinemas. In Western Europe, lesbian/gay stereotypes are widely used, not only in popular comedies and thrillers but in canonical *auteur* works: *Die Büchse der Pandora/Pandora's Box* (1929, Germany); *Roma città aperta/Rome Open City* (1945, Italy), *La Fiancée du pirate/Dirty Mary* (1969, France). They are not necessarily the same as in Hollywood, nor are stereotypes unambiguously negative, something radical gay/lesbian films have often taken up, as in *Un hombre llamado Flor de Otoño/A Man Called Autumn Flower* (1977, Spain), or *Madame X – eine absolute Herrscherin/Madame X – an Absolute Ruler* (1978, Germany). The greater number of lesbian/gay representations in Western European cinemas has much to do with identifying markets with which Hollywood did not compete: pornography and the educational film, not always firmly distinct genres. Soft-core heterosexual pornography has been a mainstay of many European industries and invariably includes lesbian sequences. Sex education films have treated male and female homosexuality and have often been enlightened as texts even when marketed as titillation, for instance *Anders als die Anderen/Different from the Others* (1919, Germany) or *Der Sittlichkeitsverbrecher/The Sex Criminal* (1962, Switzerland).

At the same time, European cinemas dealt with homosexuality in a serious manner much earlier than others. This did not only occur in films of blatant high seriousness: among the most cherishable early images of homosexuality are the male relationship in the highly strung melodrama *Geschlecht in Fesseln/Sex in Shackles* (1928, Germany) and the lesbian character in the French thriller *Quai des Orfèvres* (1947). The earliest known representation is in *Vingarne/The Wings* (1916, Sweden), with the earliest lesbian representation perhaps *Die Büchse der Pandora. Anders als die anderen* and *Mädchen in Uniform/Girls in Uniform* (1931, Germany) represent the earliest explicitly progressive treatments, a tradition taken up in the postwar years by *Victim* (1960, UK): the presence of contemporaneous, relatively strong homosexual rights movements in these countries is significant in accounting for these breakthroughs.

Government policies in many countries have facilitated *auteur* cinema, in which many more or less openly lesbian/gay directors have worked (Chantal Akerman, Pedro Almodóvar, Jean Cocteau, Rainer Werner Fassbinder, Marleen Gorris, Derek Jarman*, Ulrike Ottinger, Pier Paolo Pasolini, Luchino Visconti), as have (straight) women directors who treated homosexuality in a sympathetic, even at times envious, manner – among others, Mai Zetterling's *Älskande par/Loving Couples* (1964, Sweden), Margarethe von Trotta's *Das zweite Erwachen des Krista Klages/The Second Awakening of Krista Klage* (1977, Germany) or Diane Kurys' *Coup de foudre/Entre Nous/At First Sight* (1983, France). In recent years, the European heritage* film has been remarkably hospitable to lesbian/gay themes, as for instance in *Novembermond/November Moon* (1984, Germany), *Maurice* (1987, UK), *Meteoro ke skia/Meteor and Shadow* (1962, Greece); one might consider Jacqueline Audry's *Olivia* (1950, France) an important early example. *Auteur* and heritage cinema do not treat homosexuality as an issue or problem, but are not always lacking in anguish, as for instance in *Tystnaden/The Silence* (1962, Sweden), or melancholy, as in *Gli occhiali d'oro/The Gold-rimmed Spectacles* (1988, Italy), and few European films have had the (often bland) affirmative impulse of post-gay liberation cinema in the USA. (Richard Dyer)

Bib: Richard Dyer, *Now You See It: Studies on Lesbian and Gay Film* (1990).

SEXUALITY, EROTICISM AND PORNOGRAPHY IN EUROPEAN CINEMA

Representations of sexuality and eroticism are as old as the cinema in Europe. While 'actualities' and little comic scenes entertained audiences in fairgrounds, short pornographic movies drew a few of them into brothels. A wide underground network of porn or 'stag' films flourished, usually unknown to mainstream audiences and film history alike, except when they surfaced in 'scandalous' manifestations, as with the Romanian-born French entrepreneur Bernard Natan who directed, and starred in, a large number of them. In the 'legitimate' cinema, eroticism quickly became a feature too, in early French movies for instance and, notoriously, in the pre-World War I Danish erotic melodrama, credited with the 'invention' of the on-screen passionate kiss.

In 1935, the American authorities burned a print of the Czech film *Extase/Ecstasy* (1932, dir. Gustav Machatý), in which Hedy Lamarr appeared naked. This took place five years after the introduction of the notoriously censorious Hays Code in the US and, for a good thirty years afterwards, the cinema of Europe was regarded as comparatively free in its depiction of sexuality. Of course, such 'freedom' was, as it would be later, within the confines of dominant (and often misogynistic) representations of women as sexual icons. It was also subject to censorship laws in the European countries themselves. Germany, for example, banned *Extase*, but that was on the grounds of Lamarr being Jewish. And if, in Arletty, the French cinema of the 1930s and 1940s had an icon of 'independent' female sexuality, her brief 'nude' shower scene in *Le Jour se lève* (1939) was nevertheless excised.

The national cinemas of postwar Europe, particularly those of France and Italy, began to redefine the permissible limits of cinema's depiction of on-screen sexuality. The Italian neo-realist cinema achieved an immense international visibility based on the perceived 'realism' of its depiction of specific social milieux. Such success might equally be said to have been achieved by its depiction of female sexuality. The 'earthiness' of Silvana Mangano in *Riso amaro/Bitter Rice* (1949) and the revealing filming of Anna Magnani, not to mention the barely concealed lesbian subplot in *Roma città aperta/Rome Open City* (Roberto Rossellini, 1945), prepared international audiences for the appearances in the 1950s and 1960s of Italian stars such as Gina Lollobrigida, Sophia Loren and Claudia Cardinale.

In France, in a string of films starting with *Caroline Chérie* (1950), Martine Carol continued the line of French female stars whose presence guaranteed that their vehicles would be, as Claude Beylie wrote, 'lightly spiced with a pleasant eroticism'. If Carol and others, such as Françoise Arnoul, gave international currency to certain ideas of French cinema and French femininity, the advent of Brigitte Bardot in *Et Dieu ... créa la femme/And God Created Woman* (1956) promoted different, modern versions both of this femininity and this cinema. The same might be said, forty years on, of Béatrice Dalle, whose explosive performance in *37°2 le Matin/Betty Blue* (1985) can be read as a reprise of the Bardot sex-kitten persona, treated with *Emmanuelle*-like explicitness.

In François Truffaut's *Les Quatre cents coups* (1959), Jean-Pierre Léaud steals a publicity still of an Ingmar Bergman film showing Harriet Andersson in a revealingly off-the-shoulder outfit. It is a moment in which one European art cinema*, the French New Wave, addresses the important figure of Bergman, the most celebrated European *auteur* of the period, via the concern common to both: the 'realistic', 'adult' and hence 'explicit' treatment of sexual themes. These three terms, often interchangeable, became associated with the European art cinemas of the 1960s. It was equally the case that the 'adult' treatment of sexuality by these cinemas was accompanied by the *frisson* of the well-publicised relationships between male *auteurs* and their leading actresses, Roberto Rossellini and Ingrid Bergman, Jean-Luc Godard and Anna Karina, Michelangelo Antonioni and Monica Vitti, Ingmar Bergman and Liv Ullmann. Interestingly, the postwar rise in European art cinema was also paralleled by the burgeoning genre of pornography.

If the difference between pornography and eroticism is that between display and suggestion, the late 1960s and the 1970s saw a short-lived convergence of the two. While the sex industry in Europe had formerly restricted itself in the 1950s to low-tech 'stag films' and 'loop movies' for peep shows, and with cinema encroaching progressively upon its territory either in pseudo-documentaries on naturism, so-called 'nudie cuties' and American B-movie exploitation, the late 1960s saw a major increase in the profile of films normally associated with the sex industry.

Two moments are worth isolating in the growing explicitness of sexually oriented material – the first production of hardcore pornography in colour magazines in Scandinavia in 1967, and the international *suc-*

cès de scandale of the Swedish film *Jag är nyfiken – gul/I am Curious – Yellow* (1967), which dispensed with any documentary alibis in its straightforwardly explicit depiction of (simulated) sexual action. These two events presaged the increasing commercial importance of explicit sexual content in European cinema of the 1970s. The first half of the decade saw the great commercial success of Bernardo Bertolucci's *Ultimo Tango a Parigi/Last Tango in Paris* (1972), whose superbly performed confection of stellar cast, hack psychoanalysis and chic sodomy set a model that many *auteurs* would follow throughout the decade. Most notable among examples of this increasing hybridisation of art cinema and pornography were Dušan Makavejev's Brechtian disquisition on sexual theorist Wilhelm Reich, *W. R. Misterije organizma/ W. R. Mysteries of the Organism* (1971), Bertrand Blier's anarchic, misogynistic *Les Valseuses/Going Places* (1973); Alain Robbe-Grillet's vacuous exercise in softcore imagery and narrative origami, *Le Jeu avec le feu/Giochi di fuoco* (1975, Fr./It.); Pier Paolo Pasolini's punishing Sadian parable of Italian fascism, *Salò o le 120 giornate di Sodoma/Salò* (1975); Nagisa Oshima's brilliant, French co-produced excursion into hardcore, *Ai no corrida* (1976); and Jean-Luc Godard's highly mediated take on sexuality and domesticity, *Numéro deux* (1975).

The 'sexual revolution' of the 1960s created a climate in which the explicit depiction of sex was more acceptable to a mainstream audience. For a while, softcore and hardcore pornography flourished on European screens, especially in France where censorship began to be phased out from 1967. The most spectacular example of mainstream softcore success was *Emmanuelle* (1974), the top-grossing film of its year, making an international star of its lead actress, Sylvia Kristel. A year later, French hardcore took to similarly mainstream screens with *Exhibition* (1975). The response of the French government was not so much one of outright censorship as a fiscal and institutional one that created, in the law of 31 October 1975, the 'X' certificate to designate pornographic films, the creation of a specialised distribution circuit and the imposition of taxes on domestic pornography and a heavier tax on imported porn. While this approach kept the domestic pornography industry marginalised but financially healthy for a short period, it equally serviced the conventional film industry through the siphoning off of porn-tax income into the 'avances sur recette' funding of art cinema. However, the bubble soon burst and by the 1980s the porn cinema accounted for only 5 per cent of the national audience.

The brief foray into mainstream public consciousness that the 1970s bought to the genre of pornography, particularly in France, also saw, towards the end of that decade, the beginnings of the video boom. The European porn industries latched onto video as a means of bypassing cinematic censorship but also as a way of producing low-budget porn. While the genre of 'amateur porn' began inauspiciously in Germany in the 1970s with the so-called *Hausfrauenporn* (housewife porn), by the 1990s video had become hugely lucrative and the standard means of distribution, so that in France an organisation such as 'Nanou Contact' can organise casual sexual encounters, tape them and market them as product. Equally, the European porn industry has its own stars, many of them celebrities beyond their particular fan-base: Brigitte Lahaie and Tabatha Cash in France, Teresa Orlovski in Germany and La Cicciolina (Ilona Staller) in Italy.

If censorious worries with on-screen sexual explicitness have recently been replaced with a concern over levels of violence, it is clear that, as screens themselves have multiplied, the concern is now as much over access to such images as over their contents. The French pay-channel Canal Plus, for example, programmes soft and hardcore pornography regularly. The extension and multiplication of the audio-visual media throughout Europe with cable and satellite will doubtless revivefy the old debates. (Chris Darke)

Bib: Nick Anning and David Hebditch, *Porn Gold: Inside the Pornography Business* (1988).

APPENDIX I

European Production and Audience Statistics*

* Sources from *Encyclopedia of European Cinema*

FILM PRODUCTION FIGURES

Dates

	1945	1946	1947	1948	1949	1950	1951	1952	1953	1954	1955	1956	1957	1958	1959	1960	1961
Albania	–	–	–	–	–	–	–	–	–	–	–	–	1	–	1	1	1
Austria	1	3	13	25	25	15+2	23+5	16+3	18+10	16+6	22+6	28+9	24+2	19+4	17+2	18+2	21+2
Belgium	9	3	1	2	1	0	1	1/0	0	0	0/5	8	3	4+1	3+2	2/0	6+0
Bulgaria	2	3	4	–	1	1	3	3	1	2	4	6+1	6+4	7+2	12	11	7
Czechoslovakia	3	12	22	20	–	20	8	17	18	15	17	21+1	24+3	29	33+2	35+1	44+1
Denmark	10	13	8	8	8	14	15	16	13	14	13	17	17	14	16	17	24
Finland	21	12	14	16	16	12	18	26	23	29	29	17	20	18	17	15	20
France	72	94	72	91	99+8	99+18	94+18	88+21	64+47	52+46	76+34	90+39	81+61	75+51	68+65	79+79	69+98
Germany (East)	–	–	–	–	–	10	–	–	–	–	13	18	21	25	28	29	27
Germany (West)	–	1	9	23	61+1	73+9	57+3	78+4	89+15	94+15	120+8	115+8	96+11	98+17	85+21	85+10	69+11
Greece	5	4	5	8	13	13	15	22	21	14	24	30	31	51	52	58	68
Hungary	3	–	–	6+0	–	4	8	5	8	7	11+0	9	16	13	18	15	19
Iceland	–	–	–	–	–	–	–	–	–	–	–	–	–	–	–	–	–
Ireland	0	–	–	–	–	0	0	2	–	–	1	–	4	3	3	2	2
Italy	–	62	60	54	76	92+0	104+0	119+13	125+21	144+46	74+52	68+23	66+71	76+65	83+81	94+66	117+88
Luxemburg	–	–	–	–	–	0	0	0	0	0	0	0	0	0	0	0	0
Netherlands	2	0	1	2	2	1	0	1	1	–	3	2	2	4	2	5	1
Norway	4	6	2	5	5	4	11	10	7	10	11	9	10	12	8	8	8
Poland	0	1	2	4	4	4	4	1	9	6	9	13	10	23	15	19+2	24
Portugal	4	9	10	4	7	2	4	8	4	–	0	4	1	4	5	2	2
Romania	1	–	–	–	1	1	2	2	2	3	5	3	4	4	5	8	10
ex-Soviet Union	19	23	23	17	18	13	9	24	45	51	81+3	104	108	121	137	119	133
Spain	33	38	49	45	36	47+2	37+5	33+7	37+7	56+13	49+7	53+22	50+22	51+24	50+17	55+18	72+19
Sweden	44	42	45	32	38	36	32	33	32	37	37	34	32	29	21	24	18
Switzerland	1	0	1	1	1	0	1	2	–	–	3	3	4	3	5	4	7
UK	51	66	73	120	125	99	102	132	142	148	115	130	164	135	140	157	151
ex-Yugoslavia	0	–	2	4	3	4	6	5	9	4+3	12+2	11+1	14+2	14+2	13+2	15+1	32+0

	1962	1963	1964	1965	1966	1967	1968	1969	1970	1971	1972	1973	1974	1975	1976	1977	1978
Albania	1	1	1	1	–	–	–	–	–	3	–	–	6	10	14	–	10
Austria	16+4	13+2	11+8	11+5	7+11	7+5	2+5	1+2	3+4	2+3	4+5	3+3	4+4	2+4	3+2	4+4	1+2
Belgium	5+0	0/1	1+1	1/1	1/1	3/1	5/1	10/0	3/1	3/4	11/3	9/4	4/2	–	8/0	3/2	3/3
Bulgaria	9	11	13	11+1	12+2	12+2	13+2	13+2	14+2	17+1	22	19+1	19	22+3	26+2	19+2	30
Czechoslovakia	35+4	39	41	42+3	40	49	44+1	42+8	52+2	57+2	45+4	65+3	63+3	54+8	65+3	61+2	48
Denmark	19	21	17	18	21	20	20	20	20	28	18	20+0	22+0	16+2	20+0	16+0	17+0
Finland	19	11	9	9	6	3	12	11	9	8	8	7	2	7	9	7	10
France	43+82	36+105	45+103	34+108	45+85	47+73	49+68	70+84	66+72	67+60	71+98	97+103	137+97	160+62	170+44	190+32	116+44
Germany (East)	27	20	15	15	–	–	–	–	–	–	10+7	14+2	14+1	15+1	17+1	16	–
Germany (West)	43+18	44+22	35+42	25+47	27+33	56+40	61+46	82+39	86+27	68+31	57+28	80+18	58+22	47+26	42+18	38+14	50+7
Greece	82	92	93	101	117	99	108	98	87	90	64	44	42	38	17	17	15
Hungary	16	18+1	19+1	23	21	21+1	36+1	22+1	21+2	15+4	21	21	19+1	19	19	24+1	28
Iceland	–	–	–	–	–	–	–	–	–	–	–	–	–	0	–	1	–
Ireland	3	2	3	1	3	1	1	0	5	2	6	4	2	2	0	0	1
Italy	139+106	135+95	135+155	94+109	89+143	130+117	130+116	146+103	132+99	128+88	169+111	171+81	176+55	177+53	203+34	142+23	119+24
Luxemburg	0	0	0	0	0	0	0	0	1	1	0	0	0	0	0	0	1
Netherlands	6	5	3	1	5	–	–	–	4	4+1	6+1	8+3	8	16	8+2	7+2	–
Norway	6	6	7	9	6+1	4	7	5+1	11	7+1	8	9+2	12	13+1	14	9	7
Poland	23	27	23	20+0	25	–	–	–	24+0	27	19	19	27	20+1	–	27	31
Portugal	4+1	7+1	5+3	6	5	5+2	4	4	4	7	6	3	–	6	10	9	21
Romania	12	14	14	14+1	11+4	16	6+2	12+2	9+2	15	19	22	22	24	19+3	23	24
ex–Soviet Union	121	133	–	167	159	175	161+2	194+2	215+3	208+6	230+4	166	162+7	176+8	150+6	146+2	–
Spain	64+24	59+55	67+63	53+98	67+97	55+70	49+68	55+70	42+63	48+43	52+51	73+45	71+41	89+21	90+18	83+19	77+30
Sweden	17	21	19	25	29	23	36	28	23	17	19	15	21	25	18	26	15
Switzerland	4	2	4	10	5	2	3	5	5	6	6+2	17+3	13+4	28+2	19+1	16+4	–
UK	171	150	126	97	99	140	107	112	122	67	131	98	89	91	92	73	77
ex-Yugoslavia	22+0	14+4	17+1	18+2	17+3	33+3	32+1	27+4	23+0	21+3	20+2	20+3	14+1	17+2	14+0	20+0	20+1

Figures are for feature film production by country. 47+2 indicates films + co-productions. 5/1 indicates division of French language/Dutch and Flemish language films produced. Zero (0) indicates no films produced. A dash (–) indicates no figure available.

FILM PRODUCTION FIGURES (continued)

Dates

	1979	1980	1981	1982	1983	1984	1985	1986	1987	1988	1989	1990	1991	1992	1993
Albania	12	–	–	–	7	14	12	–	–	–	11	5	0	1	–
Austria	5+1	5+2	3+2	12+1	8+3	16+1	9+3	11+2	8+2	8+1	10+1	10+5	11	10+0	–
Belgium	8/2	4+2	1/2	4/1	4/3	3/2	6+1	4+1	7+5	4+11	10+0	9+11	3+3	3+9	4+4
Bulgaria	29	31	42	–	32	–	40	23	35	15	20	19	22	3	5+3
Czechoslovakia	47	52	48	–	66	–	50	63	55	58	70	62	17	15	20
Denmark	9+0	13+0	12+0	7+0	11+0	10+1	7+2	10+0	9+2	14+2	16+2	12+1	9+2	10+5	11+3
Finland	9	7+3	12	17	16	17	13	23+1	12	10	7+3	14	11	20	20
France	126+48	144+45	186+45	134+31	101+30	120+41	106+45	97+37	96+37	93+44	66+70	81+65	73+83	72+83	67+85
Germany (East)	–	17	–	–	16	–	16	16	5	–	–	–	–	–	–
Germany (West)	53+12	37+12	60+16	57+13	69+8	62+13	46+18	45+15	47+18	49+8	53+15	38+10	53+19	53+10	50+17
Greece	27	25	46	48	37	40	30	27	26	13	14	10	15+0	6+4	15+3
Hungary	21+5	26	25	–	25	11+6	21	26	26	14+6	37	23	15+4	17+5	9+7
Iceland	–	2	3	3	4	5	4	2+0	1+0	2+0	2+0	2+0	4	1+2	0+2
Ireland	1	5	2	1	3	2	2+0	3+1	1+3	2+3	2+1	3	1	3+1	3+3
Italy	122+24	128+32	79+24	99+15	101+9	86+17	81+8	94+15	106+10	103+21	102+15	98+21	111+18	114+13	86+20
Luxemburg	0	0	3	0	0	1	1	1	1	1	3	1	1+1	1+2	0+4
Netherlands	–	7	11	10	10	12	10+1	13+0	15+3	8+2	13	13	14	13+0	16+0
Norway	13	10	10	10	8	6	10	13	7+2	10	11	9	10	8	9
Poland	32	33+6	17+2	23+3	31+5	35	37	34	35	34	22	27	–	8+13	11+10
Portugal	6	9	6	8	4	8	8	6	9+2	16	4+3	2+7	6+3	2+6	10+6
Romania	28	32	31	32	32	–	26	30	26	23	23	4+5	15+4	12+6	10+5
ex-Soviet Union	–	156	–	–	–	–	158	142	158	153	160	300	400	65	137
Spain	56+33	82+36	92+45	118+22	81+18	63+12	65+12	49+11	62+7	54+9	43+5	37+10	46+18	38+14	41+15
Sweden	20	23+3	22+3	14+4	17+6	16+2	12	17+3	26+1	13+8	15+6	20+5	10+17	9+11	13+14
Switzerland	–	13	11	–	–	20	15	3+19	6+15	6+12	8+8	8+11	5+12	3+6	0+16
UK	77	61	66	46	56	51	53	29+6	42+6	38+2	22+5	39+8	24+22	29+13	31+29
ex-Yugoslavia	27+1	24+2	23+3	32+2	23+2	30+3	30+2	21+4	23+4	28+7	26+7	21+4	–	3	–

Figures are for feature film production by country. 47+2 indicates films + co-production. 5/1 indicates division of French language/Dutch and Flemish language films produced. Zero (0) indicates no films produced. A dash (–) indicates no figures available.

AUDIENCE FIGURES (Millions)

Dates

	1945	1946	1947	1948	1949	1950	1951	1952	1953	1954	1955	1956	1957	1958	1959	1960	1961
Albania	–	–	–	–	–	–	–	–	4.6	–	5.9	–	5.9	6.6	8.0	–	7.6
Austria	–	–	–	–	–	92.5	93.9	94.1	107.9	110.0	114.0	116.1	119.9	122.0	114.9	106.5	100.5
Belgium	–	–	–	–	–	116.4	114.1	110.4	112.2	111.4	106.0	109.7	106.7	99.9	88.7	80.0	71.7
Bulgaria	–	–	–	–	–	–	37.0	39.0	42.0	55.2	60.0	69.0	77.9	89.4	101.2	112.1	118.0
Czechoslovakia	–	–	–	–	–	–	128.0	135.0	144.0	152.0	162.6	185.5	186.2	183.3	178.0	176.5	166.0
Denmark	47.0	53.8	54.4	–	–	52.2	56.6	57.3	59.0	58.7	55.0	52.1	51.3	50.0	46.7	44.0	42.0
Finland	36.3	30.0	29.6	29.1	26.2	25.7	26.8	26.8	29.4	30.3	33.5	31.2	31.3	28.8	25.5	24.6	23.8
France	402.0	419.0	424.0	–	–	370.7	372.8	359.6	370.6	382.8	394.9	398.9	411.7	371.0	353.7	354.7	328.4
Germany (East)	–	–	–	–	–	184.0	–	–	–	–	310.0	–	–	273.1	258.6	237.9	–
Germany (West)	–	–	–	–	–	487.4	554.8	614.5	680.2	735.6	766.1	817.5	801.0	749.7	670.8	604.8	516.9
Greece	–	–	–	10.0	35.6	37.5	38.8	41.3	42.6	45.3	49.5	56.9	62.2	66.8	74.8	84.2	86.3
Hungary	–	–	–	–	–	47.1	63.0	69.0	73.0	98.0	115.8	113.6	133.4	131.0	135.0	140.1	135.4
Iceland	–	–	–	–	–	–	–	–	–	–	–	–	–	–	–	–	–
Ireland	–	–	–	–	–	46.1	47.8	49.1	50.7	54.1	50.9	52.1	49.8	45.6	43.8	41.2	38.0
Italy	–	411.0	525.0	580.0	600.0	661.5	705.7	748.1	779.9	800.7	819.4	790.2	758.4	730.4	747.9	744.8	741.0
Luxemburg	–	–	–	–	–	–	–	–	–	–	4.0	5.0	5.0	5.0	5.0	4.5	5.0
Netherlands	–	–	–	–	–	63.9	63.5	63.1	63.7	65.1	66.0	69.9	65.6	64.2	55.5	55.4	51.0
Norway	–	30.1	–	–	–	30.0	32.0	34.0	33.0	34.0	33.0	35.0	35.0	35.0	35.0	35.0	33.9
Poland	–	–	–	–	–	–	121.0	136.0	152.0	166.0	208.3	198.0	231.4	205.3	195.5	196.0	186.0
Portugal	–	17.7	20.9	20.7	19.9	20.6	20.9	23.0	22.1	24.1	25.9	27.0	27.9	26.5	26.6	26.6	26.1
Romania	–	–	–	–	–	52.4	66.0	67.0	83.0	84.0	85.4	113.0	119.0	113.5	134.1	150.3	164.3
ex-Soviet Union	–	–	–	–	–	–	–	–	–	–	2506.0	–	3063.0	3392.0	3519.9	3610.0	3849.0
Spain	–	–	–	–	–	–	315.0	310.0	314.0	320.0	310.0	324.0	360.0	362.0	365.0	370.0	370.0
Sweden	–	–	–	–	–	–	60.0	67.0	70.0	65.0	60.0	67.0	65.0	70.0	60.0	55.0	54.0
Switzerland	–	–	–	–	–	–	–	33.0	–	–	34.0	37.0	40.0	42.0	44.0	40.0	40.0
UK	1585.0	1635.0	1462.0	1514.0	1430.0	1395.8	1365.0	1312.1	1284.5	1275.8	1181.8	1100.8	915.2	754.7	581.0	515.0	449.1
ex-Yugoslavia	–	–	–	–	–	–	64.0	60.0	68.0	85.0	97.0	101.4	108.0	114.3	125.0	130.1	129.0

AUDIENCE FIGURES (Millions) (continued)

Dates

	1962	1963	1964	1965	1966	1967	1968	1969	1970	1971	1972	1973	1974	1975	1976	1977	1978
Albania	–	–	–	7.8	–	–	–	8.4	–	8.4	–	8.4	–	–	–	–	–
Austria	90.8	84.9	76.0	72.1	65.8	57.7	50.6	39.5	32.9	28.5	26.7	23.9	23.4	20.8	17.5	17.9	17.4
Belgium	63.9	52.7	46.6	40.9	39.5	36.7	33.9	31.5	30.5	29.8	29.4	26.3	26.5	24.9	23.2	22.3	21.7
Bulgaria	122.8	124.0	125.0	126.4	124.1	119.9	114.0	110.2	109.6	111.1	112.3	114.0	112.3	114.3	114.7	113.4	111.3
Czechoslovakia	152.0	140.7	134.2	128.4	127.0	118.8	118.7	120.6	114.8	110.7	98.4	89.3	87.7	85.9	85.3	86.4	84.7
Denmark	39.3	34.5	33.2	33.9	33.5	29.7	26.8	25.6	24.3	22.1	20.7	18.9	19.2	18.9	18.6	16.7	17.4
Finland	17.8	13.2	10.6	14.0	15.1	14.5	10.1	10.5	11.7	13.0	10.1	10.9	9.6	9.6	8.9	9.0	9.8
France	311.7	292.1	275.8	257.2	234.7	211.4	203.2	182.1	184.4	177.0	184.4	176.0	179.4	180.7	177.3	170.3	178.5
Germany (East)	191.2	–	140.6	119.0	–	99.2	100.6	93.3	91.4	83.4	81.5	84.5	79.5	76.9	79.7	84.1	–
Germany (West)	442.9	366.0	320.4	294.0	257.1	215.6	180.4	180.6	160.1	152.1	149.8	144.3	136.2	128.1	115.1	124.2	135.5
Greece	96.1	100.5	109.5	121.1	131.8	137.1	137.4	135.3	128.6	118.0	92.6	62.2	57.1	47.9	39.9	39.0	39.2
Hungary	122.0	115.7	111.1	106.0	104.6	96.8	84.5	82.2	79.6	79.7	74.7	74.4	77.9	74.4	73.6	76.0	71.7
Iceland	–	–	–	–	2.3	–	–	–	1.7	1.8	2.0	2.0	2.3	2.6	2.5	–	–
Ireland	35.0	–	–	30.0	–	–	–	–	20.0	–	–	–	18.0	15.0	–	–	–
Italy	728.6	697.5	683.0	663.1	632.0	568.9	559.9	550.9	525.0	535.7	553.7	544.8	544.4	513.7	454.5	373.8	318.6
Luxemburg	4.0	4.0	3.5	3.0	–	2.1	1.9	1.5	1.3	1.1	1.1	1.0	1.0	1.1	0.8	0.7	–
Netherlands	47.9	43.1	38.7	36.4	34.3	31.6	27.4	24.8	24.1	25.7	25.0	26.5	28.1	28.3	26.5	26.2	28.4
Norway	32.8	26.5	24.5	23.0	21.8	21.0	19.2	19.2	18.6	18.9	18.3	17.5	17.9	18.5	16.8	16.8	16.8
Poland	194.0	164.8	177.0	168.0	164.7	163.1	–	141.3	137.8	130.4	136.2	140.6	142.8	143.4	144.2	131.6	116.0
Portugal	25.6	24.8	24.5	25.7	26.1	27.7	26.6	26.4	28.0	27.2	28.1	28.9	35.7	41.6	42.8	39.1	34.0
Romania	181.0	191.0	181.7	204.7	216.1	209.2	203.7	200.4	198.8	189.2	179.7	177.4	182.3	185.7	191.2	183.5	187.9
ex-Soviet Union	3900.0	3900.0	–	4280.0	4200.0	4502.8	4715.0	4655.9	4651.8	4656.3	4569.0	4583.3	4566.9	4497.3	4211.0	4080.0	–
Spain	–	320.0	–	435.2	403.1	393.1	376.6	364.6	330.9	295.3	295.2	278.3	262.9	255.8	249.0	211.0	220.0
Sweden	50.0	39.5	40.0	38.2	37.3	35.4	32.6	30.4	28.2	26.0	26.7	22.9	22.1	23.7	23.7	22.5	23.5
Switzerland	40.0	39.0	37.0	45.0	34.0	32.0	35.0	33.0	32.0	30.0	28.0	27.0	25.5	23.7	20.4	21.2	20.0
UK	395.0	357.2	342.8	326.6	288.8	264.8	237.3	214.9	193.0	176.0	156.6	134.2	138.5	116.3	103.9	103.5	126.1
ex-Yugoslavia	121.8	117.0	123.0	121.2	114.6	104.9	100.2	90.3	86.3	81.5	84.2	86.3	83.3	81.7	79.7	75.8	75.4

	1979	1980	1981	1982	1983	1984	1985	1986	1987	1988	1989	1990	1991	1992	1993
Albania	–	–	–	–	–	–	–	–	–	–	3.8	–	–	–	–
Austria	17.5	17.5	18.2	16.6	17.9	16.1	17.0	12.6	11.5	10.0	11.8	10.2	10.5	9.3	12.0
Belgium	19.8	21.6	20.1	20.5	21.3	19.0	17.9	17.7	15.7	15.2	15.0	16.2	16.9	16.6	18.3
Bulgaria	109.4	100.0	91.4	92.5	93.5	–	95.5	93.2	84.2	81.0	79.0	65.0	25.7	30.0	11.0
Czechoslovakia	82.5	82.3	81.0	78.6	–	–	76.7	76.6	73.8	73.8	70.6	65.0	40.6	43.0	31.0
Denmark	17.2	15.9	16.2	14.3	13.7	12.0	11.3	11.3	11.4	10.0	10.3	9.6	9.2	8.6	10.2
Finland	10.1	9.9	9.4	9.1	9.1	7.6	6.7	6.3	6.5	6.7	7.2	6.2	6.0	5.4	5.8
France	178.1	174.8	189.2	201.9	198.8	190.8	172.2	163.4	136.7	124.7	120.9	121.8	117.0	115.9	133.3
Germany (East)	–	79.5	–	72.4	–	73.4	70.0	70.2	69.2	69.3	64.0	30.0	13.0	11.2	–
Germany (West)	142.0	143.8	141.3	124.5	125.2	112.1	104.2	105.2	108.1	108.9	101.6	102.5	106.9	94.7	57.7
Greece	34.1	43.0	40.5	35.3	35.0	22.0	23.0	22.0	22.5	17.0	17.5	16.5	6.2	6.7	7.0
Hungary	69.0	60.7	67.1	70.0	68.9	71.0	70.2	68.0	55.9	50.7	45.8	36.2	22.3	15.6	15.2
Iceland	–	2.6	–	2.2	–	–	1.4	1.2	1.3	–	1.2	1.2	1.2	1.2	1.2
Ireland	–	9.5	–	11.4	12.7	14.0	11.6	11.0	5.2	6.0	7.0	7.4	8.1	8.2	9.3
Italy	276.3	241.9	215.2	195.4	162.0	131.6	123.1	124.8	112.5	93.0	95.2	90.5	88.6	83.6	92.2
Luxemburg	–	0.8	–	0.7	0.7	0.7	0.7	0.7	0.7	0.5	0.5	0.5	0.6	0.6	0.7
Netherlands	25.8	27.9	24.7	20.5	20.2	17.4	15.3	14.9	15.5	14.8	15.6	14.6	14.9	13.7	15.9
Norway	17.8	17.5	16.4	15.1	14.8	12.8	12.9	11.1	12.4	11.5	12.6	11.4	10.8	9.6	10.9
Poland	96.2	96.9	91.1	89.4	99.7	127.6	107.0	100.0	94.0	95.3	86.4	38.0	18.0	12.0	13.7
Portugal	32.6	30.8	28.8	26.0	22.9	21.0	19.0	18.4	16.9	13.0	13.8	11.0	11.8	12.0	12.7
Romania	185.7	193.6	198.3	143.7	209.4	217.0	191.5	204.7	208.3	–	170.0	130.0	76.0	41.0	30.0
ex-Soviet Union	–	4260.0	–	4220.0	–	–	4100.0	–	3775.0	3920.2	3640.0	3500.0	2000.0	1000.0	–
Spain	200.0	176.0	173.7	156.0	141.0	118.6	101.1	87.3	85.7	69.6	78.1	78.5	79.1	83.3	87.7
Sweden	25.1	24.9	23.2	21.3	19.0	17.1	17.9	16.4	17.4	17.5	19.2	15.3	15.1	15.7	16.0
Switzerland	21.3	20.9	20.4	20.1	19.7	17.9	16.4	16.3	16.2	14.9	15.2	14.3	15.4	15.0	15.9
UK	111.9	101.0	83.0	64.0	65.7	58.4	70.2	72.6	74.8	84.0	96.0	98.2	101.6	103.6	114.4
ex-Yugoslavia	–	80.0	76.5	80.0	85.0	87.0	81.0	80.8	78.1	70.8	65.0	58.0	25.7	20.9	–

APPENDIX II

Select Bibliography for European, British and Irish Cinema

BIBLIOGRAPHY

Europe

Roy Armes, *The Ambiguous Image: Narrative Style in Modern European Cinema* (London: Secker and Warburg, 1976).

Grzegorz Balski, *Directory of Eastern European Film-makers and Films, 1945–1991* (Trowbridge, Wilts: Flicks Books, 1992).

Peter Cowie, *International Film Guide* (now *Variety International Film Guide*) (London: Andre Deutsch, annual from 1964).

Peter Cowie, *Scandinavian Cinema: a survey of film and film-makers in Denmark, Finland, Iceland, Norway and Sweden* (London: Tantivy Press, 1992).

Richard Dyer and Ginette Vincendeau (eds.), *Popular European Cinema* (London and New York: Routledge, 1992).

The European Film in the World Market (Vienna: The Austrian Film Commission, 1988).

David W. Ellwood and Rob Kroes, *Hollywood in Europe, Expressions of a Cultural Hegemony* (Amsterdam: Amsterdam University Press, 1994).

Daniel J. Goulding (ed.), *Five Filmmakers: Tarkovsky, Forman, Polanski, Szabó, Makavejev* (Bloomington: Indiana University Press, 1994).

Daniel J. Goulding (ed.), *Post New Wave Cinema in the Soviet Union and Eastern Europe* (Bloomington: Indiana University Press, 1989).

Thomas H. Guback, *The International Film Industry: Western Europe and America since 1945* (Bloomington: Indiana University Press, 1969).

Thomas H. Guback, 'Cultural Identity and Film in the European Economic Community', in *Cinema Journal*, vol. 14, no. 1, 1974.

Nicholas Hewitt (ed.), *The Culture of Reconstruction. European Literature, Thought and Film, 1945–1950* (Basingstoke and London: Macmillan, 1989).

Andrew S. Horton and Joan Magretta (eds.), *Modern European Film-makers and the Art of Adaptation* (New York: Frederick Ungar, 1981).

Mira and Antonín J. Liehm, *The Most Important Art: East European Film After 1945* (Berkeley and London: University of California Press, 1977).

David W. Paul (ed.), *Politics, Art, and Commitment in the East European Cinema* (New York: St. Martin's Press, 1983).

Duncan Petrie (ed.), *Screening Europe: Image and Identity in Contemporary European Cinema* (London: BFI, 1992).

James Quinn, *The Film and Television as an Aspect of European Culture* (Leyden: A. W. Sijthoff, 1968).

Pierre Sorlin, *European Cinemas, European Societies 1939– 1990* (London and New York: Routledge, 1991).

Great Britain

Anthony Aldgate and Jeffrey Richards, *Britain Can Take It: The British cinema in the Second World War* (Oxford: Basil Blackwell, 1986).

Roy Armes, *A Critical History of British Cinema* (London: Secker & Warburg, 1978).

Martyn Auty and Nick Roddick, *British Cinema Now* (London: BFI Publishing, 1985).

Charles Barr (ed.), *All Our Yesterdays: Ninety years of British cinema* (London: BFI Publishing, 1986).

David Berry, *Wales and Cinema: The First Hundred Years* (Cardiff: University of Wales Press, in co-operation with the Wales Film Council and the BFI, 1994).

James Curran and Vincent Porter (eds.), *British Cinema History* (London: Weidenfeld and Nicolson, 1983).

Eddie Dick (ed.), *From Limelight to Satellite: A Scottish film book* (Glasgow: Scottish Film Council, and London: BFI, 1990).

Margaret Dickinson and Sarah Street, *Cinema and State: The film industry and the British government, 1927–1984* (London: BFI Publishing, 1985).

Raymond Durgnat, *A Mirror for England, British movies from austerity to affluence* (London: Faber, 1970).

Lester Friedman (ed.), *Fires Were Started: British Cinema and Thatcherism* (Minneapolis: University of Minnesota Press, and London: UCL Press, 1993).

Jonathan Hacker and David Price (eds.), *Take Ten: Contemporary British film directors* (Oxford: Clarendon Press, 1991).

Bert Hogenkamp, *Deadly Parallels: Film and the Left in Britain, 1929–1939* (London: Lawrence & Wishart, 1986).

Marcia Landy, *British Genres: Cinema and society, 1930–1960* (Princeton, NJ: Princeton University Press, 1991).

Antonia Lant, *Blackout: Reinventing women for wartime British cinema* (Princeton, NJ: Princeton University Press, 1991).

Alan Lovell and Jim Hillier, *Studies in Documentary* (London: Secker & Warburg/BFI, 1972).

Rachael Low and Roger Manvell, *The History of British Film, 1896–1906* (London: Allen & Unwin, 1948).

Rachael Low, *The History of the British Film, 1906–1914*; *1914–1918; 1918–1929; 1929–1939: documentary and educational films of the 1930s; 1929–1939: film making in 1930s Britain; 1929–1939: films of comment and persuasion of the 1930s* (London: Allen & Unwin, 1949, 1950, 1971, 1979, 1985, 1979).

Geoffrey Macnab, *J. Arthur Rank and the British Film Industry* (London: Routledge, 1992).

Don Macpherson (ed.), *Traditions of Independence: British cinema in the Thirties* (London: BFI Publishing, 1980).

Colin McArthur (ed.), *Scotch Reels: Scotland in cinema and television* (London: BFI Publishing, 1982).

Brian McFarlane (ed.), *Sixty Voices: Celebrities recall the Golden Age of British Cinema* (London: BFI Publishing, 1992).
Kobena Mercer (ed.), *Black Film, British Cinema: ICA document no. 7* (London: Institute of Contemporary Arts, 1988).
Robert Murphy, *Realism and Tinsel: Cinema and society in Britain, 1939–1948* (London and New York: Routledge, 1989).
Robert Murphy, *Sixties British Cinema* (London: BFI Publishing, 1992).
Duncan Petrie (ed.), *New Questions of British Cinema* (London: BFI Publishing, 1992).
John Pym, *Film on Four, 1982–1991: A Survey* (London: BFI Publishing, 1992).
Jeffrey Richards, *The Age of the Dream Palace: Cinema and Society in Britain, 1930–1939* (London: Routledge & Kegan Paul, 1984).

Ireland
John Hill, Martin McLoone and Paul Hainsworth (eds.), *Border Crossing: Film in Ireland, Britain and Europe* (Belfast: Institute of Irish Studies in association with the University of Ulster and the BFI, 1994).
Brian McIlroy, *World Cinema 4: Ireland* (Trowbridge: Flicks Books, 1989).
Kevin Rockett, John Hill and Luke Gibbons, *Cinema and Ireland* (London: Routledge, 1988).